Allegiance

The Life and Times of William Eustis

Tamsen Evans George

Riverhaven Books

Allegiance: The Life and Times of William Eustis is a historical work; all materials referenced may be found in the Bibliography and Notes sections at the end of this book.

First printing

Published in the United States by Riverhaven Books
www.RiverhavenBooks.com

ISBN: 978-1-951854-24-9

Printed in the United States of America

Book and cover design by Stephanie Lynn Blackman
Whitman, MA

For all those unknown men and women whose sacrifice and commitment to liberty gave us this new nation.

Governor William Eustis, 1825

Picture Credits

Maps at the Part divisions are courtesy of the Library of Congress and include A Plan of the Town of Boston with entrenchments &c of His Majesty's Forces in 1775; West Point defenses of the Hudson Valley, 1780, courtesy of the U. S. Military Academy Department of History; and Washington City, 1824, courtesy of the Library of Congress.

Portraits:
Cover portrait: William Eustis, by Gilbert Stuart, 1804. Collection of the Shirley-Eustis House Association, Boston, MA.

William Eustis, governor of Massachusetts, by Henry Williams, 1823, Courtesy of the Commonwealth of Massachusetts Art Commission, State House, Boston, MA.

Table of Contents

PART III: FULFILLMENT, 1810 - 1825

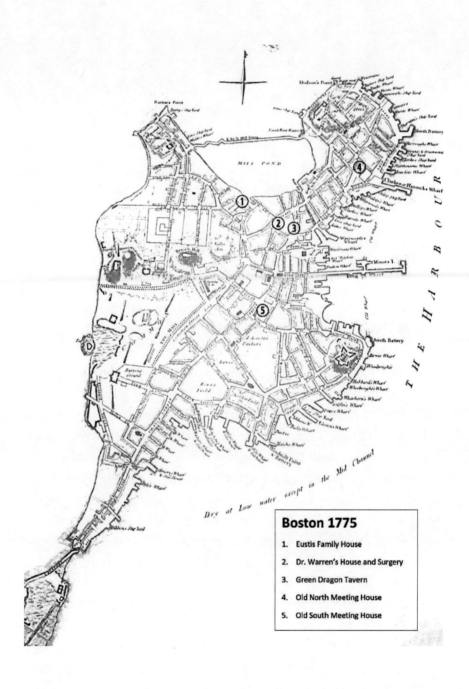

Boston 1775

1. Eustis Family House
2. Dr. Warren's House and Surgery
3. Green Dragon Tavern
4. Old North Meeting House
5. Old South Meeting House

PROLOGUE

It was not a quiet place. Boston had about seventeen thousand inhabitants, including children, crowded together in a nearly one hundred fifty-year-old town on a small peninsula. This third most populous city in America bustled with industry.[1] From dawn to dusk, neighborhood noise levels rose and fell in a crescendo of nonstop endeavors. Horseshoes and carriage wheels clattered on the cobblestone streets, a mother called out to her careless child, and peddlers cried their wares. The cooper shaved his barrel staves, the cobbler worked his skills on leather, and the blacksmith hammered red-hot iron at his forge. Shipyards bustled. Dories ferried supplies, sails, tarred rope, and cargo ranging from salted cod to apples.

Amid the noise was the stink of garbage, offal and excrement, and ever-present wood smoke. Family cows and sheep grazed on the Common, and chickens and pigs foraged in the streets. Residents roamed the town freely during the day and stepped carefully at night. With no streetlamps, no sidewalks, and no sewers, one had to walk with caution.

From the harbor, sailors could count eleven prominent church steeples spread over two primary residential areas: the North End, with its large mill pond, and the South End. The South End, with wharves along the harbor, backed onto an area toward Boston Common with a more pastoral setting featuring stately homes, gardens, fields, and pastures. Boston's central area, known as Cornhill, contained Province House, residence of the royal governor, the Town House, Boston Latin School, the merchant and financial centers, and the town's fresh-water spring. Centered on the waterfront, the Long Wharf projected nearly half a mile into the harbor, a long arm reaching for the world's business.

Many miles across the ocean, King George III ascended to the throne of the British Empire in 1761. He had little knowledge of the New World, had never traveled from England, and neither he nor his ministers understood the American people who numbered about 2.5 million. Unlike those in the mother country, these British subjects had a different vision of the New World and how they wanted to live in it. Literate churchgoing men who owned property could vote on how their colonies were run. A city like Philadelphia had seventy-seven booksellers. Although these colonists may have lacked battleships, they were inveterate seafarers, heavily involved in trade and fishing for their livelihood. And they were armed, literally, with experience and weapons following years of fighting in militias, alongside or as part of British regiments.

Neither the king nor Parliament had any concept of the size of the country—even the vertical slice of seaboard defined by an imaginary British line that discouraged expansion beyond the Appalachian Mountains. Losing these colonies meant losing about one-third of the empire. But the odds were stacked in Britain's favor; never in known history had a colony successfully thrown off its rulers.

Great Britain had gone deeply into debt fighting the French in the colonies during the French and Indian War. It seemed only reasonable to Parliament that the colonies help pay the bill for their defense. The Stamp Act of 1765 levied on these formerly semi-neglected, and happily so, colonies, mandated that every deck of cards, newspaper, pamphlet, legal paper, or document printed on paper required a stamp. For the first time, a direct tax on the residents of the American colonies impacted business activities, and it generated a fierce reaction.

Reactionary or mob behavior was not unusual in Boston. These were a fiercely independent people with ideas rooted in individual liberty and against authority. Their heritage was grounded in personal achievement, not in titled overseers and royal obligations. Many were affronted by the taxes imposed without consultation or approval from their own colonial legislatures. This would not occur in the mother country. James Otis, Jr. and John Adams, two young lawyers in town, became involved in defining the basic rights to life, liberty, and property of all Englishmen, including those in the colonies.

The Eustis family played a role in this uniquely American story, beginning in the heavily populated, working-class area called the North End. Eustis ancestors had arrived in the New World in the late sixteen hundreds and had lived in Boston for generations. William Eustis's father, Benjamin, was a carpenter, filling the family's back yard with wood scraps and shavings and the sounds of hammer and saw. He had remained in the family home, near the corner of Hawkins Street by the mill pond. Serving first as a sergeant in the colonial militia, fighting with a British artillery regiment against the French during the French and Indian Wars, he then joined his father's carpentry business.

As a solid middle-class citizen, Benjamin Eustis had building jobs all over town—from constructing the cannon platforms at Castle William (now Fort Independence) on Castle Island to framing the roof of Kings Chapel. He recorded handy references for construction inside the back cover of his account book, such as "Rule for gambeling Ruff that the Cap be 3 fifth of ye Wedth of ye House . . ."[2] In between large jobs, he kept busy making coffins, called "coffings." As a successful house wright or home builder, and as the owner of several Boston properties, he could vote.

At thirty-one, Benjamin married Elizabeth Hill, twenty-three, in

1749. Born into an established, educated family, she grew up as one of eleven children. In 1718, her father, Deacon Abraham Hill, a brick and stone mason, had brought his bride, Prudence Hancock, to the family home in Cambridge. William's grandparents' house faced a driveway leading from the road to the barn in back and had a stone wall of huge boulders and lilac trees along the road.[3] By the time of the wedding, the house had been in the possession of the Hill family for nearly fifty years.

Benjamin and Elizabeth's third son, William Eustis, was born on June 10, 1753, in the Cambridge house of his mother's parents, Prudence Hancock and Abraham Hill. Having lost her first child, Elizabeth had gone to visit her parents when her baby was due. A week later, influenced by parental concerns about infant mortality, this second living son was tightly wrapped and carried home to Boston for baptism in the wooden Brattle Street Congregational Church by the Reverend Samuel Cooper.

During her twenty-four-year marriage, Elizabeth Hill Eustis gave birth to twelve children. At the time of the birth of her first child on August 31, 1750, her husband Benjamin noted in his ledger that he paid Dr. Taylor to have her bled, a common treatment if there were complications with the delivery.[4] This first child, named Benjamin, died barely a month later. William's big brother, their first surviving son who was also named Benjamin, arrived in September 1751. It was customary following an infant's death for the name to be given to a later child. Elizabeth and Benjamin's first daughter, Elizabeth, died after a year of life in 1765 and was followed by another Elizabeth in 1766.

Elizabeth, with her growing brood, managed the needs of their ten children: Benjamin (1751), William (1753), George (1755), Abraham (1757), Jacob (1759), Catherine (1761), Nathaniel (1762), Elizabeth (1766), Prudence (1769), and Nancy (1771). The daughter of an educated man, Elizabeth instilled ideas of higher education and solid family connections in her family. She wanted her sons to be educated and taught them their letters.

Life was not expected to be comfortable, and survival was not taken for granted. Subsistence farming occupied every family during warm weather. Supplemental employment became critical in the closely settled North End where garden plots were confined, and some produce might have to be purchased or bartered. A family needed to grow and store sufficient food to last through the severe New England winters into June.

The Hills were a committed Congregational family, their beliefs grounded in Calvinism. Elizabeth's brother was Rev. Abraham Hill Jr. Two brothers-in-law were the Reverends Stephen Badger and Nathan Fiske. All were Harvard educated.

Through his mother, William was a second cousin to John Hancock, another Harvard man.

Elizabeth "superintended [William's] early years, and the excellence of her disposition and pious instruction left upon his mind impressions of her worth, that never were effaced nor impaired through life."[5]

William's father was active in the town, joining Saint John's Lodge, the first Freemasons lodge in Boston, officially chartered by the Grand Lodge of England about 1732.[6] Later, in 1756, a second lodge, Saint Andrew's, was chartered by the Grand Lodge of Scotland. As the membership in Saint John's Lodge grew more conservative and included more merchants in Boston, the members of Saint Andrew's Lodge, primarily artisans and tradesmen, became more liberal. The members of Saint Andrew's Lodge met on the second floor at the Green Dragon Tavern, owned by the lodge, in Boston's North End. Those backroom meetings and gatherings voiced the first whispers of rebellion.

PART I: REVOLUTION
1753 – 1783

"Young man, what we meant in going for those Redcoats was this:
we always had governed ourselves and we always meant to. They
didn't mean we should."
—Captain Levi Preston, Danvers Militia, to the Honorable Mellen Chamberlain
of Chelsea (c.1843).
Danvers Historical Society Collections, 68-70.

1

Counting Down to Liberty

Growing up in the center of this cantankerous Massachusetts Bay Colony, young William Eustis, affectionately called Bill, was surrounded by distractions, from swimming in the summer to skating on the Mill Pond in the winter to watching the militia drilling on Boston Common. Despite these diversions, his determined mother kept him focused on his education. She made sure he qualified for admission to Boston Latin School, the oldest school in America, and was enrolled to study Latin, Greek, and arithmetic.[1]

The school's headmaster, John Lovell, was an ardent Tory whose son James, a teacher at the school, was an equally ardent Whig. The boys' classes began at seven o'clock in the morning in the summer and eight o'clock in the winter, running until eleven o'clock when the students went to a nearby writing school to learn proper cursive handwriting. They returned by one o'clock in the afternoon and remained until five. On wintry days, students brought their sleds and, after dragging them up Beacon Hill, would slide down the hill, across Tremont Street and on past their school.

Conspiracies and plots were part of daily life. When William turned twelve in 1765, there already had been an uneasy five years during which the American colonies and their distant mother country, under a new and opinionated King George III, struggled to work out ways of dealing with each other.

The economy in Great Britain was hardly coasting. The national debt came to about $22.4 billion in today's currency. Faced with growing unrest, Parliament repealed the hated Stamp Act but reminded the unruly colonies that they still had obligations to the empire. In 1767, the Townshend Duties, named for Chancellor of the Exchequer Charles Townshend, imposed a tax on printing paper, imported lead, and tea. A new board of customs commissioners was appointed to collect these taxes and would be paid from the taxes it collected. Boston merchants, insistent on their rights as Englishmen, protested.

It appeared to the king that military force would be necessary to curtail violence, mob action, and open revolt. General Thomas Gage, commander-in-chief of His Majesty's forces in America, received orders on June 8, 1768, to put this Massachusetts colony in its place. In disrespectful response, the colony called for its towns to send representatives to a meeting in Boston's Faneuil Hall in September. After six days of discussion, the session adjourned with an agreement not to import any British goods for a year. Within hours, the sails of approaching British troop transports were rising above the horizon.

Six frigates and two armed schooners sailed into Boston Harbor that day, joining other British naval vessels already at anchor. More than seven hundred red-coated troops landed at Long Wharf and marched with drums beating and flags flying to the Town House (today's Old State House). Older Bostonians greeted their arrival with appalled silence. The nine companies of the Twenty-Ninth Regiment were particularly impressive with their Afro-Caribbean drummers decked out in yellow coats with red facings and lapels.[2] Two more regiments arrived in November. Boston became an occupied town, and a fragile standoff began.

Despite the public turmoil about the town, William had thrived at Boston Latin School. When the British troops marched up the Long Wharf, fifteen-year-old William was enrolled in Harvard College in Cambridge—the first in his father's family to attend college.[3] Scholarships were available at Harvard to help with the £50 annual tuition, reducing the amount William's parents paid to about £20 each year. On familiar ground, William happily knew the village as his birthplace and the home of his maternal relatives.

Along with studies in science, math, and rhetoric, the young men of Harvard followed the political debates concerning British taxation and the military presence in Boston even as they were translating Cicero and learning about the discovery of electricity. The senior class's decision to quit drinking tea in opposition to England's taxes impressed William and his fellow freshmen. Many of the most prominent agitators for political resistance—men such as James Otis Jr., Samuel Adams, John Adams, and Joseph Warren—were Harvard graduates, confirming the general belief that Harvard was a breeding ground for rebels.

In Boston, arriving soldiers set up their tents on the Common, an open meadow extending to the Charles River on the southwest side of town. One regiment filled parts of Faneuil Hall and the Town House, and a detachment with the artillery train from the Fifty-Ninth Regiment found housing in buildings on Griffin's Wharf in the South End. It seemed that redcoats were everywhere. Army sergeants drilled their men as often as possible in the open space of Brattle Square in front of the Eustis family's church.

One man in three was now a British soldier. Soldiers were stationed at the fortified guardhouse where Boston Neck connected to the mainland, and sentries were posted around the town, often standing silently in front of houses commandeered as residences for officers. For some it worked out. Well-connected Tory merchants won contracts to supply food and fuel to the British regulars, but working-class Bostonians faced competition for jobs from off-duty troops. Civilians and soldiers clashed frequently as each group tried to follow its own traditional way of life. Brawls broke out in taverns and on street corners. Frequently harassed, women dared not walk alone.

An immediate issue for Bostonians was how to remove this occupying force. The larger issue was the colony's place within the empire. For seventeen months, the troops and residents of Boston lived together in a strained truce until the events of March 5, 1770.

2

Fire and Ice

Shaken by Boston's ill-tempered resistance to sensible British rule, Royal Governor Sir Francis Bernard moved the Great and General Court from Boston to Harvard Hall, the newest of the five Harvard buildings, away from the military presence and unruly mobs. Despite being moved from its offices and records, the General Court refused to give up its function. And the populace still came to register petitions and voice grievances, and Harvard students became fascinated spectators. Rebellious ideas that arose in Boston spread across the river into Cambridge.

On March 6, 1770, William's second year at Harvard, students heard what had happened over in Boston the day before, during an ugly confrontation between residents and redcoats. The town was locked in winter with about a foot of snow on the ground and ice clogging its harbor. Shipping and its accompanying activities were shut down, and unemployed dock workers and restless laborers had nothing to do. After being chased away from the Custom House, a mob of men and boys returned to taunt posted sentry Private Hugh White. They threw snowballs, chunks of ice, and rocks.[1]

White called for reinforcements, and six armed grenadiers from the Twenty-Ninth Regiment surged out of the guardhouse to line up beside him. The air filled with shouting and confusion—and then musket fire. It is still unclear what prompted the general firing—the snow and ice chunks thrown by the mob or several irritated soldiers reaching a breaking point. Three men were killed. Two more lay dying on the packed snow. Six others were wounded. Someone ran to get Dr. Joseph Warren.

Ten days after what rebels were calling the "Boston Massacre," the General Court convened in Harvard Hall where James Otis Jr., another graduate of that college of liberal agitators, addressed the House of Representatives. Groups of students, including William Eustis, hung on every word. Though mentally unstable, Otis was respected because of his thriving law practice. Addressing the legislators, he spoke eloquently of the tragedy and indignity of the event and the government's relocation to Cambridge. He raged about the patriotic legislature facing unconscionable military force, the oppression of their rights as Englishmen, and misrepresentation by treacherous individuals.

Enthralled students heard that, "their country might one day look to them for support, and they should recollect that the first and noblest of all duties was to serve that country, and if necessary, to devote their lives in her cause. *Dulce et decorum est pro patria mori* [It is sweet and fitting to die for your country]."[2] The young men took to heart this and similar calls to action.

The college's Speaking Club and the Mercurial Club organized debates. Selected topics during Eustis's junior and senior years included Shakespeare's plays and passages from popular eighteenth-century British poet Alexander Pope as well as "The Pernicious Practice of Drinking Tea" and "Oppression and Tyranny." Whether debating *Hamlet* or boycotting tea, students practiced the rhetorical skills they witnessed in Harvard Hall.

William, nearly seventeen, ardently believed in Otis's patriotic call to arms. He was elected captain, the leader of the sixty-member

Marti-Mercurian Company, the student militia company appropriately named for Mars, the Roman god of war, and Mercury, the gods' wing-footed messenger. They drilled in sharp-looking uniforms of long blue coats faced in white, britches made of light-colored nankeen cotton, white stockings, and black gaiters.

By April 1771, their military training gained the attention of the House of Representatives which asked newly appointed Royal Governor Thomas Hutchinson to set aside one hundred firearms for the Harvard students' military training.[3] After each of their drill sessions, the young men would relax and pass around three or four "buckets of rum toddy." It was their time to share dreams and argue about fighting against tyranny and saving the country while drinking rum rather than tea.

Women supported the movement by drafting a pledge to abstain from drinking tea. Ultimately, more than five hundred Boston women endorsed the boycott and turned to herbal substitutes.[4] Shops that catered to a Whig, or "patriotic," clientele sold tea substitutes; those catering to Tories carried imported tea.

The period from mid-1770 into 1773 seemed remarkably calm in Boston. Governor Hutchinson had performed well after the massacre, and most everyone decided to give him the benefit of the doubt.[5] He was, after all, a native-born Bostonian. The economy had improved, and there were no perceived impositions from Parliament. Despite this veneer of peace, the spirit of revolution had hardly gone underground. The colony vigorously held to its policy of not importing British tea, and Harvard students drilled and drank rum or cider.

Besides the various distractions of their club activities and meetings of the General Court, the students attended to their classes. William read Cicero and Tacitus in Latin and Plato and Thucydides in Greek. Studying the classics, especially the Roman and Greek governments, made students more effective participants in the politics of the day and "promoted development of a character appropriate to a republican."[6]

William roomed with John Eliot, who became a well-known minister like his father, on the top floor of Massachusetts Hall, the oldest of the Harvard buildings. The entire college dined together at Commons, an abundant amount of hard cider provided with their meals. Each student brought a knife and fork which could be wiped clean on the tablecloth after dinner.

William became fast friends with John "Jack" Warren, the youngest brother of Dr. Joseph Warren, and Sam Adams Jr., the son of Samuel Adams, a Eustis neighbor in the North End.

Students had four vacations during the academic year: one week in the summer after commencement; two weeks at the end of October; five weeks from mid-January through February; and two weeks at the end of April. They were meant to go home during the spring and fall to collect a change of wardrobe suitable for the coming season—clothing that their mothers, sisters, and aunts had been sewing for them during the previous months.

Warm weather arrived in Cambridge by the end of the school year and in time for another legendary Harvard commencement. It was a fair, a festival, and a carnival combined into an exciting week that ended with graduation. These mythic commencements were known throughout the area and brought money as well as excitement to the town. When the tents started going up north of the college grounds, students, men, and boys walked over to watch.

The tents, old sails on wooden frameworks, had floors of straw and booths for vendors. There were rustic tables with pine board seats, counters for wondrous arrays of liquors, and a dance floor. Cambridge allotted better booth spaces in the prime locations on the more central Common for a fee. Musical performances were held on stages set up all over the town. Crowds of people walked or rode from surrounding towns throughout the week to be entertained. Commencement brought out "all the cheap-jacks, Indian medicine men, acrobats and public entertainers."[7]

There was some trepidation by the Harvard administration about potential turmoil during William Eustis's graduation week in 1772, not because of excessive drinking but rather due to political tensions and the students' liberal tendencies.

Differing opinions about Royal Governor Thomas Hutchinson had nearly provoked a riot the year before. Writing his history of the Massachusetts Bay Colony, Hutchinson tried to make sense of the developing events: "Americans were convinced in their own minds that they were very miserable – and those who think so are so. There is nothing so easy as to persuade people that they are badly governed. Take happy and comfortable people and talk to them with the art of the Evil One and they can soon be made discontented with their government, their rulers, with everything around them, and even themselves."[8]

The climax of the week-long festival was Commencement Day itself. William Eustis and his classmates walked silently through the heart of Cambridge with only the summons of the bell in the meeting house breaking the solemnity of the procession. The students were dressed in their best clothes: brand new coats, silk stockings, and silver-buckled shoes. Bareheaded, they all marched into the meeting house. The faculty, tutors, President Samuel Locke and his council, called Fellows, were followed by the royal governor. The gold-laced hats and red coats of the governor's uniformed escort stood out among the somber academic robes.

Some students represented the wealthiest families in Boston. Others like William Eustis's parents were from the "middling sort"—shopkeepers, farmers, and artisans able to make enough extra money to send one or maybe two sons to the college. Harvard had a "gradation" system that ranked students according to their family's social and economic standing, not on academics. They slept, sat, ate, and marched in order of this family ranking.[9] The son of a Massachusetts governor would march and sit at the head of his class. Next, respectively, were the sons of former governors, trustees, major landowners, contributors, and clergymen. Eustis was ranked thirty-sixth among the fifty graduates. Sons of farmers came last. Because of his family's limited finances, Sam Adams Jr. had to work to help pay his way through Harvard and marched last in his class of 1770. Growing republican thinking led to Harvard dropping the "gradation" system in 1773.

The graduates' families crowded into every seat in the meeting house. Those unable to find a place or denied entrance by the constable returned to Cambridge Common. President Locke occupied the pulpit, and Governor Hutchinson sat just in front in a large three-legged armchair used for all graduations. Much of the ceremony was conducted in Latin, and William had a role in a Greek dialogue. The graduates then ascended the stage in groups of four to receive their diplomas before a presidential prayer and benediction concluded the ceremony.

College bells rang out calling all graduates and guests to dinner in Harvard Hall. At day's end, the festivities culminated with wealthy merchant Ralph Inman's party for hundreds of guests in honor of his graduating son George at his mansion near today's Inman Square. Patriots and loyalists danced in lines together at the lavish entertainment.

William Eustis marched out the doors into the rest of his life.

* * *

During an impressionable nineteen years, he had heard patriotic debates and discussions about the Massachusetts colony's future that urged devotion to country. He had led his classmates in military drills in Harvard Yard. Although this "swagger company"[10] never fought together as a unit, many members went on to serve in the Continental Army.

William considered his options. There were four professions: law, theology, teaching, or perhaps medicine. He was not called to the ministry, as were his uncles, or attracted by the study of law. In the province of educated men, surgery was considered more of a

11

trade than a profession, and frequently a secondary occupation. However, he had a curiosity about the mysteries of the human body and all the ills and accidents that men, women, and children encountered.

William admired Dr. Joseph Warren and had duplicated his path through Harvard, joining the Marti-Mercurian Company and living in Massachusetts Hall. The charismatic doctor encouraged curious students' interest in the advances of medicine as well as their patriotic fervor. While a student, and with an interest in the forbidden subject of anatomy, William had joined his friends Jack Warren and Sam Adams Jr in secret meetings of the Anatomical Society, known to the "brothers" as the Spunker Club. Secrecy was required not for fraternal fun but because the members examined stolen corpses.

Hoping for an apprenticeship, William applied to study medicine with Dr. Warren.

3

Grave Issues

In 1770, about thirty-five hundred doctors were practicing throughout the colonies—and fewer than three hundred of them had university medical degrees. There were hundreds of self-declared practitioners in towns and villages who, though not graduates of a medical school, provided the bulk of care. Basic literacy seemed to be the primary qualification for a physician. Ministers often served as doctors for their communities where a healer's prayers could be as effective, if not more so, than his medical efforts.

Most students could not afford to study at the great medical institutions of Europe. Young men from the southern plantations had a better chance of being sent to England for their education than their counterparts in the north. Southern physicians frequently had studied the latest medical theories in Europe but often had not actually seen or treated a patient. The northern colonies provided apprentice-style training based in hands-on experience. Unlike in Europe, a doctor in America did everything: surgery, diagnosis of diseases, and compounding of medicines, although midwives generally handled childbirth. European universities trained their students for separate and distinct occupations: surgeons, physicians, and apothecaries.

Neither study in Europe nor attendance at Benjamin Franklin's recently founded medical school in Philadelphia was an option for William Eustis. His friend Jack Warren was already serving his first year as an apprentice to his brother, Dr. Joseph Warren. To William's delight, Warren accepted him as a student. William would overlap Jack for a year of their studies. He would be moving from the small intellectual enclave of Harvard College into the dynamic and disorderly town of Boston.

Medicine was not a very remunerative occupation and, in the colonies, was barely considered a profession. People generally felt there might be more danger from the doctors than from the disease, instead treating themselves or consulting with an herbalist. Many doctors had other careers such as the ministry, law, or politics and managed a home farm for their family's basic livelihood.

Surgery, like dentistry, was originally considered too mechanical to be true medicine, and anyone limiting their practice to just surgery or just midwifery would not be considered a real doctor.[1] Some medical practitioners emphasized a particular skill without limiting themselves. A few found they had an aversion to surgery, while others had a knack for the art of the scalpel. Those with obstetrics as a side specialty, like Dr. Warren, were considered regular doctors with a "he-midwife" sideline. Just about anyone could claim to be a doctor—except, of course, women. Although some women were sufficiently literate, the trade was considered unsuitable for women because it was believed to be dangerous to their brains and childbearing. But they could be midwives.

Dr. Joseph Warren had married eighteen-year-old Elizabeth Hooton, described in the newspapers at the time of their wedding as being beautiful and the heiress to a considerable fortune. Actively working with Samuel Adams, Warren became a leading member of the Sons of Liberty and one of the protest movement's chief propagandists.

Well-educated and urbane, the doctor was an excellent. though flowery, orator and a skilled. though bombastic, writer. He penned vicious attacks against the royal governor and passionate treatises about Parliament's various impositions. In 1769, Boston selectmen appointed Warren as physician for its eight-bed almshouse, or poorhouse, that cared for the indigent and insane. This was the nearest thing Boston had to a hospital, and it offered a range of experience for Warren's four, Harvard-educated apprentices. They included Samuel Adams Jr. and David Townsend in 1770, Warren's younger brother Jack a year later, and William Eustis in 1772.

Serving as an apprentice usually meant moving into the master's household—living, eating, and breathing the profession. William transferred his few belongings into the Warren home, a large brick house the doctor rented in the North End at the corner of Wings Lane and Hanover Street where he lived with his wife Elizabeth, and their young children, Joseph "Josey," Richard "Dick," Elizabeth "Betsey," and baby Mary, called Polly. Reflecting his position, Warren's house was elegantly furnished in the latest styles including expensive carpeting. He also had a bright red carriage that was instantly recognized throughout the town.

Just living with Warren would be an education. Everything, from unexpected injuries to long-term illnesses, arrived at Dr. Warren's doorstep. Studying the medical books in Warren's library provided the foundation for the practical experience of making house calls. The surgery contained medicinal ingredients, healing herbs, mixing apparatus, bottles, and surgical equipment. William learned to mix medicinal potions, lotions, and salves to keep the doctor well supplied.

Calomel was one of the most frequently used drugs. It was prescribed for a variety of complaints including teething or "difficult dentition." Teething was thought to be a source of many ailments and a cause of infant death. In fact, calomel, a mercury derivative, was itself a poison. Other imported remedies such as Peruvian bark, a liquid decoction, arrived in Boston from Peru in demijohns, large

15

green glass bottles protected by wooden frames. The bark made into a tea served as a common remedy for aches and pains, being similar to today's aspirin.

Boston was small enough for William to walk to the homes of patients, or they could walk to the Warren surgery. He attended the doctor in his surgery and learned to set broken limbs, treat wounds, and dispense drugs. Hovering at Warren's elbow, he was exposed to a cross section of patients from Boston's social strata, from sailors and common folk to government officials, merchants, and the wealthiest man in the town—John Hancock—to whom he was distantly related through his mother.

A distinguished-looking, slender man, Hancock had inherited his fortune from his uncle. Somewhat arrogant, accustomed to luxury, and a member of Boston's elite by virtue of his wealth, Hancock employed nearly a thousand town residents in his many businesses. He lived on the edge of the Common near the top of Beacon Hill in one of Boston's grandest, three-story houses. Conversations during these and other private consultations were informative for medical purposes and might include the revolutionary ideas and activities in the town.

Interested in preventive care, Dr. Warren discussed his ideas with Eustis, advocating for the nearly month-long process of inoculation against the often-lethal smallpox.[2] Several weeks of isolation followed the procedure while the new patient hopefully recovered and gained immunity from a presumably milder case of smallpox.

Tragedy struck during the first year of Eustis's apprenticeship when a severe epidemic of influenza swept through Boston. Apprentices and doctor worked tirelessly, hurrying to make calls throughout the town. Then Warren's wife Elizabeth, twenty-six, succumbed to the illness and died on April 27, 1773, leaving him with four young children. On Monday, May 3, 1773, the *Boston Gazette and Country Journal* printed a brief notice of her death followed by a eulogy written by her devastated husband.

Death and sorrow crept indiscriminately through the narrow streets, bringing despair to many Boston families. Paul Revere's wife, still weak from the birth of her eighth child, also died during the epidemic. The announcement of Sarah Revere's death appeared in the *Gazette* just below the notice of Elizabeth Warren's burial. While Dr. Warren attended to family affairs and the burial of his wife, Dr. John Jefferies stepped in to cover his practice and supervise his two apprentices.

With the children gone to their grandmother, the Warren home became bachelor quarters occupied by the doctor, Jack Warren, and William Eustis. There were several servants and one slave connected to the household, conveniently located just two blocks from the Green Dragon Tavern, the site of frequent second-floor meetings of the Sons of Liberty. Dr. Warren, still regularly seeing patients, plunged into these North End meetings and Lodge activities to assuage his grief over the loss of his wife, and Eustis remained busy learning the art and craft of medicine. Jack, meanwhile, planned to move to Salem in another six months, after completing his apprenticeship, to study surgery with Dr. Edward Holyoke.

Eustis learned how to extract teeth and set broken bones and amputate limbs when all else failed and gangrene might set in. He could ease pain with drops of laudanum, an opium extract, or tankards of rum or brandy. He learned to bleed a patient to balance the four *humours* in the body.[3] Since the time of the Greeks, medicine had developed no better theory than bringing the body back into balance to cure disease [dis-ease] through bleeding. Leeches could be used, particularly with children, or the doctor opened a vein in the arm with a special lancet and caught the blood in a small porringer. Bleeding was the common solution to aid recovery from illness to wounds and everything else. Sailors who crossed the equator were bled to offset any possible imbalance.

Anatomical charts or drawings helped in their studies, but Eustis and his fellow apprentices yearned for the rare chance to examine actual human bodies. Far scarcer than books were opportunities for postmortem examinations. Physicians in large towns might occasionally examine the body of a criminal or a suicide, but in New England there were strong legal and public objections to the process, religious outcries being foremost in prohibiting the practice.[4] One did not want God to have to work too hard to reassemble bodies on Resurrection Day. Despite this, as a former member of Harvard's secret Spunker Club, Eustis continued to pursue his interest at every opportunity.[5]

If the occasion arose, Eustis and his fellow apprentices went out to snatch bodies. Rather than exhume members of the community, they targeted recently hanged criminals, attempting to acquire the body sometime before or during its transportation to the burial site or immediately after it was buried. Generally, the disappearance of a criminal's corpse brought less public outcry. Yet, deceased criminals could have family or friends equally determined to keep the body away from the anatomists, as happened late one November night in 1773.

Friends, including Rev. Samuel Stillman of the Brattle Street Church, swore to save Levi Ames's body, hanged for robbery, from dissection. With their own gang of men, they intercepted the sheriff's party transporting Ames's body away from the gallows located just outside the town gates. After dark, hoping to acquire this body, William Eustis and his fellow apprentices had hurried to Boston Neck. Hours later and back home, he sat down to write about his adventure to Jack Warren, now in Salem with Dr. Holyoke.

"Dear Brother,

This may serve to inform you, that as soon as the body of Levi Ames was pronounced dead by Dr. Jeffries, it was delivered by the Sheriff to a person who carried it in a cart to the water side, where it was received into a boat filled with about twelve of Stillman's crew, who rowed over to Dorchester Point."

The apprentices followed, hoping to keep track of the body and discover where Ames would be buried. But they ran into difficulties, as described by Eustis:

"When we saw the boat land at Dorchester Point, we had a consultation, and Norwood, David, one Allen and myself took a chaise and rode around to the Point, Spunkers like, but the many obstacles we had to encounter made it eleven o'clock before we reached the Point, where we searched and searched and rid, hunted and waded; but alas, in vain! There was no corpse to be found . . . Discontented, we sat us down on the beach and groaned, &c., &c . . ..

P.S. By the way, we have since heard that Stillman's gang rowed him back from the Point up to the town, and after laying him out in mode and figure, buried him – God knows where!"[6]

4

Rally, Mohawks!

Samuel Adams would be a constant figure in William Eustis's life. Looking older than his years, Adams enjoyed singing various ballads at the nearby Green Dragon Tavern.[1] As a visionary, he saw Boston, and the rest of the colonies, as the victim of an evil plot by the British government to enslave America, drain its bounty, and enable England to sustain its lifestyle of heedless luxury and corruption.

A fervid believer in the fight for American freedom, Adams led the Sons of Liberty, their members comprising a mix of merchants, artisans, and shopkeepers. The Sons joined the nonvoting common folk in the demonstrations, processions, and mob protests that were a way of life in Boston. When circumstances adversely affected their lives, they held rallies, marched through the streets, tore down bawdy houses, and kept people with smallpox from entering their town. Not to be outdone, a supporting group of women formed the Daughters of Liberty in 1771 and attended all the men's rallies.

The Sons, with members spread throughout the town and across class boundaries, did not hesitate to take on prominent Tories including Governor Hutchinson. He had made the mistake of justifying poverty as a way of producing industry and frugality. The poor gathered in port towns such as Boston where they could get odd jobs around the docks or work on various ships. However, some of the Sons of Liberty, including John Hancock, were as wealthy as the Tory merchants. Like Samuel Adams, Hancock also resented Parliament's abuse of power in the colonies.

Dr. Joseph Warren worked with Adams. His increasing involvement in the protest activities often meant that Eustis had to keep the doctor's surgery open. He remained behind when Jack Warren moved to Salem to further study surgery with another doctor. If Warren was away, Eustis could call on Dr. John Jefferies and two former Warren apprentices, David Townsend and Sam Adams Jr.

That November, following the young men's unsuccessful search for Levi Ames's body, three ships carrying more than three hundred chests of East India Company tea (worth about $1.7 million today) sailed into Boston Harbor. The first to dock at Griffin's Wharf on the South End was the whaling ship *Dartmouth*. Her owner, Francis Rotch of New Bedford, urged unloading the chests of tea quickly because he had a shipment of whale oil ready for England. On December 2, the ship *Eleanor* docked with another hundred chests of tea. The whaling ship *Beaver* waited in the harbor, quarantined with smallpox aboard.

It seemed a simple business of unloading tea—trade as usual. Parliament, however, had changed the rules. Six months earlier, as Dr. Warren and Eustis were fighting the influenza epidemic, the British passed the Tea Act. Prior to this, tea had to pass through an English port where import duties were paid before being shipped to America. Parliament removed the duties in England, making British tea cheaper in the colonies and more appealing than the routinely smuggled Dutch tea. The Tea Act stipulated that, while duty-free in England, tea would carry a three-penny tax as an import to the recalcitrant colonies. By exerting its authority, Parliament planned to reduce its military defense debt, and the East India Company would reduce its warehouse inventory of seventeen million pounds of tea.

Tea, and later the three ships at Griffin's Wharf, became the symbol of colonial resentment with the mother country and actually helped to unite the opposition to British policy. Resistance to the tax fit nicely with lower-class resentments and transcended class structures. Although ordinary people did not pay taxes or drink tea—preferring rum, beer, or cider—they protested tea imports as a symbol of Parliament's arrogance, its persecution, and its intrusive military presence in the colonies. They started brewing other beverages made from herbs or coffee beans.

By December, the tea ships had been in port for more than a month. Bostonians, encouraged by the Sons of Liberty, insisted the tea be sent somewhere, anywhere, else and not offloaded. Dr. Warren held daily conferences with Samuel Adams while Eustis oversaw the surgery. All sought a reasonable resolution to the stalemate, but Hutchinson held his ground, insisting the tea must be unloaded and the tax paid before any ship could leave.

Everything came to a head on a clear moonlit evening in mid-December. Dr. Warren and his apprentice joined nearly two thousand others at the Old South Meeting House, the largest brick venue for meetings in town with its enormous clock and weathervane, to hear the governor's final resolution. Would he release the ships docked at Griffin's Wharf? Finally, his directive arrived restating that the tea must be unloaded and that no ship with a cargo of tea could set sail. In a previously arranged signal, Samuel Adams, who privately wondered if cheap tea really could compromise patriotism, stepped to the podium and said: "This meeting can do nothing more to save the country."[2] With those words, Boston's teapot boiled over.

Within twenty minutes, a mob of young men, mainly working-class apprentices and journeymen, wearing shabby clothes covered in dirt, feathers, and odd disguises, appeared outside the meetinghouse. With loud war whoops, they headed down Milk Street toward Griffin's Wharf. Samuel Adams, Dr. Warren, and other speakers remained behind. Only after the huge gathering had dissipated did the leading patriots stroll down to the wharf. The self-designated "Indians" were hard at work in an amazingly organized manner. Carefully avoiding any damage to the ships or crews, they dumped three hundred forty-two chests of tea into Boston Harbor. By morning, the tides and men in small boats had dispersed the tea around the harbor and its guardian islands.

Clearly, contingency plans had been arranged ahead of time. Neither Dr. Warren's nor Willian Eustis's name appears on any of the participant lists that exist today—yet Dr. Warren attended all the planning meetings. It would befit youthful Eustis's personality to at least be on the pier among the crowd of about a thousand people. His friend, Sam Adams Jr., surely was involved. There exists no completely accurate list of everyone who threw the tea into the harbor. Residents remained surprisingly silent. Boston was not the only American town to refuse tea, nor was it the most violent, but its example created a precedent for other colonies. In the days that followed, there was general good cheer throughout the town, contrasting with the anxious weeks leading up to what was called the "destruction of the tea." Paul Revere immediately set off on a ten-day, roundtrip ride to carry the news to New York and Philadelphia.

Winter yielded to an early spring. Trees budded, and residents were hopeful. The indefatigable Dr. Joseph Warren saw up to twenty patients a day. Eustis, now completing his last year as an apprentice, gained confidence in his own abilities. By taking on extra help, Warren was able to see more patients, and his account book entries reveal the different handwriting of several persons keeping the records. His surgery had an open door; it could be that some of the patients were also informants. In the doctor's logbook, one female patient is listed as "Camp Woman."[3] Was she an American spy, a British laundress, or just anonymous?

King George continued to underestimate the extent of resentment in the colony. His response arrived in mid-May. The British sloop of war *Lively* approached Boston Harbor carrying a new royal governor. Lieutenant General Thomas Gage had been commander-in-chief of the military forces in North America and as such had spent nearly ten years in New York. After receiving news of the Boston mob's action, King George summoned Gage from his family estate outside London and directed him to take this new posting. Along with being the king's governor in Boston, Gage was again given command of the British army in North America. He was careful, sensible, in his mid-fifties, and the perfect man to replace Hutchinson, who left for England. Having married Margaret Kemble of New Jersey, Gage knew the country well and understood the political situation better than anyone in England.

The nearby Warren surgery received news of Governor Gage's arrival. He officially entered Boston in a carriage he brought with him on the *Lively,* and after presenting his paperwork to the town council, he appeared on the balcony of the Town House to greet the residents. Eustis, often about the streets for Dr. Warren, could take a minute or two to join the vast crowd assembled to hear the governor read his proclamation. They gave him three rousing cheers. The people had not liked Hutchinson, had hoped for his recall, and were willing to give this new governor a chance.

The honeymoon ended barely two weeks after Gage's arrival. On June 1, 1774, the first of the Coercive Acts, the Boston Port Act, closed the harbor. Neither ships nor produce were permitted in or out. The bells of seventeen churches tolled as townspeople walked the streets in mourning attire. And if Warren, Eustis, or anyone else thought June 1 was a bad day, they soon found out that June 2 was worse. It was then that the town learned the full extent of its punishment. Not only was the town sealed off from commercial activity, but more regiments, a total of four thousand British soldiers, were on their way. On June 14, the Fourth Regiment disembarked at Long Wharf, marched up King Street, and pitched their tents on Boston Common. The Forty-Third Regiment arrived the next day. With unpleasant similarities to 1770, the Common became a barracks and training ground swarming with redcoats.

The port closed, coastal vessels carrying fuel, forage, and supplies for Boston had to check in first at Marblehead. Salem became the new seat of government, and the custom house moved to Plymouth. Bostonian life and its surroundings would remain this way until the people of Massachusetts repented and reimbursed the East India Company for the tea they destroyed. Parliament intended this massive show of strength to quell any ideas of rebellion.

Bostonians huddled in their favorite of ninety smoky taverns and talked it over. No single controlling figure existed in the town's revolutionary movement. Instead, there were seven loosely allied groups totaling more than two hundred fifty people, according to surviving lists. Membership in the individual groups was diverse, with only Paul Revere and Joseph Warren participating in five of the seven.[4]

Amid this growing resentment, Eustis approached the end of his apprenticeship with Dr. Warren. He had to decide whether to continue working with the busy doctor, join Jack Warren in Salem, or hang out his own shingle in a village farther to the west.

5

Oppose, Oppose...

British actions were creating individuals who thought differently. General Gage's strict enforcement of the Coercive Acts became the catalyst for fundamental changes in how loyal, though sometimes complaining, these British subjects were. They began to feel separate from that distant motherland—more like *Americans*. It was the *people* who decided to take up arms, and as such they were as responsible, if not more, for developments as were the more famous individuals celebrated today. The severity of Boston's punishment ended any doubts that the other colonies may have had about their relationship with the mother country. What happened to Boston could happen to them.

After the British closed the port, Gage relocated the colony's insubordinate General Court again, from Cambridge to Salem, and moved from Boston to Danvers. Other towns and colonies began to send supplies to Boston. Eleven carts of fish came from Marblehead. Two shipments of rice arrived from Charleston, South Carolina. A thousand bushels of grain were sent from Wethersfield, Connecticut.

The legendary Israel Putnam from Connecticut drove one hundred thirty sheep into town. While in Boston, the incorrigible Putnam stayed with Dr. Warren and William Eustis. A Massachusetts native, known as

"Old Put" by his men, the white-haired Putnam, fifty-seven, had fought in the French and Indian War with the famed Rogers' Rangers and had tales to tell during the long evening around the fire.

In June, Boston officials called for an unofficial, and illegal, town meeting at Faneuil Hall. The Crown's representatives were out of town, meeting in Salem. Before adjourning, the meeting issued a call to form its own Massachusetts Provincial Congress.

At the same time in Salem, meeting behind locked doors, the House of Representatives appointed delegates to attend the First Continental Congress in Philadelphia. Gage heard that something was afoot and dispatched his provincial secretary, Thomas Flucker, with a proclamation to dissolve the legislature. Flucker arrived too late, beating on the secured door as the final vote was called. Gage officially disbanded the legislature, but the congressional delegates had been approved.

And in Boston that summer evening, Dr. Joseph Warren held a candle-lit gathering at his home celebrating their coup of getting the delegation approved. Samuel Adams reported on the details, and Eustis listened to the swirl of debate and conversation. It is likely that Mercy Scollay, a Daughter of Liberty and daughter of John Scollay, chairman of the Boston selectmen, was there. By the summer of 1774, town gossips surmised that Mercy and widower Joseph Warren were the new couple to watch. Mercy Scollay, thirty-three and the same age as Warren, was considered old for a single woman but admired as "a woman of great energy and depth of character."[1]

August came around, and when the delegates left Boston, there was no slinking out of town. If they could have flown flags of defiance, they would have. In full view of British troops, Samuel Adams, his cousin John Adams, Robert Treat Paine, and Thomas Cushing boldly left in a yellow coach pulled by four horses with six liveried attendants—two white servants in front, two Black outriders, and two Black footmen in back. Massachusetts made sure it would be represented in style in this assembly of strangers from

27

the other colonies. Samuel Adams, with no money for stylish clothes, had been newly outfitted to be a proper representative.[2] Dr. Warren, for his part, saw them off from Coolidge Tavern in Watertown. With Samuel Adams away, he would have sole charge of the colony's resistance.

The First Continental Congress convened in Philadelphia.[3] Without the earlier communications among the colonies, it would have been nearly impossible to bring everyone together. Most of the anxious delegates had never left their hometowns or colonies, and they were initially nervous about traveling to the faraway territory of Pennsylvania.

An assortment of crowds, committees, conventions, and congresses—all rooted in the collective will of the majority—replaced British authority in villages throughout Massachusetts. By late summer, with their reverence for local government, rural folk had, in effect, forcibly overthrown the established government of Great Britain. By the end of the year, only Suffolk County remained under British rule. General Gage realized the full extent of his problem, and in Philadelphia, delegates to the First Continental Congress began to realize theirs.

The Congress had to convince Massachusetts that it would be supported without encouraging other colonies to take similar action. Delegates hoped to persuade Parliament that the colonies sincerely desired to remain part of Great Britain, but on their terms. Delegates, with plans to meet again, headed for their homes at the end of October.

William Eustis came to the end of his last year of study—an apprenticeship that increasingly became learning by doing. Meanwhile, Dr. Warren, the patriots' person-in-charge, had to find the time to coach his student, continue with his medical practice, and promote ideas of freedom. It became mutually beneficial for Eustis to continue with him as an assistant. He was committed to the same cause, and Warren would need ongoing support to meet all of his commitments.

With Eustis's decision to serve as his associate, Warren accepted the Boston town meeting's challenge to write a document outlining its position as a provincial representative body. After three days of writing, ducking in and out of his office to consult, Warren hurried to Milton to introduce his Suffolk Resolves. On approval, the Resolves were carried to the Congress in Philadelphia by the hard-riding Paul Revere.

Soon there would be two governments in Massachusetts: one approved by Parliament and headed by General Gage; and the new Provincial Congress headed by John Hancock and made up of the dissolved Massachusetts General Court. The first item of business was to form four committees: Correspondence, Safety, Donations, and Supplies. Dr. Warren served on all four and was president *pro tempore* whenever Hancock was absent.

Gage left Salem, moved back to Boston and Province House with its royal coat of arms over the door and an eight-sided cupola topped by a weathervane of an Indian in a war bonnet drawing a bow. He began preparing the city for a siege, strengthening the fortifications at Boston Neck with a moat, a new blockhouse, and a dozen more cannons positioned at the town gates. The Fifty-Ninth Regiment entrenched itself on either side of the Neck, forming a gauntlet for all traffic in and out of town. Gage said he was protecting His Majesty's subjects. Although the town's port remained closed, British supply ships could come and go at will. Alarmed residents thought Gage might also prevent farmers from bringing much needed produce overland into the town. In actuality, he prepared for the day when he would have to defend and hold the town for the Crown.

Eustis watched wary Bostonians prepare as well, securing muskets from the waning stockpiles of town merchants. Military stores were socked away, and Dr. Warren ordered fifteen chests stocked with medicines to be distributed in surrounding towns. To be more effective, they needed cannon—so they stole two five-hundred-pound artillery pieces that were stored in a newly-built guardhouse on the edge of Boston Common. Bringing this episode right into the doctor's surgery was William Dawes, thirty, a North End tanner and sometime express rider. He had helped several friends carry both cannon away and hide them in a wood bin under the floor of John Lovell's Boston Latin School, Eustis's former school. While carrying a cannon, Dawes had one of his shirt buttons mashed deep into his wrist.[4] Unable to extract it himself, he went to Dr. Warren's office for surgical help. No questions were asked, and neither the treatment nor the visit was officially recorded. Large amounts of goods and provisions, including four brass fieldpieces, were gradually smuggled out of town to safer storage in Concord.

The nine-member Committee of Safety oversaw military matters and served as an executive committee. Three of the members were from Boston, John Hancock, Dr. Joseph Warren, and Dr. Benjamin Church. Their most immediate concern was defense, gunpowder, and muskets. They developed guidelines for mustering town militia units, declaring that at least a quarter of each militia unit should be ready at a moment's notice—thus formalizing the minutemen, who even took their muskets to church.

The weather grew colder, and wool-wrapped farmers stockpiled provisions for what might be a difficult winter. Unconcerned, British officers enjoyed the finer and warmer things in life. They were quartered in houses around Boston, some in Faneuil Hall that was available for lodging since town meetings and assemblies had been forbidden. Without barracks, ordinary soldiers were housed in tents or empty warehouses; some with wives and children camped on Boston Common.

Confrontations and street brawls became commonplace as stressed soldiers responded to taunts from out-of-work angry Bostonians. Curfews were issued and residents had to secure passes to leave the town. Personally under siege and criticized by both patriots and loyalists, Gage wrote to Lord Dartmouth that he would need twenty thousand more troops to retake New England. And Samuel Adams in Philadelphia counseled Dr. Warren to take no overt action.

Throughout the cold winter of 1774, hardships prevailed for British and colonial residents alike. The Sons of Liberty prevented merchants from selling blankets, tools, or materials of any kind to the British army. No one, not even the unemployed, would build barracks for the troops. Rum, however, was a different matter. British orders, to ease boredom and resentment, increased the allowance of rum for all soldiers to a quart a day per six men. The locals, known disparagingly as "Jonathans," enterprisingly sold rum from American distilleries cheaply to soldiers to encourage drunkenness and desertions.

Finally, the days lengthened, the snow began to melt, and the traditional anniversary of the Boston Massacre approached. Samuel Adams, who had been welcomed back from Philadelphia in November, moderated the annual gathering on March 6 at Old South Meeting House. Dr. Joseph Warren, repeating his role of three years earlier, gave the formal address. After attending to six patients, he arrived by carriage and ducked into a house across the street to change clothes.[5]

Expectant murmurings rippled through the congregation in the overcrowded meeting house. One story claims that Warren gained access to the black-draped pulpit by climbing a ladder and going through a rear window.[6] Warren, with a flair for the dramatic, gave his speech flourishing a handkerchief and wearing a toga to emphasize his references to Roman citizens and republican virtues. His costume was likely made by his friend and expert seamstress Mercy Scollay.

Samuel Adams had invited about forty British officers to sit in the front pews. When Warren finished his performance, Adams rose to thank him for his eloquence. The British officers took offense at

31

the word "massacre," calling out "Fie! Fie!" People thought there was a fire and stampeded to the doors and jumped through the open lower windows. The selectmen managed to instill calm, officers controlled their men, and the meeting broke up peacefully, everyone relieved to have avoided a riot.

6

Listen, My Children, . . .

On the nineteenth of April 1775, just before dawn, Dr. Joseph Warren awakened William Eustis and handed over the responsibility for their practice.[1] By eight o'clock, Warren had boarded the Charlestown ferry, eager to check on reports of a fight in Lexington and to meet with his Committee of Safety at the Black Horse Tavern in Menotomy [now Arlington]. Eustis knew the British intended to march to Concord and that Dr. Warren would attend his committee's meeting, but he had no idea when Warren would return or what might be happening to his own family in Lexington. Frustrated over the lack of information, he yearned for news.

Eustis and Warren were camped out in his barely furnished house at "head of Wing's Lane."[3] Warren had emptied his luxurious brick home, loaded his good furniture into carts, and sent it to his mother at the Warren family home in Roxbury. Warren's fiancé, Mercy Scollay, took his four children to live with her in Worcester.[4] Feeling responsible to his patients despite serving as a primary leader of the rebellion and sometime president of the Provincial Congress, Warren remained in Boston with his medical associate. Their surgery became a consulting room in more ways than one.

The increasing difficulty of living in British-controlled Boston had driven Eustis's family to vacate their home several months earlier and move to the safety of the countryside in the rural town of Lexington. As more and more people hurried to leave Boston, carts and wagons filled with personal effects and furniture nearly created a traffic jam getting through the town gates.

A few weeks earlier, Eustis had warned Dr. Warren about leaving the residence after he saw some British soldiers lurking on Queen Street, around the corner from the Warren home.[2] Arming himself with two pistols, Warren said that regardless, the two of them would attend a lady in Cornhill. They strode past the officers without incident and later found that the soldiers still sought clues about the whereabouts of the two cannon stolen by William Dawes several months earlier from the guardhouse on the Common.

General Thomas Gage, head of the armed forces in the colonies as well as military governor of Massachusetts Bay Colony, learned that the Massachusetts Provincial Congress had met illegally in Concord. He also heard through espionage reports from two spies who had gone as far west as Worcester that military stores and cannon were stashed in Concord.

The British ship *Falcon* arrived on April 16 with orders from Lord Dartmouth to move against the rebels and their leaders, and Gage ordered a raid against the colonials. Gunpowder was to be captured and supplies destroyed. Despite being a military secret, Gage's plan leaked out almost immediately. Townspeople watched as the usual activities of the British garrison suspiciously shifted to signs of preparation. Warren and Eustis knew that something was up.

Everyone was watching everyone else. The British watched Boston, and Boston watched the British. Town spies were about, and seamen imbibing in taverns or soldiers visiting the enterprising local whores may well have dropped clues to the plans. Sharp-eyed boys reported increased activity in the stables. Eustis lingered and listened while running errands. By late in the afternoon on April 18, a number of rumors and reports of the suspicious activities around the town had reached Warren's surgery.

British sailors brought their ships' longboats around to the edge of the Common in Back Bay, and the seventy-gun *Boyne* and sixty-two-gun *Asia,* lowered their longboats and tied them astern. The sixty-four-gun ship-of-the-line *Somerset* took up position along the ferry track between Boston and Charlestown. No water passage would be permitted after nine o'clock, and the ferry was brought alongside the *Somerset* that evening as seven hundred elite British troops, grenadiers and light infantry, assembled on the western edge of the Common.

Through his sources, Warren heard that the British aimed to capture Samuel Adams and John Hancock who were staying in Rev. Jonas Clarke's parsonage in Lexington and to confiscate the arms and cannon hidden in Concord. Acting quickly, Warren sent for William Dawes, and Paul Revere.[5] It was well after dark, about ten o'clock, when Revere arrived. Eustis kept watch as Warren told Revere that Dawes had left earlier to alert Adams and Hancock in Lexington, riding across Boston Neck before nine o'clock when the town gates closed. As a tanner and leather worker doing much of his odoriferous business in skins and leather outside of the town, Dawes frequently passed through the gates on business. The guards knew him. It seemed likely he would get through. The forty-year-old silversmith Revere, well-known to the British as a rabble rouser, would be the backup to Dawes, rowing across the harbor to Charlestown then riding to Lexington. He left as soon as sexton Robert Newman and John Pulling, each carrying flint, steel, and a lantern, started climbing up the towering steeple of Christ Church, known as Old North, to give their pre-arranged signal to lookouts in Charlestown.

Even before the boats carrying the British regulars had crossed the river, the alarm was out in the towns to the west and north of Boston. Thanks to bonfires and a musket-firing relay system

35

organized by the Committee of Safety, the news traveled rapidly throughout Massachusetts and beyond.

In the chilly dawn of Wednesday morning in the village of Lexington, under a setting full moon, a time neither light nor dark, about seventy uneasy militiamen waited on the town green with their exhausted leader Captain John Parker, forty-five and fighting tuberculosis. The distant drums of the approaching British competed with the bells ringing in the nearby wooden belfry. No one knew what to expect.

Arriving at the green, British officers rode forward waving swords and shouting for the militia to disperse. The regulars followed, their uniforms still wet after wading ashore during their earlier landing. Shots rang out. Eight Lexington men lay dead and nine more were wounded. Neither the British nor the colonists had wanted to be the first to fire. But someone had.

The dense smoke cleared. The British troops, led by Major John Pitcairn, regrouped and marched on toward Concord. The fife and drum struck up "Yankee Doodle," a tune to taunt the colonials and restore confidence in the regulars who were now in enemy territory.[6]

On that brilliant spring morning, the trees were just leafing out. Middlesex County was an area of fields and hills and, as would become evident, numerous stone walls. The British regulars experienced mounting disappointments and difficulties as the day evolved. They had not found arms or powder in Concord, but they had suffered unexpected losses during a fight at the North Bridge. They had also encountered frequent fire from colonials hiding behind the stone walls as they marched back to Lexington to meet reinforcements and then retreated to Boston.

Hundreds of colonial volunteers arrived throughout the day from neighboring towns and from as far away as Carlisle, Littleton, and Stow. Without orders, they took up positions along the road from Lexington. Later, militia units from Woburn, Billerica, and other towns joined in.

The stylish Dr. Joseph Warren and a rustic farmer from Roxbury, militia General William Heath, met that morning in Menotomy. Offering legitimacy and some measure of organization, they worked together to form a rudimentary command structure as the British continued their retreat toward Boston. They would surround the British column with a "moving circle of incessant fire."[7] Nearly four thousand militiamen, their muskets and ancient fowling pieces loaded and primed, were hidden behind trees, boulders, and walls along the road, spoiling for a fight.

William Eustis, back in Boston, knew none of this. Only bits and pieces of information dribbled into the Warren surgery. Plagued with visitors' questions, he worried about his family in Lexington. By midafternoon, hardware merchant Moses Gill pulled up in his chaise looking for information. A member of the Sons of Liberty and heading the supply committee of the Provincial Congress' Executive Council, Gill intended to drive out to investigate and asked Eustis if he wanted to come along.

Eustis then made the single most decisive move of his life. Driven by family concerns and curiosity, he grabbed his medical kit, closed the office, and hitched a ride with Gill. The town gates were open. Taking the road through Roxbury toward Cambridge, and hearing gunfire, they skirted around an ongoing battle in which British troops fought their way back to Boston, door to door, house to house in Menotomy.

Eustis got to Lexington just as the embattled British approached the Charles River. It was dusk, about seven o'clock, and the sound and smoke of the ongoing battle resounded around the hills of Boston. Townsfolk watching from rooftops feared that the fighting would carry into the town. The exhausted British column reached the defensible three hills of Charlestown and dug in on Bunker's Hill, awaiting rescue by boat that night and into the next day. Their colonial pursuers set up camp in Cambridge and, now surrounded, Boston was under siege, and the world was utterly changed.

Reaching Lexington, Eustis found his family, checked on his ailing mother, and signed the muster roll to join Captain Parker's company of militia.[8]

7

Death and Defeat

As the sun rose on the morning of April 20, 1775, Eustis, in Lexington, grew anxious about what could be happening with Dr. Warren. Having confirmed the safety of his family, he packed some bread and cheese and began walking the fifteen or so miles back toward Boston. The loamy smell and sight of plowed fields and spring grass could not offset the horrific aftermath of the battle— trees and houses damaged by weapons fire; horses, cows, and pigs dead along the road; abandoned equipment and wagons; and small clusters of people assessing their losses. Carts collected the bodies of the ninety-five American dead. Residents of Menotomy had died in their doorways, front halls, and backyards at the hands of desperate British regulars who had fought house to house through that town.

The evening before, the colonial rebels had established their base of operations in Cambridge where Dr. Warren set up a field hospital to care for the wounded in an abandoned Tory mansion on Brattle Street. Doctors from surrounding towns came as soon as they could, and the house became the provincial government's base of operations with Dr. Warren the *de facto* leader of the patriot military effort.

By the afternoon of April 20, Eustis located Dr. Warren, who designated him as a military surgeon, "observing to him that he had already seen more practice than most surgeons from the country." Now officially Dr. Eustis, William went to work in the chaotic field hospital where he "found full demand for all the surgical skill he possessed."[1]

People were on the move everywhere. Hundreds of militiamen flooded into Cambridge throughout that night and into the next day. More than a thousand came from New Hampshire. They set up their camps and built fires in the fields and woods edging the town. Circuit riders hurried to the surrounding towns with bulletins featuring Dr. Warren's most inflammatory writing, citing "barbarous murders" by the British, urging immediate enlistment, and coming to Cambridge as quickly as possible.[2] General Artemas Ward, forty-seven, from Shrewsbury, Massachusetts, a veteran of the French and Indian Wars, presided over the first council of war that night in an attempt to organize the growing army.[3] Israel Putnam arrived, this time without sheep for market but with plenty of enthusiasm.[4]

Word of the battle had spread quickly. New Londoners heard about it by the end of the day on April 20, New Yorkers knew by the evening of April 21, and Philadelphia by April 24. The news reached Georgia by the first week of May. And when a group of western frontiersmen in Kentucky heard of the battle, they marked the event by naming their outpost Lexington.

Ten days later, Dr. Eustis became the surgeon for Colonel Richard Gridley's artillery company, part of John Parker's Lexington militia. Gridley, sixty-five, was a hero of the 1745 Massachusetts siege of the Fortress of Louisburg in Nova Scotia. Eustis's brother Benjamin became an artillery officer, and his younger brother Jacob, sixteen, became an apothecary's assistant.

As weeks passed, the rebels grew more aggressive about digging in and laying siege to Boston, intent on depriving the British of supplies. Nothing crossed Boston Neck from Roxbury—no fresh meat, no vegetables, no forage made it into the town. Toward the end of May, overly confident patriots reconnoitered all of the high ground in the vicinity and recommended building a strong redoubt on Bunker's Hill above the town of Charlestown. More cautious, Warren's Committee of Safety worried about their shortage of cannon and gunpowder.

Riders carried news to the Massachusetts delegation in Philadelphia. The rebels surrounding Boston wanted the Continental Congress to take over their impromptu army. Letters back and forth among members of Congress speculated about the most appropriate leader, and fellow delegate George Washington's name came up on several lists. Although he did not seek the position, he always wore his Virginia militia uniform to congressional sessions. Seeking Virginia's commitment as a Massachusetts ally, John Adams nominated him to be commander-in-chief of this soon-to-be-called Continental Army.

In mid-May, Boston's besieging forces relaxed their vigilance. It appeared unlikely that an attack by General Gage would be forthcoming, and farmers left to plant their crops and tend their farms. With his mother dangerously ill, Eustis went back to Lexington whenever he got the chance. But despite all efforts, Elizabeth Eustis, forty-eight, died on May 30, 1775, leaving behind her husband and ten children. The devastated family buried her behind the First Parish Church at the western end of Lexington's Village Green. Elizabeth's headstone reads that she "lived desired and died lamented." Her death left Eustis without his strongest supporter. Dr. Warren could offer some solace and security but, with the demands of the army, there was not much time to grieve. Throughout the rest of his life, Eustis would carry a piece of paper in his pocket asking to be buried next to his mother.

Although dormitories at Harvard as well as other buildings were confiscated for barracks, Eustis camped with Lexington's contingent. Conditions in the surrounding camps in Cambridge and

41

Roxbury deteriorated. Wood smoke, lice, and filthy conditions prevailed. Camp hygiene was primitive at best. Typhus and dysentery spread among the men because of a shortage of latrines. Neighboring towns sent supplies of food, including rum. Meanwhile, life in besieged Boston, without countryside provisions, meat, or forage, grew bleak.

At the end of May, lookouts sent word of more sails on the horizon. Three British generals—William Howe, Henry Clinton, and John Burgoyne—sailed into Boston harbor on *Cerberus*. It seems an odd coincidence that the three generals arrived on a ship named for the three-headed dog guarding the gates of hell.[5] Their arrival with troop transports raised the total number of soldiers in Boston to about nine thousand. The generals did not like each other very much. Clinton, for example, believed he was more competent than the other two. But they allied themselves to end the annoying colonial situation. Despite mudflats, rocks, and tidal shoals limiting mobility, British warships prepared to defend Boston against incursions by revolutionaries.

It seemed obvious to the generals what had to be done. Two strategic points around Boston, Dorchester Heights and the hills of Charlestown, were unoccupied. They decided to capture Dorchester Heights first, then take the rebel fort on the hill in Roxbury, and finally move on Cambridge and Charlestown, thereby clearing the entire perimeter. Military operations would begin on June 18.

Patriot spies alerted the Committee of Safety about the developing strategy. The committee decided the only sensible thing to do was to take the high ground first. Charlestown was closest—a natural extension of the American lines. With a population of about twenty-five hundred souls, Charlestown sat on a mile-long peninsula directly north of Boston. Land access was across a short neck at its western end where it was attached to the mainland. It was somewhat like Boston with its three rolling hills. The highest and farthest west was Bunker's Hill, about one hundred ten feet above

Charlestown Neck. The center, Breed's Hill, was about forty feet lower.

Dr. Warren opposed General Putnam's plan for fortifying the hills, citing the provincials' lack of big guns or sufficient gunpowder. Putnam prevailed, and preparations got underway quickly. Colonel Gridley's artillery company had orders to accompany the men who would construct the new redoubt.

As the sun was setting on June 16, 1775, assigned companies set out from Cambridge. In overall command was Colonel William Prescott, forty-nine, a farmer from Pepperell, Massachusetts, and another veteran of the capture of the Fortress of Louisburg thirty years before. General Putnam and his Connecticut militia joined Prescott's troops. They were a rough looking group as they marched along, the men wearing whatever they had, carrying bedrolls and assorted gear. Weapons varied from French-made muskets to long-barreled fowling pieces. Some had no firearms at all, carrying hatchets or pitchforks.

Two sergeants from Prescott's regiment led the way through the moonless night carrying hooded lanterns visible only to the men behind. Gridley's company, including brothers William and Ben Eustis, and its two horse-drawn field pieces marched behind Colonel James Frye's and Colonel Ebenezer Bridge's companies. Following them were wagons carrying picks and shovels. After a while, Putnam, never one to shy away from any action, moved forward to join Prescott at the head of the column.

Eustis, with what supplies he had gathered, dropped out of the march at the Sun Tavern, between Charlestown Neck and the western side of Bunker's Hill, to set up his field hospital. His brother continued on with the artillery.

The British had thrown up an arrow-shaped wall on the first hill during their earlier retreat from Lexington. Even though Prescott had orders to stop there, the militia continued along the ridge for another half mile. The redoubt laid out by Prescott, with advice from

Richard Gridley, would be on Breed's Hill, lower than Bunker's Hill and within a half mile of the British cannon on Boston's Copp's Hill. That was not the Committee of Safety's original intent.[6] Putnam deferred to Prescott as commander of the expedition but fortified Bunker's Hill on his own early the following morning.[7]

By daybreak, the men, having worked through the night in total darkness, discovered they had gotten themselves into a jam. They were within range of the big British guns and surrounded by eight warships that were beating to quarters and preparing to fire. And their left flank needed protection. Work still had to be done as the dawn gave way to the rising sun. Up all night, the men were exhausted and running out of water.

Prescott realized he needed a great deal more help to get the defensive works finished. John Brooks of Reading was sent back to Cambridge at about nine o'clock to alert the Committee of Safety about the predicament and immediate needs. Brooks, twenty-three, would become a seven-term governor of Massachusetts, but right now he needed a horse. Walking the nearly four miles to Cambridge would take too much time. Gridley's artillery company refused Brooks' request to use one of its horses. Brooks set out on foot. Hearing of the lack of cooperation, "Old Put" leapt onto his horse and beat Brooks to Cambridge, bringing the news to Warren's headquarters at Hastings House.[8]

A debilitating migraine had kept Warren confined to his bed.[9] Warren's former apprentice, David Townsend, twenty-two, arrived from Brighton after hearing about the impending action. Townsend likely bled Warren to relieve the headache because bleeding, especially from a vein in the nose or head, was considered a remedy for migraines. Then, after drinking a cup of chamomile tea with Townsend, Warren felt somewhat better, donned fashionable clothing, and the two set out on foot.

They stopped at the improvised field hospital at the Sun Tavern where Warren found Eustis awaiting the wounded. Townsend

44

remained to help treat several injured men who were carried in. Warren borrowed a musket and, dodging broadsides from British ships, climbed to the redoubt atop Breed's Hill.[10] Warren joined the two hundred or so sweaty, filthy, and bone-tired troops, vowing to fight as a volunteer, not as an officer. A welcome regiment of reinforcements from New Hampshire arrived under Colonel John Stark and took up the vulnerable position on the northern end of the works.

With the tide in, longboats filled with redcoats glided across the harbor at two o'clock on this hot June afternoon. Set ablaze by British cannon fire, the village of Charlestown was engulfed in flames from the meetinghouse steeple to a ship being built at the shoreline. Observers packed the rooftops of Boston and the surrounding hills.[11] No one could turn away from the sight of the impending combat.

Gridley's artillery, unnerved, did not remain on the field of battle for long. To become an officer, one had only to be related to the colonel. Hence the commission of his inexperienced son, Scarborough Gridley, as a major in the unit. Hauling his two guns away from the redoubt, Major Gridley posted them near the Neck ostensibly to cover a retreat, then he deserted them altogether. Although wounded, Colonel Richard Gridley stayed with his men.

Rebels armed with rifles proved to be a huge asset. Henry Dearborn wrote: "Our men were intent on cutting down every officer . . ."[12] That prevented the British from succeeding during their first two assaults up the hill. Their officers suffered a disproportionate number of casualties, the militia knowing how effective it would be to destroy the enemy's chain of command. Every member of General Howe's staff was killed or wounded. Even the bottle of wine carried by his servant was shattered. Howe alone survived, slightly injured in his foot.

The lack of gunpowder and reinforcements ultimately led to the patriots' defeat. Out of ammunition, Prescott's men had to evacuate

45

the fort in the face of the third furious assault which dissolved into throwing stones and fighting hand-to-hand. Mortally wounded, Dr. Warren died as the Americans abandoned, and the British captured, the redoubt.[13]

There is no evidence that William Eustis ever fired a musket. He tended to the wounded behind the lines. Some musket balls could be extracted from wounded men, but if they shattered a bone, particularly in a leg or an arm, it would inevitably require rapid amputation. Bayonet wounds, because of their irregular torn edges, were even worse—almost impossible to clean and hard to stitch. Infection was all but guaranteed. Eustis, now senior surgeon in the bloody makeshift hospital, moved quickly to save as many lives as possible, assessing the damage, performing triage among the groaning and dying men.

His brother Benjamin survived, but Warren was missing. One British officer referred to the doctor as "the famous Doctor Warren, the greatest incendiary in all America."[14]

During the days following the battle, Jack Warren, coming in from Salem, attempted to find news about his missing brother. Was Joseph a prisoner, or had he been killed? Determined to find him, Jack went to the British line at Charlestown Neck. His repeated demands for information annoyed a sentry who stabbed him with a bayonet.[15]

8

His Excellency and the Yankees

William Eustis felt a tremendous personal loss over Joseph Warren's death occurring within weeks of the death of his beloved mother. He and Dr. Warren had gone through a great deal during their nearly three years together, not the least being the death of Warren's wife, Elizabeth, and the stressful beginnings of Boston's rebellion. When he thought of Warren, Eustis recollected an incident in Boston when some British officers were overheard speaking disparagingly of the New Englanders' fighting skills. He remembered Warren exclaiming: "These fellows say we won't fight. By heavens! I hope I shall die up to my knees in blood!"[2] Dr. Warren got his wish, and young Eustis continued alone in an insecure world in rebellion.

The British had resorted to mass graves on the battlefield. There seemed no other way because there were so many dead from both sides that had to be buried quickly. And there was no body and no funeral for Dr. Warren. The immediate demands for Eustis's medical skills did not allow a moment's pause. He decided to follow Warren's example, to strive to carry on his dream for liberty, and he resolved to stay with the army until the country achieved independence. Two days after the battle, he was assigned to head an

47

army hospital located in the Reverend Samuel Cooke's parsonage at Menotomy.

The British won what is now called the Battle of Bunker Hill. It was a Pyrrhic victory with more than a thousand casualties, including ninety-two officers killed. More than four hundred rebels were killed or wounded. Having held their own for a while against the British Lion before their defeat, the rebels embraced the battle as a rallying point. It boosted their spirits and increased their determination. They also learned what they needed to do: train soldiers and form a centralized command with a coordinated strategy to carry the rebellion forward. For British generals Howe, Clinton, and Burgoyne, the battle brought the difficult realization that they would not regain control of the region quite as easily as they had thought.[3] General Gage was recalled to London, and William Howe, forty-six, his bulging eyes resembling the King's, moved into Province House as the new royal governor.

Cambridge swelled into a robust camp after the battle. The constant arrival of troops from Pennsylvania, Virginia, and Connecticut reinforced the men who had fought on Breed's Hill. Ever since the Lexington skirmish and following alerts, militia units from other colonies and towns flowed into town. Harvard College relocated to Concord and away from the chaos, turning its buildings over to the army.

All of the future leaders of the Revolutionary War assembled. Many, including Henry Knox, Henry Dearborn, Aaron Burr, Benedict Arnold, Alexander Hamilton, and James Monroe, would figure prominently in William Eustis's life. He came to know almost everyone. The crowning moment was the arrival of His Excellency, General George Washington.

President of the Congress John Hancock officially announced the appointment of Washington, forty-three, as commander-in-chief of the new Continental Army. Generals Charles Lee and Philip Schuyler escorted him out of Philadelphia on June 23. They were accompanied by music and a substantial entourage of delegates from Congress and local militiamen. Washington, an excellent horseman, arrived in the Cambridge camp on a rainy Sunday, July 2.

Eustis got his first look at the new commander-in-chief on the day following his arrival when, to the cadence of fifes and drums, the general reviewed the assembled militia. For this first military review, Washington wore his new, self-designed uniform of buff vest and breeches topped with a blue coat and yellow buttons. The New England soldiers made the best impression they could—some with muskets, some with tomahawks or knives lashed to poles. Washington toured makeshift fortifications thrown up to defend against an attack by the British who could clearly be seen barely a mile away across the Charles River.

Graceful and polished, His Excellency wore his sword and silver spurs to roam around the camp. He lived initially in Harvard President Samuel Langdon's house and then moved to a larger, more elegant house vacated by Loyalist John Vassall on Brattle Street. For all the good impressions Washington may have made on the militia, he was not particularly impressed with them. The unruly New Englanders were appalling. He wrote to his cousin, Lund Washington, in August 1775: "I daresay the men would fight very well [if properly officered], although they are an exceeding dirty and nasty people."[4] They were a mob of puritanical savages that included actual Indians. They lived in hovels and, in the case of the Stockbridge Indians, in wigwams.

The idea of arming Blacks was absolute anathema to the plantation owners of the South. Unsure about keeping or dismissing Black volunteers, Washington wrote to Congress, asking if they wanted Black persons in their Continental Army. For southerners in Congress, the fear of arming slaves overshadowed the need for volunteers. They wrote that free Blacks could be retained but no more should be recruited. Slaves were altogether excluded.[5] It was several years before free and enslaved Blacks were allowed in the fight for liberty.

It also bothered Washington that officers and their men ate and lived together without any military hierarchy. Soldiers even elected their own officers. Washington wanted Congress to appoint the officers, but designating officers went against the congressional republican ideal—a romanticized ideology of the volunteer militia being superior to standing armies. Washington would have to find a way to alter each company's strong loyalty to its hometown to a loyalty to the new country.[6] Self-disciplined and correct himself, he insisted his soldiers be instilled with personal discipline including punctual attendance at daily worship. He forbade cursing and drunkenness and required neatness among enlisted men and officers. He insisted on the best possible sanitation.[7]

The living conditions fostered contagion and infestation. Basically filthy, the camp's odorous sanitary conditions consisted of open latrines that most soldiers did not bother to use. Lice were prevalent, and home remedies were shared.[8] One recommended mixing powdered delphinium seeds with mercury in hogs' fat and spreading it on a piece of wool to wear around the waist. Smoking garments hung over a fire was also suggested.

The regimental encampments included a variety of creative dwellings as individual as the men's hometowns. As the chaplain for the Concord militia, Rev. William Emerson, wrote to his wife in July 1775: "They are as different in their form as the owners are in their dress; and every tent is a portrait of the temper and taste of the persons that camp within it. Some are made of boards, some of sailcloth, and some are partly of one and partly of the other. Others are made of stone and turf, and others again of birch and other brush."[9]

By the time Washington arrived, the makeshift army had been leaderless for several weeks. The entire structure of this new Continental Army had to be invented. Soldiers who enlisted out of enthusiasm for the cause followed the New England tradition that military service was contractual. They enrolled for short terms, sometimes only weeks, and believed they had a right to leave at the end of their term regardless of the situation.[10] They fired their guns despite the shortage of powder, argued, and fought with strangers—foreigners—from other towns or colonies. Morale was high as the siege of Boston began, but both gunpowder and discipline were lacking. A few weeks after he arrived, Washington was horrified to discover that the three hundred eight barrels of gunpowder he thought he had were actually fewer than ninety.[11]

Eustis, enrolled as a regimental surgeon for an artillery company, ran one of the many temporary field hospitals scattered throughout the area. According to custom, every company or regiment arriving in Cambridge brought its own surgeon, each with varying abilities. A large number of these doctors may have studied medicine for a winter or two with a country physician, read a medical book, and then set up a practice. Ministers often took to heart the example of the Biblical physician Luke and addressed both the spiritual and medical needs of their town's regiment. All of the independent New Englanders had been apprentice-trained, but only Massachusetts required competency examinations for its regimental surgeons.[12] Dr. Warren qualified Eustis as a surgeon. After his nearly three years of work with Warren, Eustis had more experience and education than many of his peers.

Among the applicants for medical positions in the army, James Thacher of Barnstable, Massachusetts, who became one of Eustis's closest friends, was among the sixteen young men summoned before a board of medical examiners. These examinations covered anatomy, surgery, physiology, and medicine. Six of the sixteen were found unqualified. The examiners appointed Jack, Dr. Warren's younger brother, as one of the senior surgeons in the Cambridge hospital. Eustis's friend Thacher became a surgeon's mate and later a regimental surgeon.[13]

General Washington had to devise some kind of system and structure for the medical needs of sick soldiers. Men arrived in the camp from isolated farms and villages without immunity to many diseases. Being in larger groups increased the men's vulnerability to infectious diseases. A variety of illnesses, attributed to the living conditions and association with strangers, spread throughout the camps. Among the gravest threats were malaria, dysentery, influenza, and pneumonia as well as sporadic outbreaks of yellow fever and diphtheria. Tuberculosis, often called consumption, was one of the greatest killers. And then there was smallpox.

Contracting smallpox depended on exposure, and in Europe the smallpox virus was a constant presence; its survival ensured through an endless train of victims. In America, the miles separating villages prevented the disease from spreading easily. Years could go by between outbreaks. The most recent incident of smallpox had occurred in the 1750s, so the young male population in Cambridge had never encountered it.[14] Eustis and likely most other doctors connected with the hospitals had been inoculated.

Washington grew alarmed that smallpox would spread to his men. "The small pox is in every part of Boston," he wrote to Joseph Reed in mid-December. "If we escape the small pox in this camp and the country round about, it will be miraculous."[15] When General Howe herded three hundred destitute and sick Bostonians onto boats and dumped them near American lines, Washington, fearing that they carried smallpox, sent them humanitarian provisions while carefully insulating them from his troops. After a second wave of one hundred fifty ailing Bostonians was expelled, Washington grew convinced that Howe was using smallpox as a weapon against his army.

In the late 1760s, Dr. Warren had developed a protocol for inoculationthat included a preparatory milk diet and a course of purges with calomel [mercury] and syrup of ipecac. Patients usually contracted smallpox within ten days of the inoculation and were quarantined until fear of contagion had passed—usually after another two weeks. Fortunately, it was soon determined that the debilitating preparation was not necessary, nor was the deep half-inch incision used to introduce pus from another infected patient. The process of inoculation could be taught to surgeons' mates and temporary medical volunteers, so surgeons were not using their valuable time.

At first, unsure about the procedure of inoculation, perhaps because his native Virginia had outlawed inoculations in 1771, Washington finally came to believe it would be essential to keep his army on its feet. Realizing, however, that those undergoing the process would be contagious and could spread the disease unless isolated, and that an epidemic of smallpox in his crowded camps would be disastrous, he decided on prevention. Inoculation would have to wait. He would quarantine anyone displaying symptoms in the village of Brookline or in a military hospital at Fresh Pond outside Cambridge.

Within weeks after Washington's arrival, Congress established a Continental Army medical corps called the General Hospital, not to be confused with an actual building.[16] The militia would have a corresponding volunteer medical corps with surgeons attached to each regiment. The Continental Army had its own director-general and a chief physician who appointed four more surgeons and twenty surgeon's mates to the official army hospital. A clerk kept the accounts and two storekeepers received and distributed supplies.

These positions had to be staffed immediately. Congress appointed Dr. Benjamin Church, a popular Boston physician and member of the Sons of Liberty, as the first director-general. He was supposed to instill some kind of order. It didn't happen. The colonials did not want an arrangement like the British medical system—because it was British—and created an unworkable organization. Then, within four months, Dr. Church was accused, tried, and convicted of espionage. As a mole in the Sons of Liberty meetings, Church had passed information to General Gage.

Other doctors arrived in camp with their medical bags, but Eustis had not brought much when he left Boston. Dr. Warren had carried a basic kit with him. Eustis had very little—few medicines and no surgical kit. One had to be an opportunist in this growing army.

Charming and probably cunning enough, he acquired his own surgical instruments: various probes, different size curved needles, half a dozen or so very sharp knives and scalpels, and several saws, each kept freshly oiled to prevent rust.

The Continental Army Hospital's second director-general, Dr. John Morgan, who was appointed to replace the devious Dr. Church, was a Philadelphia physician and the first medical professor at Benjamin Franklin's College of Philadelphia. Morgan was delayed for four months before arriving in Cambridge in February and then tried to bring some efficiency to the disorganized hospital organization. Limited supplies caused competition among the hospital's doctors and regimental surgeons. With no rules or guidelines in place, Dr. Morgan needed a system to require the often independent-minded regimental surgeons to comply with the hospital's regulations.[17] For one thing, he had to regulate the stores from which the regimental surgeons such as Eustis drew their supplies.

Morgan was not pleased with these regimental surgeons. After about six months of trying to get them in line, he wrote to the Continental Congress in September 1776, calling them "very great rascals." He reported that: "The regimental surgeons are aiming, I am persuaded, to break up the General Hospital, and have in numberless instances drawn medicines, stores, &c, in the most profane, and extravagant manner for private purposes."[18] Morgan finally got a regulation imposed that each regimental surgeon, including Eustis, could draw only necessities for his own medical chest from the hospital, and all other supplies had to come through each regiment's quartermaster.

9

Liberating Boston: Evacuation Day

Eustis stayed in Cambridge when Benedict Arnold's overland invasion force left for Canada to meet up with the Northern Army led by New York's General Richard Montgomery who was driving north from Ticonderoga to conquer Canada. Never a country boy, Eustis preferred more civilized living to hardships in the forest. He waved them off when the various companies set out after barely ten days of preparation. At the head of one company marched young Captain Henry Dearborn with his black Newfoundland dog.

Heroics and bad planning involving Arnold's expedition are legendary: The distance was underestimated, badly built boats fell apart, men ran out of food, shoes, and supplies, and Dearborn's dog was eaten. On December 3, at barely half strength, the Americans managed an ill-coordinated attack on Quebec. Montgomery was killed, and Arnold was seriously wounded.

Congress dispatched Benjamin Franklin to Montreal in April 1776 to save the Canadian campaign and convince the Canadians that the Americans shared their same interests. It was a hopeless task. Franklin's party discovered the American force's sorry situation and returned to Philadelphia by May. Arnold and the expedition's other survivors left Canada in mid-June.

Eustis's interests led him in a different direction. At Washington's request, Congress replaced Colonel Richard Gridley, the artillery commander, with young, six-foot-two Boston bookseller Henry Knox. An avid reader, Knox taught himself the art of warfare by reading everything about the military he could and quizzing British officers who visited his bookshop. Knox offered Eustis a commission as lieutenant colonel in his new regiment. Eustis proposed to serve as a surgeon.[1] Knox agreed. Eustis turned his hospital duties over to a recent arrival, Dr. Isaac Foster, and joined his brother Ben as a regimental doctor for the new Regiment of Artillery commanded by Colonel Knox.

For Knox, acquiring cannon and gunpowder was an urgent priority. He suggested retrieving the heavy armament at Fort Ticonderoga in upstate New York and hauling them over the winter snow to Boston for a spring offensive. It called for another expedition. Knox, twenty-five, and his brother William, nineteen, left Cambridge in November, traveling to New York City to check on any artillery pieces they might get from Fort George, then by boat up the North [Hudson] River to Albany, and to Fort Ticonderoga on Lake Champlain. At the fort, they devised ways, using sleds, horses, and some oxen, to move not just a few, but all available cannon back to Massachusetts.

While waiting, Eustis was busy trying to keep the regiment healthy enough to provide whatever support Colonel Knox would need when he returned. Emerging maladies included typhus, malaria, jaundice, and the usual respiratory ailments as well as the dreaded smallpox. Pervasive dysentery led to orders requiring soldiers to use the latrines. Dr. Thacher noted in his diary that a huge upset was created in camp in November by the discovery of an excavated casket with its body missing. General Washington issued a declaration banning all dissections. The culprit or culprits were never disclosed.

56

While waiting through the winter, those in camp talked about Thomas Paine's pamphlet, "Common Sense." Independence from Great Britain was the only resolution, Paine wrote. "Small islands not capable of protecting themselves are the proper objects for kingdoms to take under their care, but there is something very absurd in supposing a continent to be perpetually governed by an island."[3]

General Washington declared January 1, 1776, to be the first official day of the new Continental Army, which had been six months in the making. To celebrate, Washington flew the Grand Union flag, a symbol of colonial unity with its red, white, and blue British Union Jack in the upper left corner over red and white stripes. Hauled up the flagpole on Roxbury's Prospect Hill it replaced a large red flag previously flown by Israel Putnam. Washington thought he was declaring the Continental Congress's unified position. But the flag created awkward confusion because the British thought flying "their" flag signaled a surrender.[4] The patriots would have to get a flag of their own.

Every time it snowed, the Continentals' thoughts turned to the Arnold and Knox expeditions, the first to Quebec and the other to Fort Ticonderoga. The brothers Knox arrived in Framingham by January 25 with a train of forty-two sledges drawn by horses and oxen and carrying fifty-nine cannons, howitzers, and mortars from Ticonderoga. Knox had covered seven hundred miles since leaving Cambridge and returned to a hero's welcome. This astounding feat had taken about seven weeks from Knox's initial arrival at Fort Ticonderoga until he rode back into Cambridge.[5]

Now that he had cannon, Washington wanted to immediately attack Boston. He believed his army could take advantage of the frozen Charles River by walking or dragging boats across the ice. His officers argued against risking the soldiers' lives. They recommended occupying the strategic location of still-unoccupied Dorchester Heights. This high ground overlooked Boston as well as the British ships anchored in the harbor.

Although willing to attempt an occupation of the Dorchester high ground, Washington decided to keep both proposals alive. Thanks to a proposal from Rufus Putnam, the general's cousin, the militia began assembling bundles of tree branches called *fascines* and wooden cages called *chandeliers* to create cannon-proof fortifications.[6] Carpenters built large flat-bottomed boats, each capable of carrying eighty *standing* men, for an invasion of Boston. And while still tending to the usual injuries, infections, illnesses, and dysentery, Eustis and the other regimental surgeons made their preparations.

As a distraction, Henry Knox's artillery began intermittent firing from Lechmere Point. The prefabricated structures were hauled to the top of Dorchester Heights in one night on ox-drawn carts without being seen or heard. Luckily, the night proved to be perfect, the full moon dimmed by a low-lying haze. Dr. Thacher wrote in his diary, "the preparations are immense; more than three hundred loaded carts in motion."[7]

When the fog burned off the following morning, the astounded British sentries saw that two forts were occupying Dorchester Heights as if by magic. British ships lay directly in range of the Continental artillery. The patriots, crouched in the redoubts, waited to see what would happen next.

Eustis awaited the arrival of injured soldiers at a field station below the Heights. Thacher noted that the men at the top were not alarmed about the incoming cannon shot. Shipboard cannon could not be sufficiently elevated to hit the top of the hill.

Spectators began to gather. General Washington appeared, mounted on his fine gray horse Nelson, and encouraged the men, reminding all that this day—the fifth of March—was the anniversary of the Boston Massacre.

General Howe moved a force to Castle William, the fortified island in the harbor, to launch his assault from there. Then, as some would have it, God or the Fates intervened to settle the fight in the patriots' favor. An unexpected, violent nor'easter roared in, damaging buildings and driving two of the British troop transports aground.[8]

General Howe decided that merely holding Boston did nothing to regain the colonies for the Crown. The new fortifications on Dorchester Heights gave him a perfect reason to pack up and go, with Long Wharf serving as the embarkation point. The British loaded naval supplies, nine thousand soldiers, twelve hundred dependents, and more than a thousand loyalists onto available ships and abandoned or sank everything else.

When they quit Boston on March 17, fears of smallpox contagion quickly surfaced. Illness had been rampant in the besieged town that winter, and the British, cold and desperate for wood, had cut down every possible tree. Even furniture and some wooden houses were taken apart for firewood, including the wooden church where Eustis's grandparents had been married.[9] Faneuil Hall had been turned into a theater and the venerated South Church had become a riding ring.

Now, Boston could finally breathe again after three hundred thirty-three days of siege. The town was cleared within a week, and the Continental Army began a ten-day march to the south. Not sure where the British would go, Washington correctly guessed they would ultimately head for New York. He knew that if the British could get control of the North River, that all-important north-south corridor between Canada and New York City, they could potentially divide the colonies, regain New England, and end the war in their favor.

Manhattan had Loyalist sympathizers, influenced by their Dutch and British heritages. There was no open opposition but plenty of Loyalist muttering when the Continentals arrived. Residents wondered about moving out. Many men and boys, including most of the Staten Island militia, had joined the British army, and Royal

Governor Tryon evacuated to the ship *Duchess of Gordon* in the harbor.

General Charles Lee, forty-four, a skinny, beak-nosed dog lover, hastened to lay in defensive artillery in the clear area called the Battery at the southwestern tip of Manhattan Island.[10] Eustis, arriving with Knox's artillery, looked for space to establish a hospital. He immediately began attending men with crushed fingers and toes and other injuries associated with moving the heavy guns into position.

Washington arrived in New York on June 6 following a journey to Philadelphia where he found that Congress was leaning toward issuing some kind of statement about its position and that Great Britain was hiring German mercenaries. He traveled now with an entourage including a fifty-member "Life Guard."

A plot surfaced to capture or kill His Excellency, to sabotage Continental defenses in and around New York City, and to enlist Americans into the British forces. Loyalists and secret turncoats anticipated coordinating with the expected British forces. Among the instigators in one group was an Irishman, Sergeant Thomas Hickey, who had deserted the British army several years before, enlisted with the Continentals and now served as one of two men assigned from his regiment in Washington's Life Guards.

Encouraged by the British, counterfeiting coins and paper currency was becoming a lucrative sideline. For Hickey, the opportunity for "shoving the queer" was irresistible. In trouble for passing counterfeit bills, Hickey schemed to capture or kill Washington by offering His Excellency a dish of poisoned green peas, a special spring treat.[10] When the peas were thrown out a window, supposedly chickens pecking in the yard died. The story has never been proven.

Captured with several others, Hickey was accused of mutiny and sedition. After his court-martial, a crowd of nearly twenty thousand, including every colonial brigade, witnessed his execution in the meadow near the Bowery on June 28, 1776.[11] Hickey was the first and only plotter executed for the conspiracy.

"I have just now returned from the Execution of one of the General's Guard," Eustis wrote to David Townsend. Horrified that anyone could consider assassinating General Washington, "the best man on earth," he described Hickey as "Unaffected and obstinate to the last." The defiant Hickey told spectators that General Greene, unless very cautious, might yet be killed. Later, Eustis added a postscript to his letter: "Since writing the above upwards of 100 sail have arrived; we conclude that the whole fleet is there; for we have counted 140 topsail vessels; some say there are 160; people are moving out of York [New York]; and I think we must very soon come to action."[12]

The British Royal Navy had arrived in massive force. The flotilla's appearance off Sandy Hook generated a scramble of activity in the town. Lucy Knox and Martha Washington hustled out of town. Expecting total devastation, everyone who could leave did. New York's population dropped from more than twenty thousand to about five thousand. As they marched in, militia from surrounding towns saw residents with whatever belongings they could carry or load on carts going in the opposite direction.

Then, on July 2, just as the Second Continental Congress voted for independence in Philadelphia, another full pageant of British sails appeared on the horizon.

10

A New Constellation

At six o'clock on July 9, 1776, William Eustis and his comrades heard the official justification for independence, including twenty-seven grievances against the king, read on the parade ground. General Washington had ordered this new Declaration of Independence read to all brigades.

In their uproarious enthusiasm, the crowd ran down the cobblestoned Broad Way to topple and decapitate the gilded equestrian statue of the toga-clad king. The crown-shaped lead finials on the fence around the little park were sawed off and carted away with the headless sovereign and horse to a foundry in Connecticut, where the lead was melted down and molded into more than forty-two thousand musket balls. His Majesty's head decorated a pike outside the newly built Fort Washington, located where today's George Washington Bridge crosses the Hudson River.[1]

A new unofficial flag flew over Continental Army headquarters depicting a new constellation of thirteen stars in a circle on a navy-blue field in the upper left corner and incorporating the red and white stripes of the flags of the Grand Union, the Sons of Liberty, and the Continental Congress. Congress would adopt the design in June 1777.

Just three days before, on July 4, a second wave of British warships had anchored in New York Harbor, joining the armada of one hundred forty vessels already there.

The king had decided on an overwhelming show of force. Under the command of General William Howe's brother, Admiral Viscount Richard Howe, known as "Black Dick," the fleet would become the largest expeditionary invasion force ever assembled by the British Empire. British soldiers came ashore on Staten Island, established a camp, and began constructing fortifications.[2]

By July 11, a *third* fleet of one hundred fifty British ships, carrying eleven thousand more troops, arrived in New York's outer harbor. The British landing forces now totaled thirty thousand regulars, including seventeen thousand German mercenaries. General Washington, having never commanded a large force in battle, had about ten thousand men. Contagion, camp filth, and contaminated water contributed to about six thousand being too sick with typhoid, typhus, and dysentery to fight.

The British won the Battle of Long Island, fought on the southern end, at the end of August 1776. Luckily for the rebels, who had a disastrous day, General Howe called a halt, set up camp, and ordered a siege of colonial lines. Hundreds of colonials were ferried back across the river in a steady downpour to waiting doctors. After two days of rain, Marblehead's John Glover used whaleboats, scows, schooners, and skilled seamen, to transport the remaining patriots across the East River during a long, foggy, and rainy night.[3]

From September 12 to 14, after conferences with his generals, Washington disregarded his instructions by Congress to hold New York and ordered the entire army evacuated from southern Manhattan to Harlem Heights and Fort Washington. Glover's men managed to transport the troops up the North River in whatever boats could be found, from canoes to sloops. On land, horses and wagons loaded with wounded soldiers and supplies and towing artillery lumbered north up the western side of the island.

Time ran out. The American army, hindered by a shortage of wagons, was about two days shy of completing its withdrawal when, on September 15, a huge British invasion force landed at Kips Bay on the east side of Manhattan Island well south of where they were expected. If the British cut the island in half, more than three thousand Continentals, including General Putnam, his division, Colonel Knox, and William Eustis, would be trapped.

Fiercely ambitious, Alexander Hamilton, nineteen, commanded a New York artillery company. The final exodus of men from the Battery included some of Hamilton's inexperienced gunners who were injured when several of their cannon exploded. They had been firing at the sixty-four-gun *Asia* and two other ships that had sailed into the North River.

Putnam rode up and down his column of about thirty-five hundred men, urging them toward Harlem Heights. Helping move the wounded on improvised stretchers down a path to boats, Eustis came very close to being caught behind enemy lines. He and Colonel Knox seized a boat with several other men and escaped up the river. They reached Harlem Heights, long overdue and presumed lost. With Knox, a large man in the stern, and under fire, it would have been a hard row.

Eustis later sent a quick note to Jack Warren saying he and Knox were the last men out of "York" as he always knew they would be. Luckily, the Hessians "fired badly." The tone of his letter hid the truly terrifying hours of breathless exertion, but he asserted that the tale of their getaway made for a "not unamusing" story.[4] Luck again saved the Continentals. The British advance across the island was halted when several officers, including General Howe, accepted the invitation of Mrs. Robert Murray of Murray Hill (now lower Park Avenue) for cake and Madeira wine.[5]

Soon Eustis was busy in the camps around the fort where more than a third of the army lay disabled by sickness.[6] As usual, there were no provisions for the wounded or sick and little attention was given to cleanliness in the camps. Dysentery cases skyrocketed and the doctors pleaded for tents and medical supplies.

General Washington still clung to the illusory hope of driving the British back down the peninsula and regaining control of lower Manhattan. Throughout October and into November, the newly designated Northern Army spread across the northern end of Manhattan to prevent the British from breaking out overland into New England. Washington made another inexperienced decision after trying to defend Long Island. He bowed to General Nathanael Greene's desire to defend Fort Washington. By late November, the horrified Washington, having crossed to the opposite bank of the river, watched as the British won the Battle of Harlem Heights and took Fort Washington, resulting in a frightful loss of life, armaments, and supplies. Nearly three thousand Continentals were captured. Lord Cornwallis then came across the North River at dawn and surprised the vulnerable Fort Lee. Its two thousand men escaped, scurrying to join Washington's already fleeing army that he was hustling south through the province of East and West Jersey, now called the "Jersies." William's brother, Benjamin Eustis, a matross, or assistant gunner, charged with loading, firing, and sponging the barrel of a cannon, also hurried south with General Knox.

William Eustis's assignment took him elsewhere. Washington had reorganized the Continental Army's structure. There would be three regionally-based American armies: the Southern Army in Georgia and the Carolinas; the Northern Army; and the Grand Army of roughly seven divisions under Washington. General William Heath would share command with General Charles Lee. Heath was to cover the Hudson Highlands with four thousand men and Lee would remain in Westchester County with seven thousand to block access into upstate New York and New England. Eustis was reassigned from regimental surgeon under Knox to hospital physician and surgeon in a barracks hospital known as DeLancey

House in Norwalk, Connecticut, at the eastern end of the northern defensive line.

This line extended from Norwalk on the Connecticut coast west to Danbury, then across to Fishkill, New York, and the North [Hudson] River. As cold weather arrived, General Howe decided it was not worth his while to continue chasing retreating rebels and abandoned his Westchester campaign in early November. Military action now consisted chiefly of skirmishes and the back-and-forth attempts to gain control of the forts guarding the North River.

Short-staffed, the few doctors in DeLancey House were frantically busy because of border raids and the usual diseases. Although he was on call throughout the area as well as at the hospital, Eustis kept up his correspondence when he could. He apologized to Jack in October: "I acknowledge we might have written; but if you knew but half the visisitudes (this is the first time I have put pen to paper for so long a time that, by Jove, I had forgot how to spell, vi, ve, &c…) I say if you had any tolerable idea of the various maneuvers we have performed since you left us you would excuse us ..."[7] Jack had urged him to come to New Jersey, but Eustis wrote, "My duty is delineated in Norwalk." He referenced a motto he had adopted since entering the service: *"Quo fata vocant"* (Whither the Fates Call).[8]

The constant shortage of medicines and supplies compounded the doctors' difficulties. Even bedding was hard to come by. Reputedly the best-organized hospital in the army, DeLancey House became seriously overcrowded. Along with the obvious need for surgery after any engagement, Eustis longed for basic medicines and was pleased to discover substitutes for remedies that were no longer available. Their guiding light, with his signature on the Declaration of Independence and now chair of the Continental Congress Medical Committee in Philadelphia, was Dr. Benjamin Rush. He encouraged use of a recently discovered extract made by boiling down the inner bark of the butternut tree. He recommended it as a mild "yet sufficiently active" cathartic and economical substitute for jalap, an unavailable purgative imported from Mexico, useful in cases of "dysentery and bilious complaints."[9]

Eustis accepted Rush's medical theories as if they came directly from God. Believing disease was a devil to be fought, Rush thought nothing should be left to natural healing. Filled with new ideas, he urged a doctor to prepare as if going into battle and developed the theory of heroic medicine that prescribed vigorous bleeding and purgatives, sometimes with disastrous results. When his patients died, he never doubted his theories, explaining that if the procedures had been started earlier, they would have brought different results.

Washington's Grand Army retreated across New Jersey and crossed the Delaware River into Pennsylvania. The number of men available looked good on paper but, because of short enlistment periods, many were due to leave within a month. When enlistments ended, Washington's army would be reduced to about three thousand men. Desperate to accomplish something before his men departed, Washington and his generals decided to cross back over the Delaware River and pounce on the Hessian garrison in Trenton at dawn on December 26. General Howe had returned to New York for the winter, and possibly the Hessians would be at a disadvantage after their daylong celebration of Christmas.

The Continentals attempted to cross the nearly eight hundred fifty feet of the icy Delaware at two sites on a proverbial dark and snowy night. About twenty-five hundred men, including Eustis's brother Benjamin, crossed nine miles above Trenton as chunks of ice floated past. The strategy worked. Consecutive victories at Trenton and Princeton, practically miraculous, saved the Continental Army and resurrected the American spirit.[10]

In January 1777, William Eustis was reassigned from the end of the defensive line in Norwalk to the Hudson Highlands area as a hospital physician and surgeon. He was given responsibility for the sick and wounded in a New York region that included West Point, the Vails Gate hamlet in New Windsor, and Newburgh. He arrived just in time. The wounded, brought by ferry following General Heath's failed attempt to recapture Peekskill from the British, demanded immediate attention.

When spring arrived in the Continental camp, so too did highly regarded Philadelphia physician Dr. William Shippen, the third medical director-general for the army. Shippen, who competed with and hated Dr. Rush, served for the next four years, reorganizing the Continental medical system, creating North, East, Middle, and South medical districts and assigning medical officers to oversee them. Shippen directed that all new recruits be inoculated as fast as they came to camp, and General Heath reported to Washington that the Hudson Highlands "hospitals are now opened and numbers inoculated under the direction of Dr. Eustis."[11,12]

11

Trying Times

Eustis carried on, not knowing which way his or the country's fortunes would go. In August, he sent some of his patients to Danbury, Connecticut, for convalescence and included directions for their care: "You are to see them well taken care of, accommodated with suitable lodgings at night in large houses or barns – to furnish them with plenty of milk on the road, and whatever else may be necessary for their comfort."[1]

Two campaigns opened in 1777, first in upstate New York, then in Philadelphia. A British invasion force marched south from the colorful leaves and chilly winds of Canada led by the flamboyant, over-entitled but minor aristocrat General "Gentleman Johnny" Burgoyne. His mission was to divide and conquer; to sever New England and possibly parts of New York from the rest of the colonies. In New York, General Howe received royal orders to coordinate with Burgoyne and send a contingent of soldiers north. Instead, attempting to be more effective elsewhere, Howe diverted his forces to capture Philadelphia, the provincial capital and seat of the rebels' Congress. With Philadelphia in his pocket, Howe would be the hero who won the war.

Just as General Burgoyne was fighting for his life at Saratoga in upstate New York that September, Lord Cornwallis, with flags flying and bands playing, marched into Philadelphia. The British now held Newport, New York, and Philadelphia. For the Americans, the loss of their capital city was balanced by winning at Saratoga and capturing more than six thousand soldiers.

Europe followed the developments across the Atlantic. Young Frenchmen yearning to fight for glory in a noble cause and bearing promises from American diplomats in Paris appeared on Congress's doorstep and badgered members for Continental Army commissions. The very rich Marquis de Lafayette{, nineteen and educated as a knight in the royal courts of Paris, arrived wearing a uniform of his own design and with two squires. He reached Washington's camp in the middle of the fighting to defend Philadelphia. Despite Washington's objections to foreign commissions, Congress had made Lafayette a major general because of his extensive family connections and equally great wealth.

As it happened, some of these new volunteers became assets during the second milder winter in Valley Forge. The self-titled, non-English-speaking Baron von Steuben rode into camp eager to teach a proper military training regimen. There may have been some question about why he left France, but he knew how to train troops. Through interpreters, he taught the manual of arms, how to march in columns four abreast instead of the single file favored for Indian fighting, and to do more with bayonets than cook over campfires.[2]

By the spring of 1778, there was new hope and a marked change for the Americans. The Crown recalled its commander-in-chief, General William Howe, and in early June General Sir Henry Clinton, formerly Howe's second-in-command, ordered the return to New York of ten thousand troops and fifteen hundred horse-drawn supply wagons. A heartened, better-fed Continental Army, trained by von Steuben and supplied with French arms, came out of winter quarters and hounded the British across the Jersey lowlands, battled them at Monmouth, and then watched the horizon for the anticipated arrival of the French. When the French fleet hove into view by July, it proved to be a disappointment. French warships required deeper water, twenty-seven feet, than British vessels which required twenty, so they could not sail up the North River or attack New York. Instead, they sailed to Rhode Island to offer sea support to a New England force trying to evict the British from Newport.

For three years, William Eustis's itinerant lifestyle had been similar to that of a country doctor. Now that he was based in Bedford, New York, Eustis continued to ride on call throughout the region with Dr. Sam Adams Jr. and stayed in local officers' quarters. When his regiment was in the area, regimental surgeon Dr. James Thacher could occasionally join them for meals.[3] Unlike Thacher, Eustis and Adams were connected to Continental Army hospitals. Regimental field hospitals were mobile, set up in a house or some other shelter near a regiment's camp. Both groups dealt with scarcities of supplies, but regimental surgeons had to get supplies through their quartermasters who applied to the general hospitals.

The heavy mortality during the Revolutionary War was largely due to a lack of state and congressional support. Death frequently came quickly, caused by general malnutrition, polluted water, bad food, and a variety of infections. Dr. Benjamin Rush observed that "hospitals are the sinks of human life in the army."[4] An apathetic Congress, out of its depth with many of its founding leaders gone, could not comprehend the immensity and urgency of the medical situation.

Rush was convinced that the body had twice as much blood as it did and could replace its entire supply within twenty-four hours. Medicine, if administered in large enough doses, was bound to bring good results, it was believed, so the doctors applied their lancets and dosed patients with calomel (mercurous chloride, a poisonous derivative of mercury) to an unbelievable extent. The country was approaching the heyday of "heroic" medicine when physicians, in a desperate effort to relieve agony and suffering, caused more.[5]

A great admirer of Dr. Rush, Eustis followed his advice assiduously when treating his patients. As a surgeon, he might be seen with his coat stiff with the blood of past operations and several freshly waxed threads used to tie up arteries knotted through his buttonhole. Screams were part of any surgical procedure as was sawdust spread on the floor. Whiskey, brandy, laudanum (a form of opium), and nicotine from a cigar were all used to help calm the patient. It was advised to have three assistants for amputations to hold the patient down.

Women customarily nursed the sick or wounded under horrid conditions. Each of the army's hospitals was staffed by one or two surgeons, as many surgeons' mates, and several nurses who were supervised by a matron. General Washington directed that all nurses must be female. If women could not to be found for the job, he would have to substitute men from various regiments who would be "entirely lost in the proper line of their duty."[6] Washington delineated the tasks of the nurses, who received only a small fraction of the pay allocated to surgeons and mates.

Despite his need for female nurses, and his own wife's company during the winter, General Washington's ascetic opinion prevailed about the presence of women around the army. Although he was grateful that they did laundry and cooked for the soldiers, he thought women slowed the army down. When the army did move, some of the pregnant women were allowed to ride on the gun carriages, giving birth to the expression "son of a gun." Most walked with the baggage train. Americans actually had far fewer female camp followers than the British, a shortage that often resulted in neglected hygiene and an increase in disease in the American camps.[7]

Eustis gained permission to return to Boston during the early summer of 1778. He paid a visit to Dr. Nathaniel Ames in Dedham during his leave to honor a convoluted commitment involving his friend, Dr. Joseph Warren, who had been killed three years earlier

72

during the battle of Bunker Hill.[8]

Eustis took money to Ames for the care and keeping of a little girl who had been born out of wedlock to one Sally Edwards, a young woman who Warren had assisted in Boston. Mercy Scollay, Warren's fiancée, thoroughly disliked Edwards and called her a "little hussy" and a "vixen."[9]

Ames was also an innkeeper and a friend and former classmate of Warren who he visited twice during 1775, on March 30 and again on April 8. Ames took Edwards back to Dedham after his April visit. Edwards was about six months pregnant. Ames described Edwards in his account book as Warren's *"fair incognita pregnans."*[10]

Ames recorded the delivery of Edwards's baby daughter on June 28. He also noted that William Eustis would pay Edwards's bills. Eustis would assume the responsibility for paying Ames for the room, board, and clothing for the daughter from 1777 through 1779.[11] By 1778, Eustis had been paying Ames for the care of the little girl for three years out of loyalty to the late Dr. Warren. Legal obligations for supporting children usually ceased when they were four years old because they could be taken in by families as indentured servants.

Eustis first wrote to Dr. Ames from Bedford, New York, to explain that he would forward the "balance of the account" [thirty-six pounds] by way of his brother, Benjamin, who was expected to arrive in Boston soon. That was a substantial sum. Eustis either saved the money or acquired it some other way, possibly with the help on another Warren apprentice, David Townsend.

Eustis avoided becoming directly involved with the little girl in Ames's care. He apologized to Ames in his letter: "You must pardon, [my] not returning to your house but really I would not have seen the person whom I suppose you intended to introduce me to on any account; if my conjecture was wrong, I ask a thousand pardons."[12]

It is not evident what role, if any, Sally Edwards played in the

Warren household. She may have been a servant or a patient. Young ladies of the town did visit the Warren surgery unaccompanied. The paternity of her child has never been determined. Some have speculated that it may have been Dr. Warren's.

There is no explanation why Eustis would not see the child yet steadfastly pay for her support and honor his obligation to Warren. We also have to wonder why Warren's brother, Jack, did not undertake the obligation, although he had adopted all four of Joseph's children.

12

Protest and Petition

With his usual humor, Eustis wrote to Jack Warren: "The medical world goes on rather drolly." Eustis and Dr. Sam Adams Jr. were hard at work overseeing between three hundred and four hundred patients. Although the ratio of doctor to patients was about one to two hundred, he reported that the medical department seemed to be improving because of the ongoing reorganization, and he asked about Jack's participation in the "secret expedition"—the second attempt by New England militia to recapture Newport, Rhode Island. "We have information here that the French fleet have returned much shattered and one 74 [frigate] is missing." He asked if "Rhode Island [was] ours without many bloody noses."[1] They had not connected when Eustis was in Boston on leave.

Warren had been in Rhode Island volunteering as a doctor during a second attempt to drive the British out of Newport. It fared no better than the first. A severe and sudden Atlantic hurricane blew in during a sea battle between the British and French fleets, and the French suffered significant damage.

Admiral Jean Baptiste Charles Henri Hector D'Estaing's flagship lost her bowsprit and all masts, and other ships were damaged or missing. The French ships sailed directly to Boston for refitting rather than, as planned, supporting troops ashore in Newport. As soon as Admiral Howe's ships anchored in that harbor, patriot forces retreated.[2]

Eustis was transferred in 1778 from Bedford to a newly-created hospital at Loyalist Colonel Beverly Robinson's abandoned estate. It was an ideal site, about as far from a grim regimental situation as possible. Thacher described it as a "spacious and very convenient building, situated on the eastern bank of the Hudson about two miles from West Point ... on the opposite shore. Robinson's house, with the outbuildings making it convenient for a hospital; the farm and gardens are very extensive, affording excellent pasturing for horses and cows, and containing three or four large orchards."[3]

While Eustis settled his patients into adapted sheds and barns, General Washington and his army moved into their winter quarters in Middlebrook (near today's Bound Brook), New Jersey. Active fighting ceased for about five months. Instead, the focus was on survival during another fierce winter and preparations for the expected spring campaign. His Excellency and his aides went to Philadelphia to consult with a directionless, bickering Congress.

British efforts to counterfeit and discredit American-made money succeeded in damaging the economy well beyond expectations. Inflation skyrocketed, money became nearly worthless and Congress could not provide clothing or supplies for the army. They planned to call in old Continental dollars, valued at forty to one in silver,[8] and issue new ones, but army officers feared the new ones would drop equally in value. "It is not worth a Continental," they said.

The greatest danger to the patriots' cause became economic. In Paris, Benjamin Franklin had not yet managed to obtain the much-desired and necessary French assistance. In mid-January 1779, the Continentals and General Washington gave the Marquis de Lafayette a year's furlough to France to plead for support.

The campaign season opened that May with an explosive bang. British General William Clinton began early spring attacks up the Hudson River at the ferry crossing of Kings Ferry and the forts at Verplancks and Stony Point. In the midst of preparations, General Benedict Arnold arrived at Washington's headquarters anticipating his scheduled court-martial for questionable behavior as military governor in Philadelphia. To his dismay, the court-martial was called off.

Appointed the town's governor about a year earlier in June 1778, Arnold had married the lovely Peggy Shippen and began to live as the hero of Saratoga. His wounded left leg had healed badly, and he now wore a two-inch heel on that foot. He felt a distinct lack of appreciation from Congress for turning the tide of the battle at Saratoga and attempted to compensate for it with an elegant house, coach, and servants. It seemed a braggart's display at a time when many people in the city struggled to find enough to eat. Petitioned by Philadelphia commissioners to investigate Arnold for extortion and embezzlement of public funds, Congress ordered him arrested, confiscated his wealth, and requested a court-martial.

Arnold, however, was the least of General Washington's concerns. He considered West Point and the Hudson Highlands, with its fifteen-mile line of forts, as keys to thwarting British plans to divide America. This opening assault worried him. He hurried his Continentals out of winter quarters, much too focused on the renewal of action along the Hudson to take time for a court-martial. It would be rescheduled for later when the army's officers were available.

Throughout 1779, with no end to the war in sight, a constant stream of patients kept Eustis busy at Robinson House. Although soldiers could go into winter quarters after a summer of campaigning, the doctor's responsibilities changed only slightly; from treating festering wounds to remedying pin worms, piles, and fevers. Eustis often had more than a hundred patients. Transporting

77

them and keeping sufficient medical supplies on hand was a challenge.[4]

At various times, a regiment might be camped at Robinson's along with civilian camp followers and sutlers—vendors of rum, tobacco, soap, food, and military equipment. Others on the premises were skilled artisans, blacksmiths, waggoneers, laborers, and officers' servants called waiters. Women encamped with their husbands served as nurses and matrons besides washing, mending, and cooking.

"The business of this place barely forbids my leaving it but makes it probable that I shall be obliged to call in one of the gentlemen from Danbury," wrote Eustis while managing supplies and overwhelmed with patients.

Still, he found a few minutes to send financial advice to Dr. Josiah Bartlett, a surgeon assigned with Sam Adams Jr. who was still at the hospital in Danbury, Connecticut. "If you are moneyless you are in the same predicament with every officer of my knowledge in the department. I can give no directions . . . I can advise you as a friend to get rid of one of your horses and your waiter for be assured Congress will not tolerate two horses to a junior surgeon: besides it will curtail one half of your expenses. I do not expect [even] a senior will in the arrangement be allowed forage for two horses."[5]

It had been four years since these men had been inspired by the ideals of liberty and an independent republic. Throughout that time, Eustis had devoted his energy to the honorable cause of independence, but there seemed to be little progress. He no longer harbored illusions of glory. Like the other doctors and officers, Eustis often went months without pay. It seemed that his youthful motto of waiting for the fates to decide had not worked. And distressing family news came from Boston. His younger brother George, twenty-four, had died and was buried at Copp's Hill Burying Ground.

Saddened, tired, older, and frustrated by inaction, Eustis needed to do something. In October, on behalf of the military doctors in the Hudson Highlands, he submitted a petition to Congress asking that attention be paid to the lack of payment for physicians.[6] He advised consideration of the petition or, he warned, the doctors might resign. Eustis and three other officers put their signatures on the document.

Early in December, a new directive arrived from General William Heath stating that he had commandeered Robinson House for his winter quarters and the medical staff must move out. Eustis protested. Heath explained that he could not have Eustis or any other medical personnel in his household as they were too noisy, especially above the room where he planned to conduct his briefings. Heath was "astonished" that Dr. Eustis resisted moving to other quarters. He knew that when the army goes into winter quarters, military rank dictates where people live.[7] Instead, Eustis should be grateful to have used the rooms as long as he had, but now he must get out. Heath felt Eustis's protest was "indelicate" and that he meant nothing personal by moving in. It was a matter of rank and preference. The patients could remain in the outbuildings, but the house must be vacated for the next five months.

Known as the "Hard Winter," 1779-80 was one of the most severe of the eighteenth century and possibly the coldest on record—worse even than the infamous Valley Forge winter of 1777-78. Snowfall ranged up to four feet with drifts of five feet. Food shortages became commonplace. There was no meat or flour for days, and farmers refused to sell their produce for the depreciated Continental currency. Lack of food and poor hygiene led to the bleeding gums and skin problems of scurvy, compounding the soldiers' usual miseries from lice and bed bugs.

When the streams froze over, the gristmills could not function, so grain or corn could not be ground into flour. Starving, freezing soldiers plundered nearby farms looking for firewood and food. Sometimes even a horse could not get through to Robinson House. Ferries were not needed because travelers could walk across the frozen river. The danger of fire increased as people huddled around open fires inside, and the quartermaster's barracks and two redoubts at West Point burned down.

Huddled indoors, doctors hoped for a response to their petition. It was discussed in Congress in March 1780 when a congressional committee presented the results of its investigation. One report listed staff officers in certain departments and their wages and ration allowances. As a skilled senior surgeon, William Eustis was promised $120 per month and allowed one servant.

The committee, as congressional committees do, decided to study the situation further. In reality, Congress could do little to relieve the medical officers' or any officers' financial situations; it had no power to tax, and the paper money it printed was worthless. The thirteen allied colonies could ease Congress's financial problems, but they were virtually independent nations and contributed only as much as they desired.

General Washington realized that captured ground was meaningless. The Continental Army just had to survive. The British occupied New York, parts of coastal Maine, Newport, Savannah, and Charleston. Their navy blockaded ports, but they had to maintain supply lines over a vast ocean, and huge expenses increased even more. As long as the Continental Army held together, time and the country's huge interior were on the side of the Americans.

In April 1780, a fresh breeze brought anxiously awaited news from France. Lafayette sailed into Boston Harbor on the thirty-two-gun ship *Hermione,* an elegant gold fleur-de-lis painted on her stern. Governor John Hancock and Samuel Adams Sr. met the ship with the town's most prominent citizens and a thirteen-gun salute. Triumphantly, Lafayette announced that France would declare war on Great Britain and headed immediately to Morristown to tell General Washington. In Paris, Lafayette's influence plus the American triumph at Saratoga resulted in the desperately needed

French alliance and recognition that the American colonies were an independent country fighting against Great Britain, France's perpetual enemy.

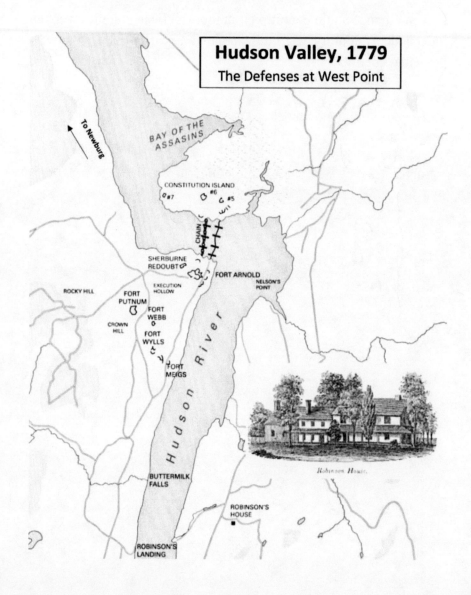

Hudson Valley, 1779
The Defenses at West Point

Robinson House.

13

Treason of the Blackest Dye[1]

It seemed to the Continentals like the just-in-time charge of the cavalry galloping over the hill, flags flying, and bugles blaring. The French were coming! In mid-June 1780, hearing of the imminent arrival of the French fleet and with instructions to consolidate troops, the British reevaluated their position, blew up their fortifications in Newport, and retreated to New York to regroup and build up defenses there.

In July 1780, news trumpeted that the French fleet under the Comte de Rochambeau had arrived in Newport Harbor bringing more than five thousand troops to establish a base there and prevent any British return. Washington was nonetheless terribly disappointed that America's new ally had not brought desperately needed arms, ammunition, and clothing. With Lafayette as translator, Rochambeau paid lip service to Washington's desire for attacking and regaining New York but explained that campaign would have to await further reinforcements.[2] Washington realized that while the French were his allies, they would do what they pleased. Lacking the means to launch an attack alone, he shifted to strengthening his defenses.

And that involved Benedict Arnold. Despite the scandals

surrounding Arnold in Philadelphia and an official military reprimand after he had been court-martialed, General Washington still had faith in him as a soldier. Arnold was by far the most effective combat general in the American army. Earlier that June, Washington had asked Arnold to assume command of part of the Continental Army. To his surprise, Arnold declined, saying his still painful leg injury made him incapable of active duty. He suggested instead that he command the garrison at West Point, a request Washington finally granted.[3]

West Point was the jewel of the Hudson Highlands and the key to preventing the British forces from dividing New England from the rest of the country. It was a mountainous area through which the Hudson River had created a deep canyon. The broad, tidal river flowed through it in tight turns before flowing south nearly sixty miles to New York. The fort was called "the American Gibraltar" because of its strength and position; and when properly manned, it could hold off an army of twenty thousand.

When Eustis approached West Point, whether by boat or on horseback, he saw buildings covering the hillside like a fortified medieval town. The entire complex included ten forts. The original stronghold, named Fort Putnam after General Israel Putnam, squatted on a natural platform of rocks at the S-curve of the river. Behind the fort, rocky ridges provided natural defenses where a range of cannons and redoubts were positioned. The entire position commanded a view of at least thirty miles in all directions.

For further defense, a huge iron chain forged of links twelve inches wide and eighteen inches long, and weighing about one hundred thirty tons, was rigged across the river to prevent ships from passing. *Cheveaux de fries,* rock-filled bins supporting vertical, metal-tipped logs, were hidden beneath the surface of the water. The chain, guarded by batteries on both sides of the river, not only worked as a deterrent but could also be brought to shore when ice clogged the river.[4]

As a resident of Robinson House, Eustis welcomed West Point's new commander, Benedict Arnold, on August 4. A short, vain man with an aquiline nose and thick unruly hair, Arnold had chosen to live across the river rather than in the great fort. Robinson House suited him. It had an attractive country setting with a view of the river and would be much more comfortable for his family. Ever cautious, he arranged for a one-hundred-man personal guard to camp in tents around the house as well as a thirty-foot, eight-oared bateau, or longboat, to facilitate his travels.[5]

Unlike General Heath, Arnold did not evict Eustis. Both men were skilled socially, and Eustis, dining at the same table, became reacquainted with stories of the siege of Boston as they spent their evenings around the hearth. Arnold's wife, Peggy, escorted by his aide David Franks, arrived six weeks later after a ten-day journey from Philadelphia with their six-month-old son, Edward Shippen "Neddy" Arnold, her luggage, her slave, and a nurse.

No one there knew that Arnold was engaged in a secret correspondence, begun in Philadelphia, with British General Sir Henry Clinton in New York. Arnold had spent months negotiating for a way to surrender West Point in exchange for money and a high-ranking position in the British army. Eustis became an innocent and astounded participant when perhaps the most famous, treasonous scheme in American history unraveled.

As usual, he took his place at the table in Robinson House on Sunday, September 17. He was seated near Arnold's aides, Colonel Richard Varick and Major David Franks, when a messenger arrived with a letter for Arnold. It had been sent ashore under a flag of truce from the British sloop *Vulture*. The letter, secretly sent by British Major John André, bore the signature of Loyalist Colonel Beverly Robinson, former owner of the house they now occupied. Arnold told them that Robinson requested a meeting.

The officers at the table urged Arnold not to respond but to discuss it with Washington that evening during their scheduled meeting in Peekskill. Washington was stopping there on his way to

85

meet with the French in Hartford, Connecticut. Washington urged Arnold to avoid any communication with the British. Arnold apparently heeded Washington's advice and sent a letter to Robinson advising him to talk to civil authorities. But he inserted a private message for André stating that they could meet secretly.

While Washington met with the Comte de Rochambeau and Admiral de Ternay in Hartford, the *Vulture* conveyed André, who was General Clinton's aide-de-camp, up the Hudson to within twelve miles of West Point. Despite various complications, Arnold met André at Haverstraw Bay where, overnight, they formulated a plan to surrender West Point. André had planned to return to the *Vulture* that night, but the ship was damaged by American cannon fire and had retreated for repairs, leaving André stranded. Arnold conducted André to the nearby home of Joshua Smith, telling him André was an American undercover agent.

On Arnold's advice, André put on Smith's old coat and breeches and, disguised as a civilian, rode overland to New York with Smith as his guide. He hid papers containing complete details about West Point in his stockings in his riding boots. Arnold provided him with a passport that allowed him to travel under the name of John Anderson, seemingly on matters of business.

André never made it back to New York. Smith accompanied him to within fifteen miles of the British lines then left him to go on alone. Three militia men stopped and searched André and, finding the concealed plans of West Point, took the British officer to their superiors. Had André been dressed in his uniform, he would have received courteous treatment, but, in civilian clothing, he was a spy. Somehow André managed to get word to Arnold that "John Anderson" had been captured.

Meanwhile, General Washington, his meetings with the French over, headed back from Hartford. Washington decided to visit West Point to review its defenses, dine with Arnold, and stay overnight at Robinson House. On Monday morning, September 25, Peggy

Arnold planned a breakfast reception for the commander-in-chief. Two aides arrived saying the general would be late because he had stopped to inspect a redoubt. Mrs. Arnold decided to remain in their second-floor bedroom. Benedict Arnold, William Eustis, and Washington's and Lafayette's aides sat down for breakfast. They had just been served when an express rider arrived with dispatches.

Arnold excused himself to read his messages in private. One gave information about the capture of "John Anderson." The other stated that the papers taken from this person had been sent to General Washington. Realizing what it meant, Arnold hurried upstairs to tell Peggy that he was leaving. When his aide, David Franks, knocked on the bedroom door to inform him that Washington's party was approaching, Arnold rushed out, saying he was off to West Point. Instead, he was rowed down river in his bateau to board the *Vulture* which was back on station after being repaired. The ship immediately sailed for New York.

General Washington, with Knox, Lafayette, Hamilton, and the one hundred sixty men in their escort, swarmed in front of the house about a half hour after Arnold left. Being told that he had gone to West Point, Washington decided to cross the river and inspect the fort with Knox and Lafayette after breakfast, leaving Hamilton behind. At West Point, the baffled officers found a deplorably maintained complex with no signs of Arnold anywhere. Returning to Robinson House at about four that afternoon, Washington was met by Hamilton who said that a courier had arrived with a packet of letters including the documents found on the captured "John Anderson." They revealed that West Point was in imminent danger.

Aghast, General Washington called in Lafayette and Knox. The men were equally horrified. Arnold was one of their own. He was a military hero. Yet, it appeared that he had sold West Point and three thousand American lives. If West Point was lost, the British plan to isolate New England could succeed. Fearing an imminent attack, and to secure the fort, Washington sent word for additional troops and rapidly made command changes.[6]

Suddenly, Peggy Arnold was heard shrieking in her upstairs bedroom.[7] Realizing that she could be a suspect, the nineteen-year-old woman feigned an attack of hysterics. Fearing some disaster, Eustis, who was in Arnold's ground-floor office checking on Colonel Varick's recovery from a prolonged bout of dysentery, rushed upstairs to see what was happening.[8]

The doctor discovered the petite blonde at the top of the stairs, her clothes and hair in disarray. She accused the men of plotting to kill her son, Neddy. Eustis, assisted by Arnold's aide David Franks and the maid, tried to restrain her. The disturbing noises continued. Varick rose from his sickbed. Eustis and the two aides, Varick and Franks, carried Mrs. Arnold back to her bedchamber, but she remained panicky and confused. Because she had asked if General Washington was in the house, and not sure what else to do, Eustis asked Varick to get him, thinking that she might wish to explain her husband's mysterious absence.

Varick brought the general up to Peggy's room. When Washington arrived, Mrs. Arnold staged another fit, denied he was the general, and accused him of wanting to kill her child. Embarrassed, Washington quickly turned and left. All the men were duped by Peggy's performance. In fact, she was well aware of the plot and had served as a willing conduit for some of her husband's correspondence.[9]

The sympathetic young men, Eustis, Lafayette, and Hamilton, conferred about what to do. As soon as they heard about Arnold's treachery, her distress made sense. There could be no escape from the scandal and condemnation for the wife of a traitor. By virtue of her marriage to Arnold, Peggy's character and reputation would be completely ruined.

As the attending doctor, Eustis needed to do something. Bleeding was a common treatment for calming hysterical women, and he had faith in the treatment for nearly everything. Obtaining her permission for the procedure, however, would be difficult. With time, her condition seemed to improve, and she stayed in her chamber, undoubtedly hoping for a chance to leave. Eustis and the two other young men went to plead her case with Washington.

Although Arnold did not take Peggy with him, it appears that he immediately sought to help her get away. While on the *Vulture*, he composed a letter to Washington soliciting protection for his wife, asking that she be permitted to leave for Philadelphia, and sent it back under a flag of truce.[10] His plea worked. Wanting to believe in the hysterical woman's innocence and to have her gone, Washington issued an order enabling Peggy to leave immediately. Robinson House became a hive of activity as Washington's aides worked to restore patriot defenses, and Eustis managed Mrs. Arnold's departure. Two days later, escorted by David Franks, the Arnolds' carriage bearing Peggy, Neddy, the slave, and nursemaid and their personal belongings left Robinson House.

A little more than a month later, on October 15, 1780, Dr. David Townsend, on his way to New Jersey, joined Eustis for dinner at Robinson House. Their visiting friend, Dr. Thacher, shared the full story of André's trial and execution After attending the hanging, Thacher's regiment had come north from the Tappan area to West Point for the winter.[11]

14

The World Turned Upside Down

William Eustis wrote to Jack Warren after André's execution. A devoted patriot, brought up to believe that honor and integrity were a person's most important attributes, Eustis felt sorely let down by Arnold's betrayal.

He had taken care of soldiers for nearly five years, doing his part but seeing no progress in the war, and then one of the country's most admired fighting men had defected. "From an unaccountable aversion to writing I have troubled neither my friends in Boston nor elsewhere with any letters this season . . . [David] Townsend has been with me for two or three days on his way to the army [in New Jersey]."[1]

In the midst of harvests and winter preparations, Eustis again put his mind to getting his patients through the winter, facing the usual shortages of supplies and money. Experience and hard reality convinced him that the war would go on and that it was unlikely he would get home for several more years. "Neither now nor at any other time have I ever despaired of the final independence or freedom of the States but I am [convinced] that new and greater exertions are necessary than have as yet been made."[2]

Washington gave up on obtaining support from an overwhelmed Congress which dealt with a multitude of new issues by referring them to committees. He appealed directly to the states for supplies; "it is in vain to think an army can be kept together much longer under such a variety of sufferings as ours has experienced."[3] Relief was not guaranteed; the states were not obligated to even respond. Even if a state did scrape up supplies, Washington had no money to pay teamsters to transport them. His own horses were starving for want of forage.

The Northern Army went into winter quarters. General Heath occupied a house closer to West Point, and Eustis remained at Robinson House with his patients. His friend Dr. Thacher was back for the winter; his regiment ordered to build a new encampment called New Windsor Cantonment two miles inland from West Point.

The usual austere living conditions, snowstorms, and meager food supplies caused Thacher to worry that another extreme winter would cause fed-up Continental soldiers to abandon their commitments and the patriots' cause altogether. The volunteer militia could go home, but Continentals could not. When their terms expired, regimental officers simply did not reenlist.

Once the New Windsor encampment was built, however, and the log houses were occupied, some took heart and soldiered on. Even so, by the early spring of 1781, when some soldiers' enlistments ended and new recruits had not arrived, the shortage of men made it difficult to garrison the forts at West Point.

Even though Congress had designated fifteen positions for the general hospital department, only eight physicians and surgeons, including William Eustis, were actually practicing in the Continental Army—hardly enough to serve hundreds of patients. Jack Warren maintained his position in Boston and ignored Director-General Dr. Cochran's orders to come to New York. With one doctor in Boston, Warren, one in Yellow Springs to the west of Valley Forge, and one in Philadelphia, only five doctors remained to tend all the soldiers in the remaining three hospitals established in the Hudson Highlands area: Robinson House, the barracks at West Point, and in New Windsor Cantonment.[4]

One monthly report for Robinson House listed forty-five new patients admitted for Eustis's attention. The other patients in residence, described by their conditions, included ten convalescents, twelve with wounds, ten with ulcers, nine with inflammatory fevers, five with nervous and remittent fevers, ten with diarrhea, three rheumatic, five "chronics" and two with smallpox. Sixty-nine patients were discharged that month, and four died. One hundred eight remained under Eustis's care at the end of the month.[5]

In March, Eustis's friend Thacher called for his help at Fort Crompond, a small fortification about eight miles from Verplanck's Point and close to British lines where hand-to-hand combat occurred on a regular basis. During a skirmish, one of the volunteer militiamen was wounded in his shoulder and lung. On examination, Eustis found that the patient had not lost a great deal of blood from the wound and recommended repeated bloodletting. He advised that in order to cure a wound through the lungs, you must "bleed your patient to death."[6] Fortunately, this patient recovered.

Downriver in New York, the British enjoyed a much more comfortable winter. Merchant ships brought supplies of all kinds including new gowns for the ladies. The birthday of Queen Charlotte in January provided an excuse for more balls and parties.

In the Highlands area, with death their shared enemy, Eustis and the four other overworked doctors sought opportunities to unwind together. Mental compartmentalizing helped to get them through the daily onslaught; divorcing themselves from their feelings seemed the only way to survive. Their inability to provide many cures weighed heavily upon them, and repeatedly losing patients meant they were defeated again and again. Fellow doctors, friends who ministered to patients under the same adversities, understood.

In April, regimental surgeon James Thacher took the ferry across the Hudson to visit overnight with Eustis. The two doctors rode to Peekskill to call on Colonel Laurence, who was confined after a smallpox inoculation, and returned to Robinson House that evening. Crossing the river the following day enabled Eustis and Thacher to enjoy a sociable evening at General Heath's quarters in West Point with Dr. Sam Adams Jr. and Director-General Dr. Cochran.[7] Barely two weeks later, feeling sick and believing in bleeding as a universal cure, Eustis sent for Thacher to come bleed him.[8]

As the war cooled in the North, it became increasingly active in the more Loyalist South where successful British armies had captured the port cities of Charleston, South Carolina, and Wilmington, North Carolina. General Washington diverted a large number of troops to Virginia under the Marquis de Lafayette and farther south under General Nathanael Greene, but he did not leave the Hudson Highlands himself. Central command and the Northern Army remained with him. If there was a chance of collaborating with the French to regain New York, Washington wanted to be there.[9] He obsessed over the ultimate capture of the fortified town as the climactic battle of the war.

The French moved closer by early July, establishing a camp in Dobbs Ferry. The French and Americans were getting acquainted— still not sure how well they would dance together. Each had different ideas about achieving their common goal of defeating the British and baffled by each other's customs. The French might bring money, but they ate frogs and snails and were Catholic. For the first time, the curious French officers had a chance to study their allies. This apparently heterogeneous, mongrel army was unlike anything the Europeans had ever seen. Baron von Closen observed: "It is incredible that soldiers composed of men of every age, even of children of fifteen, of whites and blacks, almost naked, unpaid and rather poorly fed, can march so well and withstand fire so steadfastly."[10]

Then came welcome news. Comte de Rochambeau sent word

93

that French Admiral Comte de Grasse would bring his fleet north from the West Indies later that summer to coordinate an attack on the British. Washington hoped that Rochambeau would agree to his dream of capturing Manhattan. Ever independent, Rochambeau notified Admiral de Grasse of his personal preference for attacking the British in Chesapeake Bay. By mid-August, a flurry of ideas, plans, and activities swirled around General Washington. For the next few months, he would be part of an exquisitely timed and complex game of chess played by larger-than-life personalities involving the future of his country.

Washington needed to keep British General Clinton in the dark about his plans. In hard reality, he did not have enough soldiers, and Congress did not have the money to support them. No one was contributing to the effort; no men volunteered, no states sent money. Without the French, the entire revolution would fail. Europeans were talking of mediation by unsympathetic European monarchs. If that occurred, the best the Americans could hope for was *uti possideti juris*, or keeping the land identified as the united colonies at the end of 1781, basically New England and New York but not Manhattan. Time was running out.[11]

Information arrived that the French fleet of twenty-nine ships of the line with more than three thousand troops would arrive in the Chesapeake Bay region by mid-September and remain through October. Considering that severe hurricanes had hammered the Caribbean the previous year, the admiral wanted to get his fleet out of harm's way. This news plus the arrival of desperately needed funds from the French put the Americans, as Dr. Cochran wrote, in "high Blast."[12] Washington and Rochambeau had to coordinate plans quickly.

The danger was that the British—if they knew Washington was leaving—would attack West Point. One ruse: A mailbag to be captured by Clinton with information about an allied attack on New York. Major General Heath and part of the army would remain in the Highlands to stage diversionary actions. Eustis, as the hospital doctor, would stay with them.

Wagons bustled about, and boats worked the nearby waters, laying down pontoons for bridging, hinting that an amphibious assault on Manhattan Island was at hand. Down river, Clinton built up British defenses and scanned the horizon for the French frigates.

Both Washington's American and Rochambeau's French armies marched south to Maryland and boarded assorted transports at Head of Elk, on the Elk River at the northern tip of Chesapeake Bay. They landed in Williamsburg, Virginia, three days later. Admiral de Barras's fleet off Newport prepared to sail south from Rhode Island to rendezvous with de Grasse's Caribbean fleet. The Comte de Rochambeau and others traveled south on the Delaware River. Washington rode overland via Philadelphia, checked on his Mount Vernon home and was welcomed in Williamsburg on September 15 to a review of nearly sixteen thousand assembled French and American troops.

***

Back in the Hudson Highlands, amid the distractions of creating the diversionary invasion, William Eustis received devastating news from Philadelphia. His older brother, Major Benjamin Eustis, had been killed in a duel on October 6. After being transferred to Benjamin's Fourth Massachusetts Artillery Regiment, a Captain Thomas Porter raised the contentious issue of seniority over the other regimental officers. Controversy about rank in the regiment continued for the next ten months.

Major Eustis was visiting with friends in a coffeehouse when his nemesis, Captain Porter, entered and Eustis charged: "He's nothing but a damn schoolmaster."[13] Porter asked if Eustis was speaking about him. When Eustis nodded, Porter drew his sword and struck Eustis on the shoulder—a clear challenge to a duel.

Benjamin Eustis, a man of his time, did not shy away from confrontation when defending his honor. He and Captain Porter met with their seconds at the southeast corner of Ninth and Arch Streets in Philadelphia. Porter shot Eustis through the heart. In the subsequent court-martial, convened because an officer had been killed outside of the line of duty, Porter was acquitted and later promoted to major by Congress—perhaps filling Benjamin Eustis's position.

***

The siege of Yorktown began three days after the duel. Thirty-six French ships of the line, those with sixty or more guns, stood off Yorktown in the Chesapeake Bay. The French provided about two thirds of the men ashore. The French also had provided a month's pay in cash as incentive for the Americans. When the allied siege lines—the French in position on the left and the Americans on the right—were ready, General Washington fired the first cannon to launch the attack. Cornwallis capitulated on October 17 and on October 19, 1781, to the tune of "The World Turned Upside Down," the British officially surrendered, marching out of Yorktown between two lines, each a mile long, of American and French troops. Mortified, Lord Cornwallis claimed illness and did not attend.

Couriers raced up the coast spreading the news of the Yorktown surrender. Church bells pealed in Boston in wild victory celebrations. At Fishkill, near West Point, residents had a day-long barbecue with a huge evening bonfire. A few miles up the Hudson River, at Washington's headquarters in Newburgh, New York, troops burned Benedict Arnold in effigy.

But William Eustis was not there.

While others celebrated a victory, he was riding toward Philadelphia to collect Benjamin's few belongings, settle his affairs, and seek out his grave. On October 20, he heard the victorious ringing of bells throughout the night—an odd celebration of his brother's life. Dr. Cochran wrote to tell Jack Warren that Eustis was in Philadelphia "transacting some Business on Account of his unfortunate Brothers."[14]

15

Never Ending

After its Yorktown victory, the Northern Army trudged back to winter quarters in the Hudson Highlands. Eustis awaited their return at Robinson House after returning from Philadelphia. On arrival, the Fourth Massachusetts Regiment, accompanied by his friend, Dr. James Thacher, began building another complex of huts called New Boston south of West Point.

General Washington went to Philadelphia to spend the winter talking with Congress which he found in crisis and overwhelmed by responsibility. The vision of the earlier revolutionaries seemed lost, and the founding concept of the recently-ratified Articles of Confederation—that the states would freely participate—was failing.[1] States insisted on their autonomy, even if they did not have or would not commit the funds to preserve it, and continued to fear a strong central government.

Nothing was secure or certain for the next two years. The British could break out of New York at any time. Admiral de Grasse had sailed back to the West Indies, and Comte de Rochambeau's army would leave Virginia in the spring. And the stubborn king refused to give up his colonies. Despite what was a no-win situation, and amid growing support in Parliament to discontinue this too-expensive war, George III felt his heritage and his honor prevented that. And the recently-paroled Lord Cornwallis, who was exchanged for Henry Laurens, former president of the Continental Congress and held in the Tower of London, sailed for London on the same ship with Benedict Arnold and his family.

With the return of the army, the five Hudson Highlands doctors took on the burgeoning sick list. It became, yet again, a winter of prolonged hardship, deprivation, disease, and frostbite. Everyone experienced the mixed emotions of hopes and expectations versus the uncertainty of what was really happening overseas. Smallpox again attacked the camps in early December. Several men died before General Heath issued orders to resume regular inoculations.[2] It seemed to Eustis that nothing had changed except that he no longer had an older brother, and General Heath denied him leave to visit his family.

A lack of money was the overriding concern for the Americans throughout that winter. About six months earlier, Director-General Dr. Cochran had written to Congress that no one in the medical department had received a shilling in twenty-three months. As the hospital surgeon at Robinson House, Eustis was supposed to receive $120 per month, and the chief physician, Dr. William Burnet, was to be paid $140 per month. Also on staff were two surgeon's mates at fifty dollars each, a steward at thirty-five, a ward master at twenty-five per month and one matron, Mrs. Nardy, who was paid fifty cents a day.[4] Mrs. Nardy, probably with the help of other women, dealt with practical matters of comfort and care.

Cashless, unable to raise money, and relentlessly badgered for funds, Congress voted to cut expenses and consolidate the army's hospital department. In January 1782, Eustis learned that Robinson House would be closed and medical services relocated across the river to the two remaining hospitals—one in the barracks at West Point; the other at the New Windsor Cantonment.[5] The opportunity to be with the other young men in General von Steuben's and General Gates's households might have offset the loss of his more bucolic quarters. Once reestablished, Eustis asked Washington to order arriving soldiers to be inoculated and urged that the barracks be scrubbed. "The infection is still kept up by the arrival of recruits and men,"[6] he explained.

With the onset of spring, General and Mrs. Washington returned to the Hudson Highlands, moving into Hasbrouck House, a stone farmhouse overlooking the Hudson River in Newburgh, fourteen miles upriver from West Point.

Eustis again tried to get leave. Citing the denial of his earlier request, he begged Heath's "indulgence" for six weeks to two months to visit his family. Reminding the general that he had been in camp for almost two years, he promised he would immediately return if he found David Townsend still there.[7] Eustis omitted mentioning any family-related reasons—his brother's death and the fact his father had remarried.

In April, Washington received desperately disappointing news that the French fleet under Admiral de Grasse had lost the battle of the Saintes, named for the strait between Domenica and Guadalupe. The British triumph and capture of Admiral de Grasse returned control of the West Indies and its islands to British hands. There would be no French fleet sailing north to again offer aid to the Americans.

At the same time, elated by permission to take leave, Eustis set out on horseback with James Thacher and one servant. Nasty spring weather and bad roads used up nine days of travel. They stopped for an overnight with Deputy Governor Jabez Bowen in Providence, Rhode Island, where Eustis and Bowen got into a discussion about the merits and properties of coffee. Bowen insisted it was a sedative, and Eustis argued for its stimulating effects.[8] He had given up tea during his Harvard days, loved coffee, and would be a coffee drinker for the rest of his life. The popularity of coffee as a socially acceptable drink without the dangers of intoxication had spread, and coffeehouses had opened throughout America.

Acting against the king's wishes, Parliament acknowledged that Britain's military and naval superiority would not be enough to subdue an entire continent and voted to end all aggression against America. Orders were issued to General Sir Guy Carleton to relieve General Clinton, negotiate a peace to keep the Americans in the empire, end the British military presence in America, and transport all loyalists out of the country. Carleton would undertake this Herculean task over the next eighteen months.

Despite plans for withdrawal, there was no clear resolution or end date set for the war. Despite peace negotiations underway in Paris, General Washington worried that the British would regroup. He patrolled his lines, carefully watching New York. Rumors circulated of a possible treaty, but nothing, *nothing,* alleviated the general's discontent.

Back on duty following his leave, Eustis was reaching the end of his rope. Supplies had run out, and in September his hospital began to have problems with water because a spring, the only source of water, had nearly run dry. He asked General Knox for a return of "fatigue men" and a sentry for duties such as digging ditches and cleaning. He also requested six additional guards to help ration what little water that was left.[9] Without water, they could not even clean.

And they were getting nowhere with Congress. After receiving no congressional response to their first request for back pay, and after considering applying for relief from Massachusetts, another committee was formed with Knox at its head. Eustis helped draft and signed this second petition, again begging Congress for financial relief. He wrote: "We have borne all that men can bear – our property is expended – our private resources are at an end, and our friends are wearied out and disgusted with our incessant applications." On December 5, the committee approved a draft with fourteen signatures; four generals, eight colonels, one major, and Dr. William Eustis.[10.]

They decided to send three representatives to make their case and took the time to raise the necessary money. On December 19, Eustis hosted a send-off dinner in his rooms in New Boston. His guests included Colonel Henry Jackson, Dr. Thacher, and a fiery-tempered Scot, General Alexander McDougall, commander of the First New York Regiment and New York's equivalent to Samuel Adams. Glasses were raised to a hopeful future. General McDougall would accompany this new petition to Congress in January 1783.[11]

It was another winter of widespread dissatisfaction. A large number of soldiers, their terms of enlistment over, left for home. As soldiers were mustered out, the West Point barracks hospital closed and medical care was consolidated to a single hospital at the New Windsor Cantonment. Eustis's colleagues, Doctors Burnet, Thacher, and Townsend left for home, leaving two Massachusetts physicians, Sam Adams Jr. and William Eustis, to care for the army.

Although not yet known, a preliminary peace treaty had been signed in Paris on November 30, 1782. Sitting in his snowbound quarters overlooking the Hudson and dealing with despondent soldiers and supply shortages, Washington did not learn about the treaty until February. But it was not final, so the army could not be released. The unsettling prospect rose once again that the army might be disbanded without anyone receiving their wages or pensions.

Eustis, thirty, had few expectations. His family in Boston had moved on with their lives. Other than having a place to live with his brother, he was like many officers who devoted years of service to the Continental Army. He had no immediate prospects and no savings. At various times during the previous eight years, Congress had promised officers some kind of pension. But given the irregular pay process, Eustis had doubts about receiving a pension anytime soon.

By March 1783, the situation at West Point and New Windsor had grown more volatile. Congress had taken no action on the officers' second petition. Although well aware of the looming danger, the congressmen could do nothing to mollify the spreading mutinous sentiments. They simply had no funds. Congressmen James Madison and Alexander Hamilton, who had gained a seat after leaving the army to get married and practice law in Albany, had met with the Highlands delegation to try to devise a solution. Understanding the risk of mutiny, Hamilton got New York Governor William Clinton to give land grants to the officers from New York, including the head of the Highlands delegation, General McDougall.[12] Eustis was left out.

General Washington had hoped the well-justified claims of the officers would carry some weight in Congress, writing: "The sufferings of a complaining army on the one hand and the inability of Congress and tardiness of the states on the other are the forebodings of evil."[13] Despite his concerns, he refused to become directly involved, either for the army or Congress.

A coterie of disgruntled officers rallied at Ellison House, which served as General Gates's headquarters as well as Eustis's medical office. After two years away from the army, and having campaigned for the post, Gates had recently been returned to duty by Congress without consulting Washington, and become second in command. Disliking Washington, he undoubtedly would not report any disquiet or possible conspiracy among the officers.

Eustis had friends among Gates's staff officers. One was outspoken John Armstrong Jr. who anonymously wrote two inflammatory declarations airing officers' complaints and promoting rebellion. Circulating just days apart through the Highlands encampments, each urged Continental officers to remain fully armed until Congress compensated them fairly. He presented a bleak view: "Yes, my friends, that suffering courage of yours was active once – it has conducted the United States of America through a doubtful and bloody war . . . Can you consent then to be the only sufferers by the revolution, and retiring from the field, grow old in poverty, wretchedness and contempt? If you can – go – and carry with you the jest of tories and scorn of Whigs – the ridicule, and what is worse, the pity of the world. Go starve and be forgotten!"[14]

Washington immediately took control. He denounced the first circular, cancelled its called-for meeting, and issued a personal order for officers to meet. On March 15, after the arrival of a second anonymous letter, Eustis with about five hundred other grim officers met in a cavernous new log structure called the Temple, constructed just months before for church services, meetings, and dancing. Washington normally did not attend these officers' gatherings but, making a surprise appearance, he entered the hall just after General Gates had opened the meeting. He asked for permission to speak what became known as his Newburgh Address.[15]

He began with a direct repudiation of the anonymous letters: "How inconsistent with rules of propriety, how unmilitary, and how subversive of all good order and discipline." He speculated about the unknown author: "Can he be a friend to his country? Rather is he not an insidious foe?" and surmised that the author might be a British spy bent on destroying the military. His statement drew only embarrassed and uneasy acknowledgement. Then Washington, his hair graying, his teeth rotting, fished spectacles from his pocket to read a letter from a Virginia congressman. He famously said: "Gentlemen, you must pardon me. I have grown gray in your service and now find myself going blind."[16]

There was an uneasy silence. This was a critical moment. If emotions took over, the military could assume power and force Congress to do what they wanted. If Washington had taken the lead, he could have become dictator. Instead, he refused taking any side. His desperate audience finally capitulated, the officers acknowledging that their commander had indeed suffered as well. They would not take up arms—at least not yet.

Eustis and the other officers would soon hear in April that Congress had voted to pay them five years' salary instead of a pension. With that vote, the pending mutiny by the officers collapsed. In reality, Congress' motion was completely worthless. It still lacked money to dispense to anyone, officers or men. Nor could Congress even offer certificates because it could not afford the paper to print them on.[17]

Keenly aware of anniversaries, Washington publicly announced the ceasefire on April 19, 1783—eight years precisely after those first shots were fired in Lexington, Massachusetts. He notified Congress that it would be difficult to hold the men much longer. Morale and discipline were dangerously low, and large numbers of men were becoming increasingly disruptive. Realizing that to discharge the men without pay could cause an armed uprising, Congress settled on a devious solution. Men would be sent home on furlough pending the arrival of the official signed peace treaty from London. Each soldier was awarded three months' pay. As Congress had no money, financier Robert Morris, in a move that would lead to his bankruptcy, issued $800,000 in personal notes. Many sold the notes to get home. Technically, no one was mustered out.

Their impending separation and loss of contact became a popular topic of discussion among the officers. After years of working together, bonded by a common cause, the men found their associations extremely meaningful. Eustis and Captain Christopher Richmond, a Maryland man and aide-de-camp to General Gates, talked over ways to remain connected. They decided that an association, perhaps an elite club, should be created specifically for veteran officers who had served during the war for a significant amount of time.

The men discovered within days that General Henry Knox had the same idea, so Eustis went to confer with him. By April 15, 1783, Knox had prepared a proposal, described as a rough draft, for a society to be formed by the American officers and to be called the

"Cincinnati," named after Lucius Quintus Cincinnatus, a Roman statesman, farmer, and folk hero. According to legend, Cincinnatus left his plow twice to fight Rome's enemies and preserve the republic, returning each time to his farm.[18]

Before a month had passed, the rest of the officer corps, meeting at General von Steuben's headquarters in Fishkill, approved the plan. A charter was prepared and sent to veteran officers in the thirteen states. Officers who had served at least three years or until the end of the war could become members, paying an initial membership fee and contributing one month's pay to a permanent charitable fund. As Knox had desired, membership was hereditary and passed on to the eldest male descendant. By the end of 1783, each state had adopted the idea and formed its own state chapter. There were fourteen self-governing chapters; the thirteen states and France.

The Society of the Cincinnati formally came into being with Washington as president and Knox as secretary. The Massachusetts chapter elected the secretary of war, Benjamin Lincoln, as its president and William Eustis as vice president. Nearly all of the men recognized today as Founding Fathers or considered influential in the Revolutionary War, with exceptions including Samuel Adams and Thomas Jefferson, became members of the Cincinnati, and their descendants continue the organization to this day.

16

Moving On

In June, medical Director-General Dr. Cochran informed Eustis that he would be in charge of closing the hospital at the New Windsor Cantonment. Until the British left New York, Eustis had a skeleton staff of Sam Adams Jr., two mates, a steward, a ward master, and a matron.[1]

* * *

Benjamin Franklin, John Adams, and John Jay signed the Treaty of Paris, previously approved by Parliament, on September 3, 1783. About six weeks later, Congress ratified the treaty, issued a proclamation disbanding the army on October 18, announced it would reconvene in Annapolis, Maryland, and adjourned on October 30. It was the first of November before General Washington heard that the war was over, that the army was formally disbanded, and that Congress had left town. It had made no provisions for a peacetime army or overdue pay for troops, but it had directed that all Continental soldiers who had been previously furloughed were discharged.[2] The problem of getting rid of the men may have been solved, but Congress had yet to create a peacetime structure and figure out how this confederation of states would function.

On Sunday, November 2, 1783, Washington wrapped up final

details and issued orders to release the remaining troops. Hundreds packed their gear and headed out on foot or horseback the following day. Eustis remained until the end of November, closing the hospital, disposing of supplies, and finding wagons to carry home the few remaining invalids and disabled veterans.

The Continental Army's departure was not a happy occasion.[3] Intensity and purpose had long gone. There was no parting or closing ceremony. Disgruntled officers canceled their farewell dinner, and the army just faded away. Adding insult to injury, these departing officers were denounced for forming their fraternal society named for Cincinnatus. Although it was well-intended, because of its exclusionary membership news about the Society of the Cincinnati's creation so surprised people that it was quickly branded as unpatriotic, particularly by nonmembers.

Intended as a veterans' organization for officers, it alarmed pure republican thinkers. What Washington and others viewed as an association to help impoverished officers, others saw as elitist and a dangerous source of political power. Samuel Adams said it debauched the idea of the Roman hero, and he predicted society members would try to usurp the state legislatures and the Congress.[4] Suspicious of letting foreigners into an American organization, Adams worried that a chapter in France increased the danger that French influences could creep into this country. Equally disturbed and against all things military, Thomas Jefferson thought that the society threatened the possibility of military rule.

It took time for the public to understand this new organization of retired officers. Despite dire predictions, five years later nearly half of the delegates at the Constitutional Convention in Philadelphia were members. They no longer seemed so dangerous after ninety percent of the group voted in favor of the final official document.

In New York, the last of the British transports sailed away on November 25, 1783. As soon as General Henry Knox took

107

possession of the city, Generals Washington and Knox, accompanied by New York Governor Clinton, led a grand procession down Broad Way which was lined by militiamen. Supporters scrambled to arrange a cannon salute and raise a flag on the Battery. Making it difficult, the vacating British had greased the flagpole after nailing their flag to the top.

The last thirty or so officers of the Continental Army assembled on December 4 in the Long Room at the five-story brick Fraunces Tavern, officially called the Queen's Head and featuring a sign with a picture of Queen Charlotte, King George III's wife, hanging over its door. Knox, von Steuben, and McDougall were the only diehard generals to see Washington off.[6] The rest were junior officers. Washington embraced each man, walked to a nearby wharf, and boarded a ceremonial barge before a large crowd. Oarsmen rowed him across the Hudson River to New Jersey. He formally resigned his commission when Congress reconvened in Annapolis, Maryland, on December 23.[7]

William Eustis's position in the hospital, that had offered a semblance of security and status, vanished. He had persisted through the entire war—eight long years living in deprived circumstances, doing what he could, believing in independence and in Dr. Warren's vision. Military service and his hospital position had provided male camaraderie, officer status, and substantial medical experience. Forgoing the Washington farewell, Eustis packed his meager belongings, closed the hospital door, and helped the ailing Sam Adams Jr. return to Boston.

Homecomings for the unceremoniously discharged veterans had no fireworks, no celebrations, and no speeches. No appreciation of a grateful nation. The people of Massachusetts greeted their returning soldiers with little fanfare and the officers with none at all. The people had moved on in their thinking and were not interested in commemorating a rebellion. When the veterans began to arrive *en masse* in Boston during the summer of 1783, the reaction was one of alarm. Needy veterans kept stopping at the Town House without a single month's pay in their pockets or the means to get home.

Nearly all of the four hundred officers who were serving in the military when it dissolved were in financial difficulties. They resembled Massachusetts Captain Daniel Shays whose certificate of commutation could not restore his western Massachusetts farm which desperately needed repairs and rebuilding. To pay his taxes, he sold the sword presented to him by Lafayette.

The economy, based on trade beyond the country's immediate borders, had collapsed. In Boston, the shipping and carrying trades had always provided substantial resources, but now shipyards were silent and trade all but gone. Unemployed sailors and shipwrights loitered about the wharves and slept in the streets.[8] Shipbuilding had come to a standstill when Britain stopped purchasing cargo vessels built in Massachusetts yards. All had to be reestablished with new outlets, new ports, new countries. At least traditional cod fishing remained, thanks to John Adams who fought for fishing rights and refused to accept the British demand for sole access to the Grand Banks fishing area.

The Massachusetts Great and General Court made no mention of the promised bonus of five years pay in lieu of a pension for veterans. Congress had voted to *recommend* that bonus to the states, but each state could decide whether or not to pay its veterans. Congress' initial promise of a lifetime pension at half pay had prompted an angry uproar among Massachusetts residents who would foot the bill. That October, twenty-seven towns in western Massachusetts protested that the payment was completely against the concept of a volunteer militia. Massachusetts had replaced its entire congressional delegation earlier in June because it had voted in favor of severance pay for veterans. The state also set up a watch committee to keep an eye on the new delegates lest they become swayed into promising the state's money for any similar benefit.[9]

Sam Adams Jr., exhausted and sick with a chronic cough,

traveled with Eustis toward Boston. Along the way, Eustis may have mused with Adams on their horrific as well as rewarding experiences and the intense bonds with fellow soldiers. Either they were idealists or madmen addicted to a grand cause. No one other than a fellow soldier could ever understand this experience. To be all together, men from every colony sharing the mission to create a new republic! They had believed to the bone that they were unique and could succeed, but they equally understood how the French had made it possible.

A little more than a year before, the Continentals, hoping for positive news about a peace treaty, knew there still remained the possibility that the British might come out of New York. Deciding on a distraction combined with a farewell to the French, General Washington and the boisterous General Knox had arranged a grand *fête* in June 1782 to celebrate the birth of the Dauphin—the new son of King Louis XVI. A French officer and chief engineer, the Chevalier de Villefranche, designed a huge arbor six hundred feet long. More than a thousand soldiers then worked a week under French supervision to erect it using tree trunks for pillars and branches for the roof. Decorations inside included French and American military colors and emblems, with various weapons, muskets, and bayonets tied to the pillars. French and American officers with wives and invited ladies dined together in the huge leafy shelter, ending their meal with thirteen toasts, the firing of cannon, and fireworks. Eustis attended with fellow doctor James Thacher. A splendid ball followed as the finale. General Washington enjoyed dancing and partnered with the plump Mrs. Knox.[10] It was the closest anyone had come to celebrating their success.

America would create a free republic, its people able to choose their own government. But how would that work? The officers at West Point, gathering at various dinners, had speculated about the future of this new country and the most pressing question of all; How to govern this new confederation? The Confederation

Congress seemed to lack the vision.

Should people rely on the Congress to adapt the present system or hope a new individual might come along as leader? Perhaps it should not be one individual. Maybe three would be better. Some officers were more comfortable with military discipline and thought that General George Washington would make an excellent king. They could have their own King George. Others abhorred the idea, including Washington himself.

For the exhausted Dr. William Eustis, the next adventure was just beginning.

PART II: FORGING A COUNTRY
1783 ~ 1810

*We exhibit at present the novel & astonishing Spectacle of a
whole people deliberating calmly on what form of government will
be most conducive to their happiness ...*
—George Washington, Aug. 29, 1788
Cited in Edward J. Larson, The Return of George Washington, 339.

Louisiana will go all well—we have purchased a bargain ...
—William Eustis to Aaron Burr, November 12, 1803.
Special Collections, Louisiana State University.

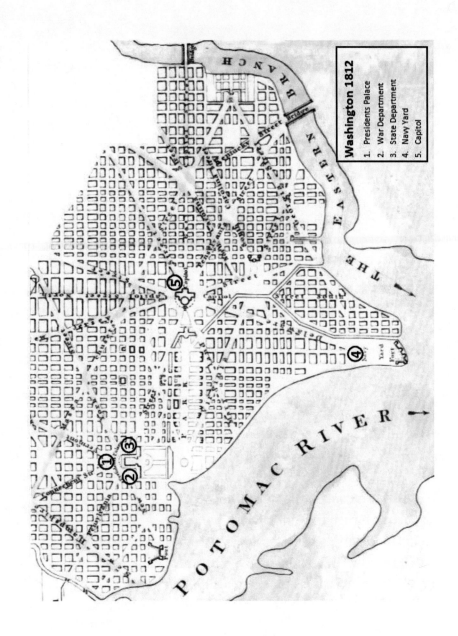

17

Democracy Run Riot

William Eustis found himself at a crossroads, with no clear sense of what to do in the postwar world, when he got home. His physical and mental recovery from total exhaustion required not only time and self-acceptance but a jumpstart combining new interests, improvements in the local economy, and especially, four years later, a farmers' revolt called Shays' Rebellion.

* * *

Eustis moved into his family's house "near the Mill Pond."[1] The family moved to its present house on the northwest side of Sudbury Street in 1767. It was a working-class neighborhood of shops, mills, and craftsmen's yards as well as homes. Sudbury Street led to a large pond on the north side of the peninsula created when Bostonians constructed a dam across a small bay of water. Rising and falling tidal action turned the mill wheels.

Eustis eagerly sought an appointment as a surgeon at Boston's new Foundling Hospital. His education and eight years of experience as an army surgeon made him well qualified. The board of directors concurred. But it never happened. Reluctantly, Eustis declined the subsequent offer, citing lingering illness. It took several years to completely regain his health.

114

This inability to work—the result of long service in appalling conditions—reminds us of post-traumatic stress symptoms today. Haunted by whispering ghosts, lost friends, and the needs of dying patients, he required years to feel stable again. Some five years later, claiming that "poor health will no longer hinder me from accepting it," he solicited the board at the Foundling Hospital for another appointment.[2] He was turned down.

Eustis spent time with his friend Sam who was suffering from a type of tuberculosis often called consumption. Sam lived with his father, Samuel Adams Sr., on Winter Street, not far from the Eustis house. The elder Adams was concerned about his son's friend, proposing that Eustis spend the winter of 1785-86 in the South, perhaps Virginia, "hoping in a warmer Climate to recover his Health which he lost in the service of the united [sic] States."[3] The senior Adams wrote a letter of introduction for Eustis to Richard Henry Lee of Virginia, a fellow delegate from the Continental Congress.

That fall, despite Samuel Adams's introduction, Eustis instead decided to visit with former army associates in a house in rural Petersburg, New York, loaned to him by William North. Several of Eustis's closest friends, equally directionless, were also trying to work out how to live in the peacetime world.

He wrote to North, who remained a close, lifelong correspondent, of his hope "that from pain & distress I am removed to a state of ease & happiness – from a view of defeat & imposition I have a prospect of health & I now expect some tolerable share of enjoyment."[4] North came to visit him in Petersburg and talked of his own decision to move near Albany permanently to establish a homestead. He planned to buy land, start a farm in Duanesburg, New York, and in 1787, he would marry Mary Duane.

In a later letter, Eustis confided that his health still varied. "Since your last visit in New York I have sustained more pain than I would have been willing to bequeath to anyone of my worst enemies – but I am clearly of candid opinion . . . I shall keep the house some weeks longer & then see some of your friends."[5]

* * *

The Confederation Congress had tightened restrictions on who could receive pensions, and Massachusetts enacted even more stringent laws. Everyone receiving pensions in the past had to reapply. Invalids or disabled soldiers were required to obtain certificates from army officers testifying to their service and from doctors verifying their disabilities. Once back in Boston, Eustis and his colleague, Dr. David Townsend, accepted jobs with the Commonwealth of Massachusetts to review veterans' applications to determine who had legitimate claims.[6]

Eustis's old friend, Dr. Jack Warren, had left the war effort after two years and was satisfactorily ensconced in a burgeoning practice. His household on School Street teemed with children and six servants including three free Blacks. After working at the army hospital in Boston instead of returning to the Hudson Highlands, Jack had stayed involved with the Massachusetts Medical Society and founded Boston's medical society.[7] The society's first meetings at the Green Dragon Tavern became the basis for the first medical school at Harvard College. Jack, one of its three instructors, lectured on surgery. Shortly after he returned, Eustis applied to Harvard for one of its first master's degrees.

Loosely linked by the 1777 Articles of Confederation, each of the thirteen states was a separate republic. Each made its own laws, determined its own taxes, and printed its own currency. Some states even levied tariffs on imports from other states. Two distinct philosophies had gradually emerged about the kind of government the unprecedented and still unstable republic should have. Political discussions expanded and evolved into two separate points of view.

Although Eustis had called Jack Warren "brother" years before, as adults their friendship cooled, strained by their growing differences about how the country should be run. The "conservatives," including Warren, wanted a strong central

116

government. Others, Eustis and fellow "republicans," favored limited central power and a state's rights to self-government. It may have been based on personal experience; Eustis had little faith in the Confederation Congress and little access to cash, his personal finances mirroring the lean economy of his state.

Nearly two years after his return to Boston, and with no response to his two congressional petitions, he wrote to Society of the Cincinnati cohort Henry Knox about a way to "promote the pecuniary interests of the Revolutionary War officers" and suggested a meeting of the society to see if it would send a "memorial" to Congress asking that officers be paid the interest due on their notes [IOU certificates] issued at the end of the war. He cited particularly those notes on which four years interest was due. He probably held some himself.[8]

In western Massachusetts, limited access to cash fomented anger and a rebellion by farmers. The state had refused to adopt any form of paper money. Taxes, bank loans, and debts had to be paid in hard cash, and the state dealt in whatever specie was available, usually Spanish. Taxes along with an economic depression hit especially hard in the part of the state where there was so little cash that no matter how hard small farmers worked, they found it nearly impossible to pay their debts. Country folk faced foreclosure and jail, and they pleaded for relief. When the legislature refused to respond, the farmers took matters into their own hands. Some formed armed bands and closed several courts to prevent hearings or more foreclosures. Massachusetts Governor James Bowdoin sent troops to reopen the courts.

Inadvertently, Daniel Shays became a leader in the farmers' movement. Formerly a captain in the Fifth Massachusetts Regiment, Shays had fought with distinction at the Battle of Saratoga. Lafayette honored him with the ornate sword that Shays later sold to save his farm. In September 1786, Shays and about five or six hundred farmers and veterans rallied to close the debtors' court in

Springfield. Called out to protect the court, the militia watched as the farmers chased the circuit judges and clerks out of town. A letter calling for resistance and signed by Shays was circulated, associating his name with the rebellion.

Henry Knox, newly appointed by Congress as secretary of war, rode out to investigate and happened to witness the militia's apparent inability to stop the mob's action. He realized that the country's only arsenal, containing nearly fifteen thousand muskets as well as artillery, a foundry, and gunpowder, was right there in Springfield. He brought exaggerated accounts of nearly fifteen thousand rebels under arms back to Congress and urged an immediate armed response.[9]

With the crisis at its height, Congress, meeting without a quorum in New York, voted to increase the federal army by two thousand troops. Actually, the lack of a quorum made no difference because Congress had insufficient funds and could not have paid for troops anyway. It considered asking General Washington to go to Massachusetts. Then, in a moment of brilliance, the Congress realized the mess could be referred to the Massachusetts state legislature because, after all, the rebellion and the armory were in their backyard.[9] The state's militia leaders felt otherwise. Why should they protect a federal installation when not a single federal soldier guarded it? The Massachusetts state treasurer could not even borrow money to supply its own volunteer army. Everyone was broke, and yet here was a situation where something had to be done.

In Boston, despite being sympathetic to the farmers' financial predicament, many people, including William Eustis, were outraged at this open resistance. Eustis did not believe that armed rebellion would solve anything. He condemned the farmers' actions. A republic should not permit armed insurgencies, and it could not allow this farmers' movement to continue.

The Society of the Cincinnati provided the solution. Major General Benjamin Lincoln, president of the Massachusetts chapter, rallied the Boston militia. Using his own money, and with help from other wealthy Bostonians, he mounted an expedition to Springfield.[11] Former Continental Army officers joined Lincoln. As the society's vice president, Eustis signed on as chief physician and surgeon for £15 a month.

Four months later, in January, Daniel Shays and his army of nearly fifteen hundred farmers marched on the arsenal for the third time to capture some of its stockpiled weapons.[12] General William Shepherd fired two rounds of grapeshot from the arsenal, killing three of Shays' men. When Eustis's division arrived three days later, the protesters had dispersed, and Shays was negotiating with General Lincoln. The next afternoon, Eustis, while riding with a group of militiamen, came upon a small gathering of men and, with the advantage of surprise, immediately led a charge against them. The farmers either fled or surrendered to the militiamen so quickly that there were no injuries.

Eustis, writing to Henry Knox from a camp in Hadley, stated he was so tired that he was feeling barely effective. He was intrigued by Colonel William Hull joking that he "will carry more in his head than we can probably crowd into his pockets . . .." This overly confident colonel would come back into Eustis's life many years later as General Hull during the War of 1812. "Colonel Hull knows everything – he has acted as prime minister & the secrets of state are as common to him as hard fare is to a soldier." stated Eustis.[13]

The rebellion ended when the Massachusetts militia surprised and surrounded about one hundred fifty men during a blinding snowstorm. Many insurgents fled to Vermont, and Daniel Shays retreated across the Connecticut River to West Springfield. Most of the leaders were captured and jailed. Federal troops arrived to man the arsenal by March. Although two ringleaders were hanged, Shays and others sentenced to death were later pardoned by Governor John Hancock.

Despite his very minor role, Eustis gained some notoriety for helping to rout one rebel group. Although his services as a doctor were never needed, he returned to Boston with an enhanced reputation, a little money in his pocket, some good stories, and, after nearly four years, a renewed interest in shaping the country's future.

Now in his mid-thirties, Dr. Eustis was handsome, well-mannered, educated, and recognized for his contributions during the Revolutionary War as well as Shays' Rebellion. Although his status as an eligible bachelor was widely known in Boston, it was town politics rather than marriage that interested him. For the next twenty-five years, Eustis remained single and active in local, then national, arenas of social, political, and civic activities.

18

E Pluribus Unum

Shays' Rebellion sparked the whirlwind for redefining the nation in 1787-88. The American dream of a republic—a government without hereditary rulers, with all power coming from the people—was not working.[1] Would it follow the pattern of previous republics and fall back upon a powerful leader to instill order? The country's lack of effective government became an international embarrassment. Abigail Adams, in London with her husband John Adams, ambassador to Great Britain, wrote to her cousin saying the United States had a humiliating reputation abroad. It had ". . . no Head, no Body, in short not capable of entering into any treaties, or giving authority to them."[2]

Something had to be done.

Congress altered an economic conference already scheduled for May in Philadelphia into a convention to revise the Articles of Confederation. Problems that needed to be resolved included protecting of the nation's interests in trade. The country could not safeguard its own shipping. All thirty-one vessels in the navy had been sold, and the navy had ceased to exist. And questions about ensuring access to the Mississippi River arose as Americans moved west.

The convention got underway in Philadelphia in May 1787 at

the State House (today's Independence Hall) after most of the fifty-three delegates had arrived. Elder statesman Benjamin Franklin traveled in a sedan chair carried by four inmates from the Walnut Street jail.[3] The convention began with a startling concept introduced by Virginia—that the *people* would become the component parts of the national republic rather than the *states,* making the government *of, by, and for the people.* Events progressed from there.

Without informing Congress, the convention threw out the Articles of Confederation and started from scratch. Keeping the shutters drawn to ensure secrecy, the delegates hammered out compromises and agreements in Philadelphia's summer heat for the next three and a half months.

A late compromise situated the nation's new capital on the Potomac River in a newly-created District of Columbia. This was a concession for southerners in exchange for their agreement to back Alexander Hamilton's financial plan. An earlier agreement counted an enslaved person as three-fifths of a white person to raise the southern population count and increase the South's representation in the House of Representatives. And until a capital city could be built, the federal government would immediately move from New York to Philadelphia—presumably a more civilized, less corrupt place.

During their final session, Benjamin Franklin invited all delegates to sign the document. The Confederation Congress in New York received a copy of the proposed Constitution and sent it to the states for their approval. For some, the mere fact that two luminaries, Franklin and Washington, were part of its creation and had signed the document gave sufficient reason for ratification. Not so New England.

Governor John Hancock delivered the new Constitution to the Massachusetts General Court in a joint session of the House of Representatives and the Governor's Council in October. They scheduled a ratification convention for January 1788 in Boston. With three hundred sixty-four delegates, it was the largest convention held in any state. In the contentious Bay State, signatures of famous people were not enough. Residents were highly suspicious of giving Congress power to overrule states and, especially, to have unlimited power to levy and collect taxes.[4] Hadn't they fought against taxes?

William Eustis was not a delegate to the commonwealth's convention. Instead, he tended to the dying Sam Adams Jr. Now thirty-seven, Sam had never recovered his health after contracting a form of tuberculosis referred to as a scrofulous disease. In the senior Adams's Winter Street home, the young men talked about their wartime adventures, the current politics of change, and their unease with a strong central government. Sam Jr. died eight days after the convention began.[5] Lieutenant Governor Samuel Adams Sr., one of the twelve delegates from Boston, left to bury his son, and the convention adjourned so that members could join the funeral procession.

Not only was Samuel Adams in mourning, but the grieving Governor John Hancock did not attend the convention, having lost his last surviving child, nine-year-old John George Washington Hancock, in a skating accident. A few days later, General Benjamin Lincoln, president of the Society of the Cincinnati, also buried a son.

The convention changed locations several times to seek more appropriate space and finally found it in the Congregational Church, whose pastor was a delegate, on Long Lane.[6] Visitors arrived early each day, filling the galleries to see what would happen and listen to the speeches. Those supporting ratification came from the towns along the coast. Those suspicious of these new developments came in coaches, wagons, or on horseback from the towns in the western part of the state.

The lack of a Bill of Rights proved to be a significant issue for the opposition who worried it would be British rule all over again. When it came time to vote, it was breathtakingly close. Even with the backing of Boston's major revolutionaries, the new Constitution was ratified by just ten votes. The decision made, however, bells rang out all over Boston, and the people poured into the streets. In celebration, Long Lane was renamed Federal Street.

And they were off! After ratification, the flurry of activity that followed throughout the states was unprecedented. Senators and representatives had to be elected before a presidential candidate could be selected. Old friend Henry Knox, now secretary of war, offered William Eustis the position of chief surgeon of the army hospital in the new federal government. Ambivalent about a return to the military, Eustis declined, preferring the status of a political position. He won election as one of Boston's seven unpaid state representatives to the state legislature with two hundred twenty-one votes.[7] Only James Bowdoin and Christopher Gore garnered more. Eustis would be reelected for the next ten years while continuing to practice medicine for his livelihood.

Eustis's mother had been a significant figure in his life. Therefore, caring for his distant friend Bill North's mother concerned him. He sent updates on her condition, "I visited your mother Sunday [and on the Friday before] I saw her because of a pain in her head which the unusual cold weather had given to old people in particular – this pain has been severe & affected her eyes . . . with moderations of weather she will grow better . . . she is a good woman & her love & confidence in you would carry her thro' fire & water."[8] Eustis even offered comfort when Mrs. North's cat died.

A year later, when "she was seized with a stroke of the palsy," he called in Dr. John Warren. The mother died, however, and Eustis informed North and offered his deep sympathy then dealt with the disposal of her belongings, asking, "how is it that the dirty things of this world intrude themselves into consideration of a higher nature & yet you must be told that Mr. Geyer will by my desire give place to her furniture – the disposal of which will wait your direction."[9]

While Eustis cared for Mrs. North, made his rounds visiting patients, and gained his footing as a representative at the State

House, the newly formed Electoral College gave all of its votes to George Washington as president and to John Adams as vice president. In early March, Washington departed Mt. Vernon for memory-filled New York, riding in a yellow coach through a three-hundred-mile-long tribute.[10] Wearing a ceremonial sword, he took the oath of office on April 2, 1789, on a second-floor balcony at Federal Hall, and a new era began.

With a long-range perspective, Washington decided to visit all of the former colonies in a grand review to bring the states together.[11] He would begin with New England, mapping out a month-long tour and traveling with three aides and six servants. Bostonians, thrilled to learn they would be the first major city to host the new president, crafted their celebration.

Appointed to the committee responsible for the ceremonies, Eustis nonetheless paid attention to educational issues. Initially, the town meeting had assigned Samuel Adams to assess the town's needs for public schooling. As a result, the General Court passed an Education Act in 1788 requiring all towns with at least fifty families to maintain a public school, and Adams had to work out how it would be done in Boston. Boys would attend school year-round; girls for six months. Girls would be taught reading, writing, and spelling, but boys also would learn mathematics and science.

Adams, now lieutenant governor to John Hancock, became chair of the new school committee, called the Committee of Twelve, with a representative from each of Boston's wards. Adams represented the ninth ward and selected Eustis for the fifth ward. They were tasked with the "instruction of youth of both sexes and for reforming the system of public education."[12]

In October 1789, as Washington approached, Eustis traveled with two other representatives to Spencer, Massachusetts, to greet and inform him of arrangements for the grand entry parade. Just as the president feared, elaborate celebrations were planned for his five-day visit. Washington usually traveled in an open carriage, but

125

he gave in to expectations, noting in his diary that he found, "this ceremony was not to be avoided though I made every effort to do so . . .."[13] Fully kitted out in his Continental Army regalia astride a white horse, Washington entered Boston on a cold, windy, overcast day.

The welcome procession involved the entire Society of the Cincinnati. As the Massachusetts chapter's vice president, Eustis, carrying a flag of white silk with the Union cockade, led local Continental Army veterans in the opening procession. Schoolchildren lined the streets in front of tradesmen holding white silk banners. Church bells rang, cannon were fired from the French fleet in the harbor and from Dorchester Heights, recalling the British evacuation. The streets Washington traveled across Boston Neck to the old State House were renamed Washington Street in honor of his visit. Declining to visit private residences, he stayed at the Ingersoll Inn on Court Street.

As the parade approached the State House, there was an enormous arch, designed by local architect Charles Bulfinch, crowned with a canopy and laurel wreath inscribed "Boston relieved March 17, 1776." Lieutenant Governor Samuel Adams welcomed the president on an elevated reviewing stand. There was an interesting bit of business between Washington and Governor Hancock, who wanted the president to call on him. Still peeved that Washington had been given the generalship of the Continental Army and then the presidency of the country, Hancock wanted to make it appear that he outranked the president on his own turf. Equally cranky because of a head cold and eye inflammation, Washington insisted on his rights as chief executive of the unified nation. A day later, Hancock, suffering from gout, made a public display of coming to welcome him.

They kept the president busy. He sat for a portrait and received maritime honors aboard the French flagship in the harbor. He attended a concert in the former King's Chapel, renamed Stone

126

Chapel, toured developing industries, and attended services at both Trinity Church and Eustis's Brattle Street Church. With the exception of one exclusively male dinner at Faneuil Hall for one hundred-fifty gentlemen, as the visiting heartthrob Washington spent evenings at dinners attended by the fashionable ladies of the town. Eustis and all state dignitaries were always in attendance. After five days of intense activity, the exhausted president headed north along the coast accompanied by four hundred cavalrymen. Tired of the festivities, he looked forward to relief in Portsmouth, New Hampshire, where he might go fishing.

Later, while a gratified Boston recovered, the Eustis household suffered tragic news. Nathaniel Eustis in Petersburg, Virginia, wrote to his brother William of "our dear beloved Betsy" dying at twenty-three on Dec. 9, 1789, in Norfolk, Virginia.[14] Nathaniel wanted William to pass his sympathies to their father, "the old gentleman." William's younger brother Abraham had died in Petersburg, Virginia, only the year before on December 24, 1788.

19

1790s: A New Country

The federal government moved from New York to Philadelphia. It would relocate to Washington City in 1800, allowing ten years to build the capital. By far the largest city in the United States, Philadelphia was comparable to London or Paris—ideal as the new nation's political, economic, and cultural center. Years later, the first major boulevard in Washington City, initially a woodland path, would be named Pennsylvania Avenue in honor of this first capital.

The 1790s became a decade of new beginnings. As a rising civic leader, William Eustis practiced medicine, served as state representative, and participated in an increasing number of activities connected to the welfare of Boston's residents. He maintained his independent thought in the legislature and fussed over details in any proposal. His desire for accuracy, perhaps from his medical training, led him to vote against bills in which the wording was not as specific as he desired or gave too much power to too few people.

Boston held to its sedate, morally proper values. Beginning in January 1790, and raising a certain amount of alarm, ideas for a theater crept into conversations. It was the only coastal city without one. Even Norwich, Connecticut, and Portsmouth, New Hampshire, had theaters. Voters at the town meeting considered repealing a

1750 statute that banned theatrical performances. Some argued that they were damaging to industry and frugality. Others argued that plays need not be like the licentious English stage productions and that some theatrical performances could serve educational purposes; that they might be a deterrent to immorality, improve manners, and bring society together. Eustis remained suspicious of theatrical influences.

Harrison Gray Otis gave a lengthy oration in the legislature about the evils of such performances. Minding their republican virtues and aligning with Otis, William Eustis and Lieutenant Governor Samuel Adams voted against a theater in 1792. Two years later, following revisions to the petition, the Federal Street Theater, designed by Charles Bulfinch, rose in the South End.[1]

Along with his work as a legislator and service on a committee to help the town's poor, Eustis sought a job at the almshouse where the town's nearly three hundred indigent poor lived, six or seven people per room. His application reminded the Board of Overseers that he was now sufficiently recovered to undertake a position,[2] and he secured the appointment for "Doctoring the State's poor" including "Inoculating with the Small Pox 87 persons on Castle Island."[3] Eustis wrote to Bill North about his new job: "I have not wealth nor much [of a] practice but I have health & a pretty good conscience. I shall have about £100 a year & the surgeoncy of the castle [the island fort in Boston Harbor] £50-."[4]

Recognizing his experience as a former hospital director and surgeon, as well as his work at the almshouse, the legislature asked Eustis to study possible sites for constructing a hospital. Finding that the almshouse yard was too small, the committee sought another site. To Eustis's satisfaction, construction on a new hospital and almshouse in an isolated area of Boston's West End began within three years.

All things seemed possible as the Massachusetts economy improved significantly with growth in overseas trade and shipping.

Ships sailed from the Bay State's harbors to ports around the world. On a single day in late October 1791, more than seventy vessels, coastal sloops, and trading schooners sailed from Boston. Among them was the *Margaret*, commanded by Captain James Magee, bound on a voyage of "observation and enterprise" to develop the fur trade on the northwest coast and then in China.[5] Magee would become important to William Eustis many years later when the captain sold his house.

Politics seemed the way to personal advancement, and he continued with his civic duties and served as a director of the Massachusetts Mutual Fire Insurance Company and the Boston Bank. As vice president of the Massachusetts Society of the Cincinnati from 1786-1810, he was invited to deliver the Fourth of July speech for the society in 1791. He was nervous about it: "I never came to the smell of gunpowder with half the reluctance & loss of appetite that proceeded this oration." Confiding in Bill North: "They heard me with great attention & after the most agreeable clap of my whole life – my chagrin was infinite that I had not made it a good thing & improved the opportunity. . . .. I am lazy & dissipated."[6]

He penned a congratulatory letter to Bill North on his marriage to Mary Duane. Moving to upstate New York, North had carved a farm out of the wilderness at the edge of a small town and married a local girl, taking his proper place in society as a married property owner—something Eustis was not ready to do.

Eustis served as a representative for the First District — Suffolk, Middlesex, and Essex counties—for the next nine years. He joined the Freemasons' Lodge of Saint Andrew where his mentor, Dr. Joseph Warren, had been heavily involved during the days of revolution. His initiate's vows pledged he would live his days in honor, integrity, and service to his fellow man. A man's sacred honor and his "word" were all he would take from this world. At times, politics annoyed him: "If you get into politics, remember what I say to you – you will be teased, mortified & anger'd infinitely beyond any pleasure to be derived from that kind of life."[7]

With the Constitution written and ratified and the federal government established in Philadelphia, Americans contemplated what they wanted their country to be—what image it would have, how it would work. In 1792, there were no national parties; no party platforms, no coordinated campaigns. Presidential and vice-presidential candidates ran separately as individuals. The two-party system began to emerge as two philosophies evolved. Anti-Federalists supported the idea of power being held by the states, listened to Thomas Jefferson, and became Jeffersonian-Republicans. Others, called Federalists, wanted a strong central government. They supported George Washington and Alexander Hamilton.

Aristocratic "English" versus revolutionary "French" principles set the two factions apart. Federalists were stereotyped as Anglophiles who lived in luxury and supported a central government as a more entitled, educated class of Americans. The Jeffersonian-Republicans, Eustis among them, were admirers of the simple country ideals of French philosopher Jean-Jacques Rousseau and favored a social contract among honorable men in a free society created through common effort.

Most Massachusetts residents were Federalists, reflecting the trade-based merchant economy of the Bay State in line with John Adams and his son John Quincy Adams. They supported Hamilton's argument for a strong national currency backed by a government that paid its debts. What was good for business was good for Massachusetts.

William Eustis backed Thomas Jefferson and the Republicans who were generally more prevalent in the South. With different needs than the North and fearing outside control, the southern states rallied behind the idea of states' rights and the autonomy to operate their own governments, be responsible for their own debts, and have the freedom to establish their own laws. They were opposed to maintaining standing armies during peacetime.

Political factionalism influenced daily residential life. Many a Federalist Bostonian, man or woman, would shop only at a store owned by a Federalist or visit a doctor whose political philosophy agreed with theirs. Federalist Dr. Jack Warren was known for resisting such polarization, yet somehow everyone also knew where he stood.

Eustis could not agree with Warren. His ambivalence about the Federalists might be explained by his wartime memories of congressional ineffectiveness and the lack of support for the medical community. He allied with his longtime friend, Dr. David Cobb, now a new Massachusetts congressman.[8]

Bringing joy to the Eustis household, William's youngest sister Nancy, often called Anne, married Henry Sherburne Langdon of Portsmouth, New Hampshire, in May 1792.[9] Langdon was the nephew of John Langdon, the governor of New Hampshire who had signed the Constitution. Although it required a two-day trip each way, the Eustis and Langdon families began frequent visits back and forth.

When the December 1792 campaign season began, Eustis was backed for state representative by the *Columbian Centinel,* citing his qualifications as "agreeable deportment, extensive information, firm and honest principles, his attachment to the interests of this state, and his truly republican regard for the national government."[10]

20

Striving toward a New Century

In 1793, the new French Republic declared war on longstanding enemy Great Britain. They would remain adversaries until the British won the Battle of Waterloo in 1815. Americans wanted nothing to do with another war. Leery of a French call for assistance, President Washington issued a proclamation of neutrality stating that since King Louis XVI was dead, the new United States would not become allied with the new republic.[1]

The United States craved recognition and freedom to trade, but both Great Britain and France stopped American ships, seized the cargo, then sold the captured ships. American crewmembers who could prove their U.S. citizenship were deposited at the nearest port, but British-born subjects were pressed into service with the Royal Navy. In a matter of months, two hundred fifty American ships had been stopped. Americans called it the Quasi War and talked of who they would end up fighting, the British or the French.

Responding to this continuous foreign harassment, Congress declared an embargo on trade with both France and Great Britain. American ships could not carry goods to France, Britain, or their colonies. Congress erroneously believed that American products would be so valued that Britain and France would accept the rights of neutral trade in order to have them.

William Eustis supported American neutrality, speaking in favor of the embargo at a town meeting in Boston's Faneuil Hall.[2] He argued that an embargo was preferable to war, particularly because this country was so ill-prepared. Bostonians listened, and the meeting adjourned with a resolution advocating careful caution. The embargo indeed threatened their shipping livelihood. *O Grab Me*, they called it, which was "embargo" backwards. But Bostonians would wait and see what happened.

David Cobb was Massachusetts' first congressman-at-large in Philadelphia. Eustis had known him for years, first as a member of Washington's staff, then as major general of Massachusetts' militia in 1786. They both had ridden out to provide medical care during Shays' Rebellion. Hoping that the embargo might work over the short term, Eustis explained his position to Cobb. Despite "the discontent, the murmurs of unemployed seamen, the chagrin of owners blown up by the idle, the clamorous & unprincipled which are to be found in every society," Eustis could "derive a consolation from the embargo which is considered a prelude to more serious resentment on the part of the country . . . the measure appears to be a good one."[3]

He reversed his position less than a month later after witnessing the disastrous economic crash in Boston. The loss of its maritime livelihood made the town impatient for a stronger resolution and, although opposed to rash moves, Eustis reflected its growing frustration: "D—n ye pimping restrictions, confiscate their [British] property & declare war."[4]

Within a day or so, however, all of Eustis's political considerations were overshadowed when his family suddenly needed his doctoring skills. What could and should have been a joyful family occasion became one of its darkest times.

Described as "the beautiful Miss Prudence Eustis" in the *Columbian Centinel*, Eustis's baby sister, who was eighteen years

134

younger than he, had married Francis Amory in 1792. Prudence, twenty-five, gave birth prematurely two years later and the baby, possibly stillborn, did not live. Young women knew the risks of childbirth; that even if their baby survived, they could not assume they would. And now Prudence lay dying.

Eustis tried everything he could to save her. He described his desperation to David Cobb on March 10 and the "horrors" of his inability to save his sister.[5] The family likely gathered around her bed, praying, and looking to him for a miracle. For a short while they thought she might recover. But she continued to weaken. Then she died.

The foremost killer of young women was childbirth and the potentially deadly accompanying childbed fever. Within a few days of giving birth a woman might feel the first chills that could spread throughout her body with shocking speed, and often she died. Not knowing about bacteria or microorganisms, doctors were unable to determine its cause. In the 1850s, Boston's Oliver Wendell Holmes Sr. finally discovered that childbed, or puerperal, fever was contagious. Before washing hands and sterilizing instruments became mandatory, a doctor could easily spread the disease from patient to patient.

Eustis fell into a black hole. His medical competence had been his identity, and nothing is more disheartening to a physician then a problem he cannot solve. An unspeakable tragedy, Prudence's death flashed him back to his days during the war and his earlier, often futile, attempts to save his patients. About a week after Prudence died, deeply depressed, he scrawled a barely legible letter to Cobb, referencing life in general, and the dark "hated" world.[6] This loss of his young sister carried Eustis further from medicine and toward politics where, no longer an innocent in the world, he could feel more effective. By the end of March, he wrote: "My contempt for the [medical] profession has derived a strong addition from the late unfortunate issue."[7]

Working through his grief, Eustis transferred his anger to the mistreatment of his country. "I feel most sensibly the indignity continually shown to our flag. Flag, did I say – shame on the word, an old rag hoisted by the most errant pirate that ever infested the ocean could not be less respected than the American stripes . . . so long as injuries are tolerable we ought to endure but there is a point beyond which endurance ceases to be a virtue."

He did not trust the British, and the French seemed only marginally better. "That we have nothing to expect from the honor or justice of G. Britain we must see by this time if we keep our eyes open . . . should [Great Britain] flourish in distressing our commerce, by G— I should be willing to try what efforts could avail in the contest. At least I would demand restitution & in the alternative of a refusal I would [ask] the French what we could rely on from them in case of the worst . . . At any rate 'tis our duty to be prepared for the contest."

Eustis fussed over the health of his friends. He ended his letter to Cobb with a classic piece of advice frequently given to others, including Thomas Jefferson: "I prescribe for you a ride every morning before breakfast & every evening before sunset. They will do you more good than all the prescriptory of the college of Philadelphia." Based on Eustis's advice to ride horseback to cure his bowel problem, Thomas Jefferson rode daily for several hours throughout his two terms as president.

Eustis added a postscript to his letter with an affectionate reference to the aging Samuel Adams, now up for reelection for governor, ". . . the Old Patriot will have a large portion [of the vote] which I confess myself old fashioned enough to be pleased with – There is a violence of decorum in dropping this old political horse."[8] As it happened, both Samuel Adams and Eustis were reelected to their respective positions as governor and state representative.

The public called for action against Great Britain, but Eustis worried that the "monstrous expense of calling them [the militia] into actual service almost frightens me: my hope is that every necessary preparation will be made, and that no great personal service will be required till the enemy are almost at the gate . . . The government was not made for you or me or A or B but for the whole, & if I am not mistaken they [the people] like it & will support it . . .. My idea is to make us strong as we can & speak <u>bold</u>."[9]

The family celebrated the marriage of William Eustis's younger brother Jacob to Elizabeth Saunders Gray in August 1794. For many more years, William would share their household and partner with Jacob on moneymaking schemes. Jacob was a merchant involved with various commercial trading deals; an office on Boston's wharves marked his growing success. Jacob and Elizabeth named their first son George, for the Eustis brother who had died in 1779, and their second son after his Uncle William.

After Prudence died, Eustis often made the two-day ride to Portsmouth, New Hampshire, to visit with his sister, Anne Eustis Langdon, who offered a sympathetic ear. In December, while traveling to Portsmouth, Eustis rode through villages and towns, witnessing the hardships caused by the embargo. "On the road I find everybody [no, not everybody] violent for everything revengeful & satisfactory . . . my fervent prayer is that we may not have occasion to use it—you must go on cool & withstand the shock of momentary opposition to measures [the embargo] bottomed on solid & lasting interest of the country. . .."[10]

Despite the embargo, Bostonians boldly forged ahead to improve their city. In February 1795, Eustis was appointed to a ten-member committee that was allotted £8,000 to purchase a piece of land "sufficient in size and location to build a larger state house."[11] Shortly thereafter, the committee, acting for the city of Boston, conveyed to the commonwealth a John Hancock-owned lot on the top of Beacon Hill and turned to Charles Bulfinch for the appropriate domed design.[12]

For the next five years, Eustis watched the new home for the state government gradually rise on Beacon Hill. Before any actual building could begin, a level surface had to prepared by reducing the summit by about sixty feet. Workers shoveled enormous amounts of dirt and rocks into horse-drawn carts that were trundled down the hill and dumped into the Mill Pond. Near the end of the decade, to Eustis's satisfaction and Massachusetts' pride, a large structure of red brick with a classical dome and side extensions rose on top of Beacon Hill.[13] On January 11, 1798, Eustis and his fellow politicians in a solemn procession carried the nearly five-foot-long gilded wooden fish known as the "sacred cod" that was wrapped in a flag from the old State House to hang in the elegant new House Chamber.

Special envoy John Jay negotiated a treaty to end the country's ruinous embargo. It was an utter failure. Eustis, having originally backed the Treaty of Amity, Commerce, and Navigation, felt betrayed by the outcome. He spoke during a public protest at Faneuil Hall in July 1795 and was subsequently appointed to a committee to prepare an address to the president expressing disapproval of the pending Jay treaty. But by April 1796, despite vigorous protests, the Jay treaty squeezed through Congress bundled with another treaty with Spain that allowed Americans free access to the Mississippi River. It seemed that trade along the Mississippi outweighed New England's trade across the Atlantic.

In a popular toast of the day, President Washington was hailed as "the man who unites all hearts," yet he decided not to become a king.[14] In 1796, every newspaper in the country printed his farewell letter announcing he would decline a third term. After nearly twenty years, American would face the painful reality of life without George Washington's guidance. The nine-year-old country would hold a contested national election—for the first time.

The Constitution stipulated that a qualified voter in each state could cast two votes for two people, each bearing equal weight, in presidential elections. The presidency was awarded to the man receiving the most popular votes, the vice presidency to the second-place finisher.

The country's 1796 election had two opposing factions: Federalists and Jeffersonian-Republicans. The Republicans chose Thomas Jefferson as their candidate. Federalists backed Vice President John Adams. Despite their mutual respect, Adams and Jefferson promoted opposing visions for the country's future. Not only were their ideas of government opposite, so was their behavior. Historian Joseph Ellis notes that Adams's style was to confront, shout, and rant about an issue, whereas Jefferson's was to evade, maintain pretenses, and work through deception.[14] The Republican's candidate for vice president was Eustis's friend, Aaron Burr of New York. The Federalists promoted Thomas Pinckney.

The election for this country's second president was punctuated with loud, accusatory rhetoric, flamboyant displays, and frequent claims of imminent disaster. The concept of a "loyal opposition" did not exist. Warring bands of believers made political alliances, and dueling personalities fought it out in barely civilized fashion, fortunately with dialogue and arguments rather than guns and swords.[15]

The electoral votes were tallied in February 1797. John Adams won the presidency. His chief rival, Thomas Jefferson, became vice president. Adams took the presidential oath of office in Congress Hall in Philadelphia in March. Vice President Jefferson had been sworn in upstairs in the Senate Chamber. Washington was greeted with applause by the dignitaries who gathered before the ceremony. It was a remarkable moment with Washington, Jefferson, and Adams, together in the same room.

It was not quite as exciting in the Massachusetts election in which Acting Governor Samuel Adams was elected governor after John Hancock had died in office. William Eustis had decided to run for the state senate. Securing 1,513 votes was not enough. He lost the race, declaring: "Perhaps if we had more charity one for another parties would never rise so high, nor the publick welfare sink so low."[16]

He would be reelected annually to both the House of Representatives and the school committee, remaining one of seven representatives from Suffolk County.[17] He hated the combative partisan campaigns: "After all 'tis a poor business, this of life where we live & prey one half of us on the other."[18] Then melancholy news arrived of his younger brother Nathaniel's death at thirty-four, the third Eustis sibling to die in Virginia.

21

Business & Burr

Ever since the two men had met during the early days of the Siege of Boston, Eustis had kept in touch with Aaron Burr, son of Rev. Aaron Burr, president of Princeton College, and grandson of Rev. Jonathan Edwards, noted preacher and philosopher. These religious antecedents, plus his own graduation from Princeton, gave Burr a certain pedigree and confidence.

Much like Eustis, Burr was handsome, witty, and impeccably dressed. As middle-aged men, they shared a similar nature as *bon vivants*. Three years Burr's senior, Eustis matched the New Yorker's interest in smart, accomplished women. Their correspondence discussed politics, election results, and, occasionally, mutual female acquaintances. Some of Burr's letters, using code words or initials, are nearly impossible to interpret. Intercepted letters threatened both personal and political reputations and, suspicious by nature, Burr guarded against any letter going astray or that could be read and published by others.

Both Eustis and Burr were Jeffersonian-Republicans and Francophiles. Burr wrote about the anti-France "posturing" of the Adams administration. How, he asked, could the United States, a country without a navy or army, hope to intimidate what was at that time the greatest military power in the world—post-revolutionary France? Napoleon, having risen rapidly, would become First Consul in 1799. Burr disagreed with the Adams administration's intent to borrow money, in his view "a ruinous system of loans," for new armaments. He did not believe "the bold language of the President, and the fierce speeches of [Federalist senators] . . . may intimidate the French directory so that they [surrender to] our Magnamity [*sic*] and Justice and submit to such terms as we shall see fit to impose."[1]

The two men had ups and downs in their friendship. At heart, Burr was an opportunist. If something interesting developed that might prove advantageous for him, he responded, whether a friend was coming to visit or not. Eustis, who traveled to see Burr in Manhattan in November 1796, arrived after two days to find Burr was not at home. Furious, Eustis left in a huff. Burr subsequently apologized profusely: "You drove off while I was in sight of the house – If you can apologize for me, you are the best of men, the most forbearing of friends."[2]

Politics, elections, investments, and employment may have occupied both men, but discussing the ladies was their avocation, especially Burr's. They kept track of each other's acquaintances. Burr cautioned Eustis in June 1797 about "two ladies," saying they are "mere adventurers," but begged Eustis to report on their connection to his "pleasure and happiness."[3]

That July, Eustis wrote back about one L.S. Eager to know when this woman would return to New York. Burr assured Eustis that he would not prejudice his interest. "You have excited my curiosity to an extreme. How could such an animal be months in my vicinity & I not even hear of her?"[4] As it happened, Burr began a romance with Leonora Sansay, a woman he met through Eustis, likely the L.S. of earlier letters. Mme. Sansay later married an older French merchant in 1800—supposedly after her romance with Burr ended. Yet it appears that Burr became the couple's marriage counselor as well as lawyer and continued as Mme. Sansay's intimate friend.[5]

There were few people with whom Aaron Burr felt comfortable discussing his liaisons. Among them were his uncle Pierpont Edwards and William Eustis.[6] Burr wrote to Eustis in June 1800, urging his friend to pay his respects to a Miss Susan Binney who was visiting in Boston, "if you have not forsworn all Virtuous women."[7] Susan Binney, twenty-three, about half the age of the two men in their late forties, was the daughter of Dr. Barnabas Binney, a prominent Philadelphia physician. Burr teased Eustis, calling him "cold and perverse" for not sharing an account of his time with the young woman. Eustis corresponded with Susan Binney for several more years.

Although keeping up with Aaron Burr's social life may have kept him amused, Eustis needed more than a medical practice to maintain his lifestyle as a gentleman. He urgently sought more income and various ways of improving his position. One popular trend was land investment.

Eustis visited Henry Knox at his new home in Thomaston, Maine, to scout for acreage to buy. He wrote to Bill North about thinking of him when seeing "a new world unfolding itself thro' the woods of Maine to the majestic waters of the rivers, bays & oceans."[8] He did not invest there, but he did in Boston, buying a wharf with buildings in November 1797 from his brother Jacob and his wife Elizabeth for $2,000.[9] The wharf, near Hartt's Shipyard, where the *Constitution* was being rigged, seemed to be a good location, not far from the Long Wharf with important wagon access to Ann Street.

William partnered with Jacob two years later to purchase a store and land on Union Street near the wharf.[10] The store, rented to various tenants, would be a steady source of income over the next twenty-five years. At the same time, he invested in another small wharf, again on the "northward side of Boston," paying $243 to John Taylor of Virginia.[11]

His legislative duties, investments, and doctoring

notwithstanding, Eustis still worried about money and securing his proper position in the world. Looking for further business opportunities, he tried being an *auchtioneer*, certified and licensed by Boston's selectmen.[12] He advertised in the *Columbian Centinel* on November 2, 1799, that he had taken over an auction house and would be available for transacting business as an auctioneer and commission merchant. There were many advantages: working with Jacob's import and export business, increasing his income, and gaining further introductions and political connections around the town.

Like most Americans of the day, Eustis was a self-made gentleman. He confided in Bill North: "I am consoled & indeed exult that no man can accuse me of anything little, mean, selfish, dishonorable or dishonest. I have a pride over those who think me a neglected man [unmarried] and who I really believe have a sort of pity for me measuring my mind by the little standard of their own which I am obliged to conceal – my pity is for them."[13] Politics forced him to mix "with men who are not so good or well-meaning as myself." He speculated that he might attract more political attention if he rode about the town in an elegant coach. Perhaps he had not attained a higher political office because he lacked a fortune. "It was once objected to me when a candidate that I did not live in a splendid house like the other gentlemen."[14] He believed he was more focused as a candidate, perhaps more knowledgeable and attentive than some who had been elected to office.

Both William Eustis and Aaron Burr were interested in women's education. Eustis had served on the Boston school committee since its inception. The prevalent education for girls offered reading and basic writing combined with social and household skills. Burr had become deeply involved in his daughter Theodosia's education, ensuring that she was schooled in subjects such as languages, the sciences, and mathematics that were normally reserved for young men.

Influencing both men was a daring and controversial publication, *A Vindication of the Rights of Women,* written in 1792 by English author Mary Wollstonecraft. She argued for equal education for girls, writing that it was the consciousness of "always being a woman" that inhibited women from becoming fully functioning human beings. "Women are systematically degraded by receiving the trivial attentions which men think it manly to pay to the sex, when, in fact, men are insultingly supporting their own superiority."[15] It was eye-opening material, and Aaron Burr considered it a book of genius.[16]

Wollstonecraft's writing concurred with the republican ideal of virtue as more than moral behavior, including being public spirited and striving for the common good.[15] Republicans believed the American republic would not long survive unless its citizens were virtuous in their public and private lives. The teaching and practice of virtue began in the household, the realm of women who thereby had a crucial role in shaping the future citizens of the new republic.

There was even talk within educated and upper-class communities about women having rights. It was all hypothetical, as it was difficult for women to have "rights" when they were legally dependent on men. Women could not own property or handle investments or money in their own right, but enlightened treatment of women indicated a sign of civilization.

A revealing collaboration between Aaron Burr and William Eustis in the field of education involved their altruistic action on behalf of Susan Lewis, daughter of Maria (Lewis) Reynolds. Mrs. Reynolds's social reputation had been ruined because of her affair with Alexander Hamilton. Burr had served as Mrs. Reynolds's divorce attorney and later acted as a guardian for her daughter, Susan. Burr implored Eustis to risk his own political reputation by finding a residential school for his ward. "I repeat & do assure you, she is to my belief, pure and innocent as an angel."[17] Aware of his public reputation, he assured Eustis that Susan was not his own illegitimate offspring, and Eustis located an appropriate boarding school in Boston.

* * *

The sand in the century's hourglass was rapidly running out when unexpected news swiftly circulated from Mount Vernon. While overseeing his plantation, George Washington had ridden out in sleety weather and returned home soaking wet with a sore throat. Three different physicians had been called, and he had been bled repeatedly. He died on December 14, 1799, at sixty-seven, of "quinsy," a streptococcus infection. When the news reached Philadelphia on December 17, people gathered to ring the Liberty Bell. Black fabric was draped on Washington's church pew and on the door to the presidential mansion.

22

The Election of 1800

After a decade as a state representative, Eustis decided politics would take precedence over medicine. He ran for the United States Congress in 1800. Although Eustis was never wholly accepted by Boston's Federalist gentry, people living elsewhere considered him a suitable candidate.[1] While Eustis hoped to be elected in Massachusetts, the nation at large followed its third presidential campaign.

This race, arguably one of America's more significant and bitter presidential contests, attempted to shift the country from one party's control to another—Federalists to Republicans. It had never been done. Federalists John Adams and Thomas Pinckney, second-term candidates, ran against Republicans Thomas Jefferson and Aaron Burr.

Political groups and newspapers did the campaigning; not the candidates themselves. Demonstrating eagerness or making promises to constituents, it was believed, indicated a candidate's essential unfitness for office. But if he remained aloof, the public could trust that he would not abuse the power given him. It was this reputation for honesty and integrity that qualified a man for the office, not a craven exhibition of personal ambition.

There were no boundaries between acceptable rhetoric and outright slander. The American people had never before experienced so much vilification, rumormongering, and mudslinging. Tempers ran as high as differences ran deep. The 1796 campaign may have seemed contentious, but nothing prepared anyone for this second round. Newspapers, openly allied with political factions, whipped up public frenzies of fear and alarm. A Federalist newspaper in New York predicted Jefferson's victory would bring a flood of French and Irish revolutionaries, "the refuse of Europe," into the country to launch a Jacobin-style reign of terror. Jeffersonian-Republicans struck back, accusing Federalist John Adams of being a monarchist, a warmonger, and a secret agent of the British.

Federalist and Yale College President Timothy Dwight warned that if Thomas Jefferson won, "The Bible would be cast into a bonfire, our holy worship changed into a dance of Jacobin frenzy, our wives and daughters dishonored, and our sons converted into the disciples of Voltaire and the dragoons of Marat."[2]

With single-minded focus, Federalist Alexander Hamilton campaigned against Aaron Burr, accusing him of being unbalanced, lacking in moral values, despising democracy, and being an "American Catiline." (A Roman conspirator indicted by Cicero, whose crimes included incest and murder of his sister, wife, and son.)

There were hard feelings even *within* the Federalist Party.

Congress assembled in January 1801 to read the Electoral College vote from the previous fall. Adams was not present, and Jefferson, assuming he had won, announced the results. Shockingly, there was a tie. He and Burr had seventy-three votes apiece. Adams had sixty-five and Pinckney sixty-four. Although it had been more or less understood among Republicans that Jefferson would be president and Burr vice president, now a winner had to be determined by the House of Representatives. The tie would not be resolved easily.

The bitter campaign continued until the House gathered on February 10 to select the next president. Without the possibility of litigation or prosecution for defamation of character, speeches and newspaper articles became even more outrageous, aggressive, and insulting. Jefferson was portrayed as a dangerous atheist. Handbills accusing Burr of being a deviant, preying on the female population of Washington City, were widely distributed. Hamilton announced he would support Jefferson over Burr as the lesser of two hated evils.

Burr wrote to his friend Eustis: "The handbills were numerous . . . to vilify A.B. was deemed of so much Consequence, that packages of them were sent to various parts of the Country." Although his friends urged him to publicly deny these accusations, Burr refused: "I always presume that my friends will treat as false, everything said of me, which ought not to be true."[3]

Some fellow Republicans thought that Burr had guaranteed that should he be elected president, he would resign in favor of Jefferson. The Federalists considered supporting Burr simply because he was not Jefferson—and because Burr had a military record and Jefferson did not. Rumors circulated that if Jefferson was not selected, Virginia would leave the Union. Burr, not expecting to be in such a strong position, stayed away from Washington City and waited to see what would happen.

The office was Burr's to lose. If he had campaigned, it is likely he would have become president. By his own standards, however, he acted correctly, disdaining competition with Jefferson. Although he never negotiated for the presidency, Burr did send a letter to the House of Representatives stating that he would indeed accept the job if the House so decided.[4] Hugely annoyed that Burr had not graciously retired, Jefferson, who was prone to hold grudges, began a lifelong vendetta against him.

Burr again wrote to Eustis about accusations that he had broken his word to Jefferson, saying that the Federalists completely ignored his disavowal of any agreement with Jefferson.[5] They would believe what they wanted, so why should he issue yet another statement? Negotiations in the House of Representatives continued for a week. As it happened, the Federalists were not sufficiently united to make Burr president. Some sided with anti-Burr Hamiltonians

It took six days and thirty-five ballots before Delaware withheld its vote based on the possibility that Jefferson would strengthen the navy. Actually, Jefferson hated the idea of any navy and did not acknowledge any such deal. On February 17, 1801, however, Thomas Jefferson was elected on the thirty-sixth ballot and became the third president, and Aaron Burr was declared vice president. It was less than three weeks before the inauguration.

In Boston, William Eustis, forty-seven, defeated Josiah Quincy for the Suffolk County seat in the United States House of Representatives. The newspapers called the election a "triumph of republicanism." Campaign literature had touted Eustis as a tradesman's son, and "a friend to the Constitution, but...not a friend to a Standing Army, heavy taxes, Land taxes, a War with France, or eight percent loans."[6] As a candidate, Eustis attempted to unite moderates in both parties, carefully incorporating centrist Boston Federalists.[7] Riding on the incoming wave of Jefferson's Republican popularity, he garnered 48 percent of Boston's votes with big majorities in the surrounding towns to become the only Jeffersonian-Republican sent to Washington from Massachusetts.[8]

The *Constitutional Telegraph* hailed the election and congratulated "every genuine *whig* of '75 that Eustis [was] chosen representative to Congress from the federal district." It noted with astonishment that upwards "of eighteen hundred independent citizens could be found to support a candidate whom all the Tory papers had announced as the enemy of a Washington and an Adams."[9] The campaign did feature some questionable behavior. Henry Jackson reported to Eustis's friend David Cobb that, in Boston, "The votes exceeded four hundred more than was ever known to be given in the town. I suppose that near one thousand votes were illegal."[10]

William Eustis joined eleven other Massachusetts representatives elected to the Seventh United States Congress. Eustis chortled to Bill North after the election: "You a Senator & I a member of Congress!"[11] Less enthusiastic, outgoing president John Adams wrote to Abigail from Washington that he felt depressed about the election and probable divisions in the country, noting in a postscript, "Eustis won."[12]

Fisher Ames and Federalist Christopher Gore, both Boston lawyers, politicians, and Eustis's contemporaries, did not know quite what to make of his politics. Although he was a Republican, some of Eustis's opinions reflected Federalist thinking. "Eustis will have a difficult game to play. If he spiritedly supports revenue, a navy, and credit, what becomes of Jacobinism [Republicanism]? If he joins in demolishing them, what becomes of his Boston support?"[13] Ames had known Eustis for many years; his father being Dr. Nathaniel Ames of Dedham to whom Eustis had paid child support for the young daughter of Sally Edwards.

Nevertheless, Eustis had won his first election to national office representing the people of Suffolk County and would go to Washington City where inaugural ceremonies were scheduled for March 4, 1801. He had one obligation first—a trip to Albany.

Five months earlier, Aaron Burr had asked Eustis to evaluate his barely eighteen-year-old daughter Theodosia'sprospective husband, Joseph Alston, twenty-two, a slave-holding rice planter and an aspiring politician from South Carolina. Craving assurance that the young suitor was a worthy companion for his precious daughter, Burr implored Eustis to "analyse and anatomize him Soul & heart & body so that you may answer me all questions which I may put to you."[14]

Burr, his daughter, and her friend, Natalie Delage, left New York for Albany in January 1801 to prepare for Theodosia's wedding.

Burr, feeling upbeat, wrote to inform Eustis of their arrival, looking forward to time to talk personally, referring to his intended rice-planter son-in-law as "the Rice." He sent directions to his rented house on the corner of Market and State Streets, noting they would have Eustis's room ready. Burr relayed that while he was on legal business in Albany that morning, the "girls" openly rebelled and, despite his belief that he rented "pretty decent lodgings," had re-furbished half the house before he got home.[15]

On February 2, as an informal member of Burr's family, rather like an older uncle, Eustis attended Theodosia's small evening wedding to Joseph Alston. Once Theodosia was married, both men had barely a month to get to the capital for the opening of Congress. Eustis, likely traveling down the Hudson River, arrived in brand new Washington City with two weeks to spare. Burr followed about a week and a half later.[16]

Eustis needed to locate a place to live in Washington, learn how to get along, find his desk in the House of Representatives, and make friends. He would be living for five to six months in the nation's new capital which was still in a wilderness. Unsure about expenses, he worried about giving up his medical income. He had discussed his apprehensions with Burr at Theodosia's wedding.

* * *

The 1801 inauguration was America's first peaceful transition from one controlling party to another. The incoming Jeffersonian-Republicans were committed to liberal principles of international commerce that they thought would promote peace everywhere. They believed that republics were peaceable by nature and neither needed nor could afford a traditional army and navy. Federalists thought the government should be strengthened in the European manner and be ready for war.

Eligibility to vote now included taxpayers as well as property owners. The republican principles involving common people meant these people could be and were elected to office. Republican leaders in the North made speeches, held rallies, and wrote pamphlets repeatedly appealing to mechanics, laborers, and farmers to elect men of their own kind—as had happened with William Eustis. Public opinion soon became the foundation for government, society, and culture.[17]

John Adams wrote to fellow Boston lawyer William Tudor about Burr's success. "That he should have the Same Number of Votes with Mr. Jefferson Shews the astonishing force and Energy of Party Spirit. Mr. Hamilton has carried his Eggs to a fine Market. The very Man, the very two Men of all the World that he was most jealous of [Burr and Jefferson], are now placed over him. . .. I am anxious for two Men in Massachusetts Lincoln and Eustis for both of whom I have long had a great regard."[18]

23

A Capital Life

Vice President Aaron Burr went to Washington only for the months when Congress was in session and otherwise practiced law in New York. Shortly after Congress began its new session, Eustis received an update about Theodosia along with some advice in Burr's usual cryptic style.

"You can afford to abandon the practice of Physic and if this be true, it is a duty you owe to yourself, to your friends & to your Country—by the first I mean W.E. & all the sex . . . by the second A.B. [Aaron Burr] and T.B. [Theodosia Burr] And by the third + + + + + [a personal code]. But now for the Calculation—

You have I know some income independent of your Drs profession . . . .

Say . . . 350 –

Six Months pay in Cong . . . 1080 –

Allowance for Travelling . . . 270 –

$1,700 – which will or ought to support any Bachelor in the U.S.—During the Six Mo. Residence in Washington, you will not, without the aid of Gambling, be able to expend more than $600.—This Calculation

goes for two years only—long enough in Conscience—If
you choose to survive that, and to quit Cong. —the thing
will be easy and leaves no room for hesitation or anxiety
. . ." [1]

Although Eustis had no intention of losing money at gambling
or the horse races, life as a congressman would not be simple. Not
only did he need to support himself, but he was in a tricky situation.
He had to walk a tightrope between his friend, Aaron Burr, and
Burr's enemy, President Jefferson. And he worried about where he
stood with Bill North, who had arrived in town as a member of the
opposing Federalist faction.

Eustis wished everyone could leave their politics out of personal
friendships. "There had been a villainy in this business [politics]
which takes from me all patience – If you want to defray the
Constitution & substitute a golden calf – strange & mad as the
project in my view, no idea that you had grown so bad could enter
my head. This has nothing to do with friendship or society – it is or
ought to be an abstract business concerning which men equally good
may differ as well as about their wigs or their breeches . . .." [2]

Living in Washington City was a challenge. The federal district,
located between the Potomac and the Anacostia Rivers, had been
selected by George Washington. Now, ten years later, the capital,
rising out of the swampland, was still undeveloped and barely
settled. The summer heat was terrible and the mosquitoes worse.
Travelers might ask for directions only to find they had reached their
destination. The federal government had moved in during the
previous autumn while the nation considered who would become the
next president.

For Thomas Jefferson, an independent country presented the
perfect opportunity to create an idyllic society in the ideal rural
setting. As secretary of state under Washington, he had general
supervision over the design of the new capital. Pierre Charles

L'Enfant, a French-born civil engineer, created the basic layout for streets and avenues, the Capitol building, and the President's House. Although it was called a city and looked pretty good on paper, it was hardly that. Jefferson envisioned the Rome of the New World, but when people arrived, they saw a vast construction site of unfinished neoclassical temples. Name changes seemed important. Goose Creek, renamed the Tiber for Rome's river, meandered through the center of the settlement. The high rise of ground intended for the Capitol building became Capitoline Hill. Other than high hopes and visions, there was nothing matching the splendor or refinement of European capitals.

When the federal government arrived, one hundred nine houses had been built of native brick or stone. The total population numbered fewer than four thousand people with two hundred thirty-three males owning property, a noticeable contrast to the two former capitals, New York City and Philadelphia, both with populations well over forty thousand. Counting Eustis, the government numbered one hundred six representatives and thirty-two senators with assorted federal employees and officers. They joined 2,464 white people, six hundred twenty-three enslaved people, and one hundred twenty-three free Black people.[3]

It was completely rural. Cows grazed in open areas, chickens and hogs rooted in refuse, and bullfrogs croaked along the Tiber. Roads meandered into trails, and houses were spread far apart. Instead of wide boulevards and magnificent buildings, there were cleared fields.[4] Venturing forth on the unpaved pathways, inhabitants risked life, limb, and carriage. Scattered throughout the area were discarded piles of construction debris, shacks, clusters of boarding houses, and backyard privies. Very few men chanced finding their way between buildings after dark.

The presidential residence rose a mile and a half from the half-built Capitol, down a straight woodland path called Pennsylvania Avenue. Dolley Madison, wife of the fourth president, James

Madison, finally finished and decorated the residence. Two brick buildings, one for the Treasury Department and another for the Departments of State, War, and Navy, were on either side.

Hardly anyone could say anything flattering about Washington City. For those elected to Congress, it became "this city which so many are willing to come to and all so anxious to leave"[5] and described as "mostly houses with no streets and streets with no houses."[6] Gouverneur Morris, a congressman from New York, arrived the same year Eustis did. He wrote to a friend: "We want nothing here but houses, cellars, kitchens, well-informed men, amiable women, and other trifles of the kind. . .it is the very best city in the world for a *future* residence."[7]

There was no central point for the town such as a village common or church.[8] Instead, there were three small communities: one near the executive mansion, one on the opposite side of the Tiber around the Capitol, and the third near the Navy Yard on the Anacostia River. The Supreme Court justices met in the basement of the Capitol during their two months in town.[9] A flagstone walkway had been started from the President's House, sometimes called the Palace, toward the Capitol; and a footpath strewn with stone chips had been started from the Capitol toward the President's House. But the pathways did not connect.

In the morning, legislators walked down to the Tiber River to fish or hunt ducks before Congress convened at about eleven o'clock. It then "rose," or adjourned, for dinner at about three o'clock. There were two places of amusement: a racetrack and a theater that featured revues.[10] Horse racing, the "sport of kings," was a southern gentleman's entertainment, and Washington was a southern town.

Eustis moved into Mr. Pontius Stelle's hotel on First Street between A and B Streets, one of eight boardinghouses clustered near the Capitol that provided short-term accommodations for congressmen.[11] The neighborhood provided all of the essentials congressmen needed: a tailor, a shoemaker, a washerwoman, a grocery store, and an oyster house.

On March 4, 1801, after being sworn in as a freshman congressman, Eustis witnessed Jefferson's inauguration and the transfer of power in the Senate Chamber in the completed north wing of the Capitol. Aaron Burr was sworn in as vice president before Jefferson.[12] Senators crowded over to one side. Eustis and the other representatives were wedged into the other side. Many remained standing so that the ladies in attendance could sit. When control of the government peacefully shifted from one party to another, it proved that this uniquely democratic nation with a popularly-elected government could actually function.

The ceremony over, Jefferson walked back to his boardinghouse and sat down to dinner with about thirty fellow boarders. He continued to live at the boardinghouse for another two weeks before moving into the President's House. An American aristocrat, Jefferson fancied himself a simple child of nature rather than what he actually was—a grandee, a slaveholder, a gourmet, a hedonist, and a clever, ruthless politician.[13] His was a life of careful contradictions. A romantic, he kept a lock of his dead wife's hair wrapped in a page from their favorite novel, *Tristram Shandy* by Laurence Sterne, in his desk.[14]

Jefferson's friend, fellow Virginian James Madison, became secretary of state, and his wife, Dolley, who was seventeen years younger, became Jefferson's official hostess. The Madisons moved into a house on F Street in the village area around the President's House. The cabinet also included financial wizard Albert Gallatin of Pennsylvania as secretary of the treasury and, remaining as secretary of war, General Henry Dearborn. Throughout Jefferson's two terms, the cabinet's decisions were not reached through consensus but by vote in true republican fashion with the president having one vote.

Eustis, with his charismatic personality and irreverent wit, met and befriended people of all ages from all over; North, South, the seacoast, mountains, and the frontier. Many came from different cultures and ethnic backgrounds. They had different standards of behavior. When the work day ended, the congressmen retreated to their regional residential groups. Many were like Samuel Adams who considered himself a citizen of two countries, Massachusetts and the United States.

For Eustis, boardinghouse life was a combination of college dormitory, political club, and hotel. It was familiar ground, much like his experiences at Harvard College and in the Hudson Highlands. Residents were summoned to the long dining table by a dinner bell. They gathered around the evening fire after dinner. Manners were informal. Men removed coats and boots to be comfortable. Very few politicians brought their wives to Washington. In this man's world, without a household to run, there was nothing for women to do.[15]

Eustis worked at his desk among other congressmen in the chaotic House Chamber. Comings and goings were constant. Author James Sterling Young offers this description: "Some [congressmen] gave audience to the speaker of the moment; some sat at their desks reading or catching up on correspondence; some stood chatting with lady friends invited on the floor; others dozed, feet propped high. Page boys weaved through the crowd bearing messages; pitchers of water...bundles of documents, calling out members' names, distributing mail just arrived on the stagecoach. Quills scratched . . . newspapers rustled, desk drawers banged, feet shuffled through a sea of documents strewn on the floor. . . and bird dogs fresh from the hunt bounded in with their masters."[16]

Congress had no established rules in 1801—no one with authority to stop debate, no party leaders, and, consequently, no particular spirit of conciliation or deference to the opinions of others. There were no limits on the number of times a member could speak about a bill. Orations depended on one's stamina and could last for two or three days. The boardinghouse groups generally voted as blocs, and political factions did not have broad control. Party affiliations were not officially recognized, yet holidays, militia meetings, funerals, parades, and every form of print reflected partisan ideas or causes. The Republicans made the Fourth of July, with its celebration of Jefferson's Declaration of Independence, their paramount holiday. The Federalists countered with major celebrations for George Washington's birthday on February 22.[17]

By September 1801, Eustis acknowledged that those first months in Washington had not been easy. Compared to Bill North in the Senate, he felt he had a harder time in the contentious House. ". . . you have rode at easy anchor on a tranquil sea – and may the good god preserve you from the rude buffeting which have beaten back some of your friends . . .."[18] He puzzled over how to interact with friends in the political world; how to separate party issues from personal friendships. Conflicted about how to maintain a friendship with anyone in the Federalist Party, he wanted to know if North, a Federalist, could remain a friend. He tried to explain: "I go . . . by myself, expecting neither joy nor comfort of any kind excepting in one man [Jefferson] of whom you do not think well – will you pray for me? Or are you poisoned?"[19]

24

Whiskey and Reelection, 1802-1804

After the summer recess, Congressman Eustis rejoined Washington City's mostly male society. Still watching over his deceased son's friend, elderly Governor Samuel Adams gave him a letter for President Jefferson; "Doctr: Eustis will be so kind as to deliver you this letter —I am perswaded, you will find him a man of a candid and fair Mind and liberal sentiments."[1]

And his constituents sent letters—some encouraging, some with despairing pleas due to a sinking economy. One petitioner desperately hoped for compensation because of his "exertions in Canada" during the Arnold expedition in 1776.[2] His only reference was Colonel Burr, now the vice president. Another wrote pleading to be retained in the diminishing army. Jefferson, who believed in a volunteer militia, had reduced the country's standing army to twenty-five hundred men.

David Townsend sent news that Massachusetts' critical seagoing trade had slowed considerably with very few ships transporting goods and tobacco to France and England. He urged Eustis to remain independent from any partisan alliance, "in spite of all party considerations in the face of calumny . . . 'tis certain your best judgement is your surest guide."[3]

Looking ahead to his spring return to Boston, and contemplating another run for office, Eustis considered changing his residence. Moving back in with his brother would not suit his image as a congressman, so he wrote to a Hudson Highlands friend, General Henry Jackson, asking for advice about sharing a residence or finding a place to live. A real estate investor who was developing Beacon Hill and a lifelong bachelor, Jackson lived on Tremont Street as a companion for socialite Hepzibah Swan while her estranged husband, James Swan, resided in Paris. The two knew everything and everybody in Boston, and Jackson owned a boardinghouse.

Jackson sent Eustis encouraging suggestions about making a complete change, and although his boardinghouse had no room available, he suggested other solutions. Eustis might find a country place from April through October within ten miles of Boston, and for the four winter months he should find lodging, preferably two rooms, in town at a "reputable" boardinghouse or with a private family. He urged Eustis to come to see him when he returned to "dear Boston."[4]

Reality intruded, however, and Eustis went back to his family home to initiate his campaign for reelection. His Federalist opponent, John Quincy Adams, had returned to Boston after serving as U.S. minister to Prussia. Both men became personally and actively involved in the campaign. In Eustis's opinion, "The ostensible difference between the parties is that one [Democratic-Republicans] would treat first & fight afterwards if necessary – the other [Federalists] would first fight & then treat."[5] He maintained good relations with the Boston Federalists, who considered him socially respectable and a moderate among Republicans. Secretary of War Dearborn decided that the congressman had "a great deal more *prudence* than I had heretofore given him credit for as a politician."[6]

Vice President Aaron Burr, knowing he would not have a second term, considered running for governor of New York. Threatened in their quest to control that state, DeWitt Clinton and Alexander Hamilton ramped up their efforts to destroy Burr's reputation, defeat his efforts to win the governorship, and remove him from New York politics. James Cheetham, editor of the New York newspaper *American Citizen*, consistently attacked Burr with scurrilous articles including threats to publish a list of the twenty top prostitutes in New York City who all claimed Burr as their favorite customer. Although not in New York, Eustis was known as a friend of Burr's and became a target, accused of ulterior motives and being under Burr's influence whenever he spoke in Congress.[7]

Summering at Monticello, Jefferson carefully monitored the various midterm campaigns. He did not mind invective or innuendo written against his vice president. In fact, he encouraged it. But Eustis, running for reelection in Boston, was another story. In August 1802, Jefferson wrote: "I always expected the New York schism [among the Republicans] would produce a boisterous struggle... The manner in which Dr. Eustis and Mr. Bishop have been spoken of is neither just nor judicious."[8]

That summer, various women had maintained contact with Eustis by mail. Miss T. Law, a friend of Burr's, sent a note, probably at Burr's instigation while she was visiting at his house, with a poem she had written. Miss Law thought authors of the nasty political attacks on Burr and Eustis were "knaves" and knew George Clinton was being suggested to replace Burr as vice president.[9] She hoped Eustis might make something of her poem, perhaps even a song.

In Massachusetts, as the well-known son of John Adams, John Quincy Adams had every reason to believe he could win the race for Congress. He had an extraordinary background in international statecraft beginning at the age of eleven when he joined his father's mission to France. He was brilliant, haughty, very proper, and, with his heritage, would not be easy to defeat.

Eustis gave his campaign a different political spin, focusing on local issues, not just on the political differences between Federalists and Republicans. He cast Quincy Adams as an outsider who had lived much of his life abroad and barely knew the commonwealth. Local Boston newspapers cited the doctor's age, experience, knowledge, and moderation as the principal reasons to reelect him.

Eustis played to his constituents as a man of the people. Close acquaintances called him Bill. There is a story that he traveled with a keg of whiskey under the seat of his wagon and offered refreshment to those who turned out at his campaign stops. It seemed that listening to verbose politicians during the summer could be thirsty business. Americans drank far more whiskey, which was plentiful and cheap because of large crops of grain and low taxes, than did Europeans. Americans in 1802 consumed nearly three times the quantity of spirits as they do today; more than at any other time in American history.[10] People took dram breaks instead of coffee breaks.

After the campaigning was over, and on the eve of the fall elections, Eustis returned to Washington City for the opening of Congress. His brother Jacob, an outspoken Republican, suggested that if William was defeated, it might prove a blessing in disguise if only to convince "all half ass'd politicians that . . . there must be a *radical* change in the offices and in the presses."[11]

The congressional election was breathtakingly close in Suffolk County. Quincy Adams gained a majority of votes in Boston itself, but Eustis carried the district. The final tally was 1,899 votes for Eustis and 1,840 for Adams. Eustis won his second term in the House of Representatives by fifty-nine votes.[12]

Quincy Adams believed the weather was a critical factor in Eustis's victory.[13] On election day, a torrential rain pounded on slate and shingled roofs and flooded cobbled streets, making the trip to the polls seem more trouble than it was worth. Many Federalists, thinking Quincy Adams would win, stayed home, while Democratic-Republicans, committed to their underdog candidate, braved the storm and voted. The Massachusetts legislature

164

appointed John Quincy Adams to the United States Senate the following year. State legislatures appointed their two U. S. senators until a constitutional amendment ratified in 1913 mandated their popular election.

Once Eustis was back in Washington, Susan Binney, who Burr called "La Bin," continued her correspondence, sending several letters to him. He had asked her to perform a "commission" for him—purchasing a token of his appreciation for young Miss Law, who had sent Eustis a poem.[14] Miss Binney considered many options and sought Eustis's opinion on the merits of buying a necklace. For nearly three months, she seemed unable to carry out the task without writing frequent letters.

It appeared that Miss Binney was also campaigning for Eustis's attention. Teasing him about keeping his knife (probably a penknife) hostage, she said she would return it only if he offered reasonable terms. She reconsidered the gift of a necklace for Miss Law and, by December, had decided she would instead purchase a pocketbook (a sewing kit), reasoning that: "A pocketbook is fit for a young lady who is never more safely engaged than when learning the uses of a needle."[15] Despite the flirtations, Eustis was not interested in marriage.

After Eustis had left for Washington, his brother Jacob shipped his "great trunk" down the coast on the sloop *Caroline* and attempted to sell his horse for $150.[16] Living in a different boardinghouse, the Francis Hotel, Eustis reported back that the winter in Washington was "less disagreeable than the last – [he was] better lodged & fed . . . I am more at ease . . .."[17]

Jacob sent disturbing news in December 1802. The "new low building" opposite their store on Union Street had burned to the ground. The store would require at least fifty dollars in repairs. Jacob had discovered that their insurance allowed a 50 percent payment of the amount insured toward the damages and applied for funds "on the spot." Insurance representatives inspected the store the following day but to Jacob's dismay said the damages amounted to only thirty dollars. Jacob felt this was a personal "mortification" by uncivil people. He hired Ames Levi, a brick mason, to make repairs. The insurers then, citing their confidence in Levi's estimates, awarded Jacob fifty-six dollars.[18]

Eustis had not followed Burr's advice to give up medicine entirely. Although not considering the practice as a source of income, he remained available to friends and acquaintances, responding when Joseph Wheaton asked him to attend "our old General Shepard," saying the general had no confidence in any other doctor.[19]

For income during this congressional term, Eustis would sell produce shipped to him by Jacob. The business worked fairly well at first. Jacob generally sent salted or dried fish and beef packed in barrels. A shipment at the end of December included ten bushels of potatoes, cheese, beef, and fish.[20] Worried about spoilage, Jacob decided not to ship cider, the weather being so warm, he wrote, that "it would be throwing away money."[21] Knowing of his brother's interest, he also sent news of another attempt to build a hospital and its possible location. Ever frugal, they both agreed that their cousin, Joseph Eustis, a builder, should be asked to present a proposal because he would employ "good republicans from Charlestown who could do the work cheaper."[22]

Their transactions did not always go smoothly. Jacob had shipped three hundred pounds of flour but, unable to sell the flour after a month and without warehouse storage, Eustis had to figure out what to do with it.[23] He lacked confidence in his brother's evaluation of risk and worried that the circuitous voyages intended to avoid British detection yielded uncertain results. Their ventures were costing more than they were worth, so Eustis decided to stop being Jacob's local agent and asked about the precise amount owed for the flour.[24]

In Washington City during the first decade of the new century, mature single men were part of the evolving social scene. Eustis at forty-nine was not alone. Jefferson had been a widower for nineteen years when he became president. It had been seven years since Aaron Burr lost his wife, Theodosia. Typical was New York Federalist Congressman Egbert Benson, well known for his conviviality and Epicurean taste. He was described as an "invincible bachelor" because he lived to be eighty-seven and never married.[25] Unmarried older men suffered little if any stigma among the social elite in cosmopolitan cities.

The capital's social life revolved around Dolley Madison. The Madisons opened their doors for what Dolley called "drawing rooms" on Wednesday evenings at their F Street home. Politicos, including William Eustis, would attend evening teas after their midafternoon dinner. It became the essential way to meet, greet, and find out what was happening around the town.

The minister from Great Britain, Anthony Merry and his wife Elizabeth, arrived in Washington City in 1803. Jefferson did not think much of the garrulous Mrs. Merry, dismissing her as a "virago."[26] The mild-mannered Ambassador Merry was scandalized when Jefferson hosted a dinner for Napoleon's brother Jerome and his new American wife, Elizabeth Patterson. Mrs. Merry, convinced that she ranked higher on the social scale than the other women, felt grievously insulted when Jefferson escorted Mrs. Bonaparte to dinner. Some said the president simply delighted in beautiful Mrs. Bonaparte who wore nearly transparent dresses that only slightly covered her breasts. Several prominent American ladies refused to attend events for the Bonapartes until she wore more clothing.[27]

Posing as the common man, Jefferson changed the social role played by the two previous presidents. He made no public appearances other than his daily horseback rides which Eustis had recommended for his health. Rather than hold parties, he hosted small dinners for those who interested him or advanced his interests. Eustis regularly attended those dinners.

Jefferson said he brought congressmen together, "to get to know one another and have opportunities of little explanations of circumstances, which [if] not understood might produce jealousy and suspicions injurious to public interest."[28] The president held these dinners nearly every night during the five months that Congress was in session. Cabinet members were not invited. During the evening, Jefferson would single out certain legislators for confidential consultations and requests to assist him with passing particular bills. Politics were not discussed during dinner, but guests would leave with an idea of the president's preferences and a sense of personal obligation and appreciation for his attention.

Guests sat at a round dining table with no place of honor for Jefferson whose nondescript dress made him appear to be a simple country gentleman. Without wait staff, Jefferson served everyone himself from a dumbwaiter installed in the wall. His French chef, however, created the gourmet meals accompanied by fine imported wines. Neither the clamor, the wine, nor the food at boardinghouse tables were remotely comparable to these intimate presidential dinners.

25

Beyond Measure

During the 1802 fall session in the House of Representatives, an uproar developed over how Spain was enforcing new regulations for shipping on the Mississippi River. Although Spain's King Carlos IV had given the vast territory of Louisiana to Napoleon, the French had not yet arrived. Angry congressmen from Kentucky and Tennessee urged that New Orleans be taken over by force. Somewhat jaded, Eustis thought the flamboyant warmongering was overdone, and that "the subject of New Orleans is rendered most prominent by people wanting to hear fine speeches."[1] He could not abide irresponsible threats of war.

Controlling the river would solve the problem. Congress approved spending $2 million to purchase New Orleans and, if possible, West and East Florida. Modifying his ideas, Jefferson expanded the power of the presidency and dispatched James Monroe to inform his diplomats in France that he would be interested in buying the "island" of New Orleans.

Monroe arrived in Paris in April 1803. He was dumbfounded when informed that Napoleon wanted to sell the entire Louisiana Territory. Napoleon had realized that France could not defend the huge North American territory acquired from the Spanish. It seemed likely that the Americans would take advantage of his focus on fighting the British and move in—and he needed money. In fact, Americans were already moving in.

Monroe did not dare wait out the months it would take for instructions to arrive. He and Robert Livingston, the American minister to France, made a deal on the spot to purchase an estimated eight hundred twenty-five thousand square miles of North America for $15 million. They did not know how it would be paid or even what the boundaries were, other than it was the land Spain had given to France in 1801. Monroe and Livingston put pen to paper and the United States doubled in size. And on the Fourth of July, when Jefferson announced that Napoleon had sold the entire District of Louisiana to the United States, his reelection was guaranteed. Furthermore, thanks to Secretary of the Treasury Albert Gallatin's superb money management, the Americans paid cash.

Planning for an expedition to find out what was in those vast reaches of the West was already underway. Congress had set aside $2,500 to explore the unknown and uncharted territory along the Missouri River to its source, and Jefferson selected his personal secretary and fellow Virginian Meriwether Lewis to lead this scientific expedition.[2]

Lewis, twenty-eight, was a family friend. He had done a tour of duty in the Virginia militia and served on the western frontier in Ohio and eastern Minnesota. The president began to personally instruct him in botany, geography, mineralogy, astronomy, and ethnology.

The timing of the Lewis expedition could not have been better. Jefferson had commissioned Lewis to lead an expedition *before* acquiring the Louisiana Territory. When news of the purchase reached America, Lewis was in Pittsburgh, Pennsylvania, arranging for supplies and construction of a thirty-foot keel boat. His mission became the Corps of Discovery, charged with exploring not just the newly-acquired land beyond the headwaters of the Missouri River but down the Columbia River to the Pacific Ocean. Jefferson added

William Clark, who Lewis had met at a military post in Ohio, as co-captain or second officer.

When the expedition's expenses surpassed what Congress had allotted, Jefferson arranged for a secret appropriation and opened the coffers of the War Department, instructing Secretary of War Dearborn to pay Lewis an eighteen-month advance on his salary.[3] Offering her support, Dolley Madison sent a plea to affluent families in Washington. Her lady friends made sure the expedition had all of the equipment it needed.[4]

The president had to be nearly desperate to approach Mrs. Madison. Only men had any political standing in Jefferson's America. Women were expected to be good republican mothers and wives. Lacking any identity, women could not legally handle money, own property, or vote. They had little political influence other than by indirectly manipulating their men. Jefferson worried about the female exercise of this "unnatural power" in unofficial or social settings. Amazingly, he trusted Dolley, who carefully flew under the presidential radar.

Late in October 1803, Eustis attended one of Jefferson's dinner parties "at 3 p.m. or whatever later hour the house may rise."[5] As at all of Jefferson's dinners, conversations were nonpolitical and wide-ranging. The Corps of Discovery's preparations, expedition, river transport, and availability of land were surely discussed in anticipation of its departure scheduled for the following May.

The medical preparations would interest Eustis. He admired Dr. Benjamin Rush, the chief adviser about the expedition's supplies and remedies. One of Rush's patent medicines, believed to be good for most of mankind's ills, was plentiful: fifty dozen of Rush's Pills generally called "Thunderclappers."[6] They were a combination of calomel [a compound of six parts mercury to one part chlorine] and jalap [a powdered purgative], each pill a laxative of explosive power. The results were awesome. The pills remained the treatment of choice for syphilis until the advent of penicillin during World War

II.

The addition of the Louisiana Territory to the United States triggered a huge land grab; speculation became rampant. Petitions for land grants poured into Congress from men hoping to strike it rich. Elbridge Gerry, who was elected governor of Massachusetts in 1810 and vice president to James Madison in 1812, wrote to Eustis asking if he would be "deeply engaged in the important concern of Louisiana."[7] Gerry wanted to know the value of his shares in Louisiana real estate and requested a diagram of his lots. Others wrote to offer Eustis helpful advice about Louisiana. General Joseph Sullivan recommended General William Hull as governor of the new territory, citing the advantage of having a man from New England. He thought that "our people" would be more inclined to go to Louisiana, and the bond of union would be strengthened.[8]

* * *

Knowing that Aaron Burr was interested in proposed changes to the presidential election process, Eustis cautioned Burr not to expect immediate results because the December horseracing season had started and there were difficulties in the Senate. That chamber's ceiling had fallen down. In further social updates, William couldn't resist telling Burr about the arrival of a new lady, a Miss Wheeler, saying he had "no foot to stand on" to get an introduction. But he wondered "who can the intended be? So beyond the reach of conjecture and so charming."[9]

Distracting Burr with talk of the ladies, Eustis did not reveal that he would speak in Congress against the proposed Twelfth Amendment that provided separate Electoral College votes for president and vice president to prevent the problems that had occurred in the election of 1800. He believed the amendment as written would not restrict the House's choice to the top three presidential contenders and that it could give undue leverage to a Speaker of the House who might be acting as interim president in the case of a delayed election.

Eustis's speech drew favorable interest. A fellow Massachusetts congressman, Rev. Manasseh Cutler, wrote: "Dr. Eustis did well and deserves much credit for the decided part he took [in the debate]. He gave the [Democratic-Republicans] more trouble and excited more apprehension, than all the opposition besides . . .. But there is no man . . . who is so much feared, so much courted, and so much dreaded. Whatever may be his real principles, he has done more, in checking, opposing, and defeating their wild measures, than all the minority. It happens almost daily, and I do believe he is, incomparably, the most useful member within our walls."[10] When the vote was called, despite Eustis and several colleagues voting against it, the Twelfth Amendment passed.

That winter, a snowstorm swirled through the capital. The Potomac was "sealed in ice from shore to shore and the cold greater than is generally known in this part of the country." Eustis could barely get through the snow after twisting his foot. Maintaining his humor, he commented that "he was not reconciled to this place or this business & yet bearing all with becoming patience"[11] He hated cold weather.

One thing he could do, in keeping with his support for the welfare of women, was respond to a request from old acquaintance Paul Revere. Revere asked that a pension be issued to Deborah Sampson who, disguised as a man, had served as a soldier and been wounded in the Revolutionary War. Revere reported that she was now in bad health and in desperate financial straits. Eustis added Deborah's name to the Massachusetts invalid pension rolls with a retroactive allowance to 1803.

When the spring thaw arrived, Eustis sent love and sympathy regarding his sister-in-law Elizabeth's severe "indisposition," often an indication of pregnancy. Memories of his inability to save his sister Prudence years before flooded over him when he reassured his brother that, in Dr. Jarvis's hands, she would have less medicine and would be cared for better than if he were there. "He trusts more in dame nature than I do."[12]

Eustis, insecure financially, was usually just barely able to pay his debts. By the end of the spring session, he asked Jacob to send $500 to him in "post notes" [money orders] and made arrangements so that if the notes arrived after Congress adjourned and he was on the road home, the package would be forwarded to him. Two weeks later, when the funds had not arrived, Eustis wrote again, hoping the money would reach him in Washington or on the way home when he visited friends in Philadelphia or with Aaron Burr at his home, Richmond Hill.[13] Eustis made it to Boston in time to bid farewell to his father, Benjamin Eustis, who died at age eighty-four in May and was buried at the Copp's Hill Burying Ground in Boston near his son, George.[14]

* * *

Aaron Burr realized he would not be on Jefferson's ticket for the next presidential election, so he ran for governor of New York. As old friends, during Eustis's visit with Burr on the way home, Eustis and Burr likely discussed the recently intensified Hamiltonian attacks stimulated by Burr's campaign. After Eustis left, Burr discovered he had lost the election but would remain as vice president for another nine months. There are theories about what finally pushed him to respond to years of Hamilton's vituperative insults. A Hamiltonian diatribe at a dinner party, overheard by a guest and later published in the *Albany Register,* could have been the spark.

Hamilton had gone into his usual rant, insisting that Burr was dangerous to the future of the country, but it was the word "despicable" that set Burr ablaze, bringing him out of his election-loss lethargy. He decided to end Hamilton's constant harassment once and for all and leave for the Southwest as a soldier of fortune. On June 18, Burr challenged Hamilton to apologize for his insults or answer in a duel. Reluctant to fight, Hamilton, with a military reputation to protect, would not back down from his accusations or negotiate any apology. He had been challenged eleven times before and all had been settled without resorting to pistols.[15] He had, however, lost his son to a duel in 1802.

After more than three weeks of negotiations with no positive results and no forthcoming apologies. Hamilton finally agreed to meet Burr at the Weehawken, New Jersey, dueling ground on July 11, 1804. Hamilton wrote the night before the confrontation that he decided to throw away his shot and take the noble stance as he had advised his dead son, Philip. Burr also wrote final letters and planned to leave small tokens of affection to his friends and family, including a painting of himself for William Eustis.[16]

Aaron Burr won the duel. It seemed no one could forgive him for killing Alexander Hamilton. Rarely did a duelist who killed his opponent find himself prosecuted for murder as Burr and the two men serving as his seconds were in both New Jersey and New York. Hamilton's wife, Elizabeth, and other supporters sought revenge and staged an elaborate military funeral and procession, insisting their hero was murdered. Burr headed south to survey the Spanish possession of West Florida but returned to Washington when Congress convened in November to continue his duties as vice president.[17] The House of Representatives took no legal actions, but there were consequences. Now a political pariah, Burr had no future in New York or in politics. History began to pass him by.

Eustis, in Boston, campaigned for another term in Congress and visited his sister Anne Langdon Eustis's family in Portsmouth, New Hampshire. He spent time with Woodbury Langdon and his clever daughter, twenty-three-year-old Caroline.[18] Democratic-Republicans in Boston supported his bid for reelection and attacked his Federalist opponent, Josiah Quincy, as being anti-Republican, anti-Jeffersonian, overly ambitious, and tinged with the same monarchical inclinations of Hamilton.

On November 5, 1804, voters chose Quincy, and Congressman Eustis returned to Washington City to finish out his term. He marked this moment in his life by commissioning artist Gilbert Stuart to do his portrait.[19] In 1803, the artist, his fame preceding him, had moved from Philadelphia into a two-room studio off Pennsylvania Avenue in Washington. Dignitaries flocked to have their portraits painted; among them Thomas Jefferson, James and Dolley Madison, Dolley's sister Anna Payne Cutts, and Jerome Bonaparte. Stuart's flattering portrait of Eustis highlights his youthful appearance, possibly better than he looked at fifty-three.

Both Eustis and Burr ended their time in Washington in March 1805. Unsure of what Burr might do, Eustis and Madison, among others, reconsidered their association and made choices to protect their own futures. Eustis and Burr went their separate ways. Burr set out on another scouting trip down the Mississippi River, and Eustis headed north to Boston.

The country was at peace and prosperous when, radiating success, Jefferson began his second term. Although a member of the Virginia slave-owning aristocracy, he presented an image of republican simplicity and modesty.

26

Uncertainties of Life

Eustis sought a new direction, a new purpose, and a new chapter in his life after losing his congressional seat. He arrived in Boston to find that his brother Jacob, perhaps sympathetic to his dilemma, had remodeled his quarters, raising the roof in his part of the house to make three rooms "not very large but where one might get a nap . . . and then the salt water you know is near."[1]

Renewing political connections, he remembered President Washington's perambulation through New England and urged Jefferson to come north on a similar journey, saying it would offer great support and encouragement for local Republicans. Come this summer, he entreated. "Among all the uncertainties of life, that of life itself is not the least and if in a disposition *carpe diem.*"[2] But it was not Jefferson's style, and he would not ride north.

Instead of beginning another medical practice, Eustis attended meetings of the Massachusetts Medical Society. The Harvard Corporation appointed him to the Boylston Committee to determine the college's medical prizes to be awarded in 1805.[3] He offered medical advice freely to friends. "I advise you to eat more milk – to leave wine for old age," he wrote to Bill North, explaining, "I am a good physician and this very morning I have been desired to go to a

Mr W of Salem to save him when no other can – but I do not practice."[4]

Along with his voluminous correspondence, Eustis followed the international news. In England, Dr. Edward Jenner had discovered that an inoculation with cowpox could give immunity against the dreaded smallpox in a safer process than the usual inoculation with the live smallpox virus. The serum administered was referred to as a vaccine because of its bovine origins. The process was called a vaccination. American cows did not have cowpox, so the inoculant was imported from England on cotton threads inside feather quills.

Dr. Benjamin Waterhouse was the exclusive Boston importer and controlled the vaccine's distribution, advertising it as a "kine pock inoculation" and the greatest blessing ever bestowed on man. When the Massachusetts Medical Society raised questions about who had authority over the vaccine and who could properly use it, Dr. Waterhouse pressed charges against the society for interfering with his business. He claimed he had the sole right to approve the doctors who administered the serum and, despite saying he was importing it as a charitable measure, he demanded a percentage of their fees. Many in the medical community had differing opinions. It appeared there might be political overtones in the accusations. At its annual meeting, the society appointed Dr. Eustis, as the most prominent politician in the medical profession, to investigate.[4]

Eustis began gathering information, prompting Waterhouse to protest that the society had no right to inquire into his business. The society in turn refuted Waterhouse's accusations that its members did not believe in the vaccine. Although bits of the controversy had seemed political, Eustis's investigation revealed that Waterhouse held a monopoly on importing the vaccine and sold it for profit.[5] The society then secured the vaccine from Europe through different channels despite the cantankerous Waterhouse's protests.

In October 1806, Henry Knox's son wrote of the death of his father, Eustis's longtime friend and a much-admired veteran of the

Revolutionary War, at his home in Thomaston, Maine. Eustis relayed the sad news to Bill North that "our friend Knox...died after an illness of a few days of a mortification caused by swallowing the bone of a chicken – this is inconceivable because on Tuesday preceding Friday, the day on which he died, he walked down on board a packet or coaster & told the Capt. he had swallowed the bone but had taken it away from the rectum without surgery and probably with his own fingers . . . he was amiable estimable affectionate and kind – his talent to make others happy was peculiarly his own and he had more of it than any man I ever knew – he is universally lamented."[6] Eustis and Knox had escaped from the British together nearly thirty years earlier, rowing up the Hudson River.

* * *

Meriwether Lewis sent reports about the progress of the Corps of Discovery's expedition to President Jefferson who kept Eustis informed. The reports included stories of wintering with the Mandan tribe and stated that a number of Indians would come to Washington. Eustis relayed the news to Bill North.[7]

Americans celebrated at the end of September 1806 when the young men arrived in St. Louis. In December, three and a half years after he left, Lewis came to Washington with an entourage. Much to Jefferson's delight, they brought a treasure trove of specimens for his inspection and collections and the Mandan Indian Chief Big White. Congress discussed compensation and land grants for all the members of the expedition except York, Clark's slave. Within two months, Jefferson nominated Lewis to be governor of the Louisiana Territory and Clark as superintendent of Indian Affairs. Some six months passed before Secretary of War Dearborn began pestering Lewis for an accounting of the expedition's expenses. In the glory of it all, those details had been set aside.[8]

Fascinating stories about his former friend and ally Aaron Burr came to Eustis's attention. Burr had achieved celebrity status.[9] Starstruck newspapers speculated about this man of mystery who

179

was frequently out of reach somewhere in the wilderness. Many wondered if he would capture and rule a new empire in Mexico. A newspaper loyal to Jefferson reported that Burr had received a shipment of six thousand muskets. Nothing was based on fact, and Burr said not a word.

Returning to the frontier had seemed Burr's only recourse after the death of Hamilton. Toward the end of his term as vice president, he made several expeditions down the Mississippi River, studying its western banks and the newly-acquired Louisiana Territory. Although reviled in the North and East, Burr was hailed as a hero in the western territories, admired as an independent thinker and an outdoorsman.

Among the more bizarre characters Burr contacted in his travels was General James Wilkinson who would later become a problem for William Eustis and James Madison. The consummate survivor, Wilkinson managed to outlive every other Revolutionary War general and lived the good life far above his paygrade by secretly serving the Spanish government as Agent 13.

The president became his protector and supporter. Pleased with his gifts of Indian artifacts and mineral samples, Jefferson in 1805 appointed Wilkinson governor of the Louisiana Territory for two years, replaced later by Meriwether Lewis. Congress raised alarms about Wilkinson's activities including reports that he had received — literally — barrels filled with pesos as a Spanish spy. Jefferson dismissed all such reports as politically-motivated abuse, and the new governor went to St. Louis. Having Agent 13 as governor of a bordering territory and in command of the United States Army was worth a great deal to Spain.

Uneasy about possible Spanish attacks, Secretary of War Dearborn ordered Wilkinson to travel downriver from St. Louis and defend New Orleans. The general considered all of his options and came up with a plan that was personally more favorable. Arriving in New Orleans, he declared martial law and set up extraordinary defenses, announcing that Burr planned to attack New Orleans with eight thousand to twelve thousand men. It created an impending calamity, pleased Jefferson, enhanced Wilkinson's position, and distracted everyone.

Burr learned that Jefferson had ordered his arrest as a traitor when he landed in Vicksburg, Mississippi, in January 1807 with nearly eighty men—possibly planning to start a township.[10] A grand jury in Washington, Mississippi, found no grounds to indict him. Once released, Burr said good-bye to his men and immediately headed into the wilderness. Jefferson, however, would not drop the charges and encouraged pursuit.

That April, Eustis heard from Dearborn that Burr had been recaptured and had tried to escape. "Col. Burr after forfeiting his bond to the guard at Natchez by an escape was taken up in a shabby disguise a few miles from the Spanish boundary on the Mobile [River in today's Alabama]." Then, Dearborn wrote, "in a small village in S. Carolina where some people had assembled he [Burr] leaped from his horse, ran towards the people, announced himself and claimed protection, but the guard cocking their pieces and threatening to fire if he did not immediately return, he returned and proceeded on the journey."[11]

Eustis followed the latest Burr news in the *Boston Gazette.* Chief Justice John Marshall had announced "there is no probable ground from the testimony for believing Colonel Burr has been guilty of treason . . . [but] probable grounds of a misdemeanor in setting foot in or preparing an expedition against Spanish settlements."[12]

Avid readers followed the evolving story. Eustis wrote to North: "What think you now of Burr – They seem to admit Mexico to have been the object. God grant New Orleans may not be proven to have been the first branch."[13] Eustis knew that if the investigation proved that Burr had threatened New Orleans, as Wilkinson claimed, it would prove he was a traitor. Burr was taken under heavy guard to Richmond, Virginia, to stand trial. Wilkinson's efforts to move the focus away from himself plus the hostility of Thomas Jefferson figured in the prosecution. The president could not forgive Burr for the presidential election debacle. In a possibly illegal pretrial move, he wrote a letter to Congress declaring Burr guilty of treason.

Chief Justice Marshall, a Federalist and certainly not Jefferson's friend, presided over what was more spectacle than trial.[14] As the chief witness and Jefferson's toady, Wilkinson entered the courtroom to testify dressed in a self-designed gold-braided uniform and wearing a sword. Despite immediate issues over the sword in the courtroom, the general prevailed to offer evidence for four days. Burr's defense team shifted the trial to an examination of Wilkinson's own questionable actions. The jury found Burr not guilty for lack of evidence in September 1807, and he immediately left to spend three years in Europe.

* * *

In the chill of December, Boston's Republican congressional delegation petitioned Congress to appoint Eustis as surgeon general to the Boston Marine Hospital, replacing the contentious Dr. Waterhouse.[15] The congressmen had discovered to their alarm that Waterhouse was not a qualified surgeon. Dr. Eustis, they stated, was more qualified to serve as their *chirugeon*, adding that he was certainly the most respectable and popular man in New England. They expected Congress to award the appointment to Eustis because it was the wish of all Republicans in Massachusetts.

27

Preparations for War

In Boston, William Eustis studied the available newspapers and military accounts every day. He was as interested in Napoleon's exploits in Europe and Russia as in Burr's trial in Virginia, and he tracked the military actions on his own map. He thought King George III was definitely insane and that the United Kingdom, which he still called Great Britain, should declare a regent. To his regret, he confessed, "I am only a 'soldier' in theory."[1]

For their part, the British believed they were fighting a just and necessary war on behalf of *all* civilized nations. They stood as the last bastion between the self-proclaimed emperor and his ambition to conquer the world. To a segment of the British public, Americans, who were claiming neutrality, were unprincipled savages eager to enrich themselves in the wartime "carrying trade" while the United Kingdom fought to hold back the Corsican tyrant.[2] While not acknowledging it, British interests stood to profit from a limited war with the Americans. Condemning captured American vessels in Admiralty prize courts enabled the sale of cargo and ships. Proceeds subsidized a broad constituency, including every man in the Royal Navy, from admirals to seamen, plus a hierarchy of lawyers and judges. British merchants and shipowners stood to gain substantially by the suppression of a maritime rival.[3]

The British needed crews and impressed, or kidnapped, every British-born seaman they found on American ships. If possible, American sailors carried a document proving their citizenship. Secretary of State James Madison issued sternly-worded protests to the United Kingdom. But the British ignored the protests, and it seemed that unless they changed their ways, another war between the United States and the United Kingdom was inevitable.

In much of his correspondence, along with concerns about a potential war or ongoing politics, Eustis offered medical counsel to friends. As usual, he recommended horseback riding, one of his universal remedies for good health. "If you are healthy it will keep & confirm you, if an invalid it will make you healthy. It helps the wind & the water the functions of all the alimentary organs & particularly that tube of 15 or 20 yards which begins at the mouth & ends at the last ends of the most vulgar conversation."[4] Believing in the curative quality of milk, he recommended it to Bill North: "If you find me amiable, ascribe it to a milk diet for 25 days for a bad cold."[5]

In June, the *Chesapeake,* one of the original six naval frigates commissioned by President Washington, sailed for the Mediterranean to deal with Barbary Coast pirates. The British warship *Leopard* accosted the frigate looking for men not far outside Chesapeake Bay. The American captain refused to let the British board, and the *Leopard* fired two broadsides of solid shot and canister from about two hundred feet away. When the third broadside struck, the *Chesapeake,* totally unprepared, lowered her colors. The British boarded and claimed four sailors. With three dead and eighteen crew wounded, the damaged *Chesapeake* wallowed back to Norfolk under improvised rigging.

Americans were clamoring for retaliation, but Congress was on summer recess. Madison hurried to Washington from his home, Montpelier, and sent an irate communication to London demanding that the kidnapped sailors be returned. More than anything, he dreaded sending the country into war, still hoping that discussion and negotiation could bring about a conciliatory response by the time Congress reconvened. There was none.

American opinion was divided on what might happen during the war between France and the United Kingdom. As a Francophile, Eustis thought that the French would win unless "Bonaparte meets with ill luck which is next to impossible."[6] After Napoleon's probable victory over Great Britain, there would no longer be sea battles, and American seamen would come home. Eustis did not see how Napoleon could lose because he seemed far too effective against the British in his land battles. Some months later, with France still not victorious, Eustis remained disturbed by British animosity and the attack on the *Chesapeake* but continued backing Madison. "I cling to the idea of peace from hope from fear from love of country from personal considerations from pride of opinion from everything that we animate or interest."[7]

Pacifists at heart, Republicans believed almost anything was preferable to a war. In December, despite heated objections from New England merchants, Jefferson signed an Embargo Act. This sweeping prohibition against all American ships sailing for Europe became the great mistake of Jefferson's second term. He thought that the embargo, and preventing sailors from going to sea, would protect them from impressments and would pressure the British into accepting the American position on neutral shipping.[8] Experienced only in southern, self-sufficient plantations, Jefferson underestimated the rest of America's reliance on overseas trade and overestimated the British dependence on American commerce.

American merchants floundered during the economic disaster. Activity in the seaports ceased that spring; no fishnets were drying, no men were packing salted fish into iron-hooped barrels; no carts were hauling produce on or off ships at the wharves; no rope or canvas or supplies were on sale. Unemployed seamen wandered the waterfronts. Exports piled up in warehouses, scarce imports were sold for high prices, wages fell or were not paid.[9] Smuggling became rampant with federal enforcement nearly impossible.

Inland states also suffered. Vermont's economy depended heavily on agricultural exports to Canada, and its citizens rose up in a general rebellion. They built rafts defended by men with small arms and cannon to transport goods on Lake Champlain. Jefferson issued a proclamation that the Lake Champlain region was in a state of general insurrection.[10]

Despite his experience with previous embargoes, Eustis tried to be optimistic, hoping there would be a "satisfactory adjustment." American exports plunged from $108 million in 1807 to $22 million in 1808.[11] The federal government's fiscal surplus, dependent on customs revenues, vanished. Now, even if the United States wanted to go to war, it could not afford to do so. Eustis's defense of the embargo won him more friends in Washington than in Boston. He saw what was happening: "Embargo never fails to beget discontent and grumbling in the seaports." But he tried to believe that this one would be of short duration and end well. "I have never abandoned my hope of peace."[12]

Three months later, Eustis worried increasingly about the likelihood of war, doubting that the country had a strong military leader. "We are taught we need for our guide men of knowledge, virtue, honor . . . I have cast about among our friends for a skillful chief. I see none to compare with old George especially for this crisis . . . I remember I asked a Virginian in Washington whom they intended to give us from there for our next Pres'."[13]

By April, Eustis was questioning how effectively Jefferson had handled the *Chesapeake* affair. He wrote to Secretary of War Henry Dearborn suggesting the United States might send a signal to the United Kingdom that Jefferson would rescind his embargo if the British offered reparations for the *Chesapeake*; but perhaps it was too late for anything positive to develop. "Sometimes I think a war

186

with some foreign nation preferable to this perpetual conflict at home."[14]

He informed Dearborn that his nephew, Abraham Eustis, had decided to join the army and "will break his mother's heart."[15] He had known Dearborn ever since the Siege of Boston and wondered if Dearborn had any insider information. "Who is to be vice president? . . . if there is peace it is no great matter, if war so many heads will not ache for us [the Republican Party] under it." Always fishing for work, Eustis speculated that he should try becoming an army contractor or something that would make him rich in a short time, ". . . for I am old [at fifty-five]."[16]

Escaping the summer heat in Boston, Eustis was visiting at his sister Anne Langdon's house in Portsmouth when an invitation arrived offering the job of undersecretary in the War Department. Dearborn wrote that he could not handle the job alone. Eustis accepted. It may seem an odd choice for a doctor to embark on a career in the War Department, but he fit the mold of the previous two secretaries, both educated as physicians in Massachusetts and possessing a keen interest in military affairs.

About six months before Eustis received Dearborn's job offer, he purchased the family homestead on Sudbury Street from his brother for $3,100.[17] The Eustis brothers did not register the change of home ownership until more than a year later. His address for the next fifteen years continued to be the crowded house still occupied by Elizabeth and Jacob, their four children, and two servants.[18] Eustis either visited in Portsmouth or lived in rented quarters in Washington for more than six months each year. In Boston, it was considered proper, less scandalous, for a bachelor to live with a family or in a suitable boardinghouse rather than alone. So Eustis, practical and conforming to custom, saved the cost of separate housing and servants.

Toward the end of summer in 1808, he boarded a coach and rocked on south to Washington City to become Dearborn's assistant.

Offices for the Departments of War, Navy, and State were in a two-and-a-half-story brick building on the corner of Chestnut and Fifth Streets, diagonally across from the President's House. As a member of the executive branch, he would live in the village surrounding the president's residence.

Washington City had made considerable progress toward becoming a capital city. A road now linked it to Alexandria, Virginia, and there was more of everything: shops, hotels, and boardinghouses. Senators and representatives brought their wives for the "season." Living in boardinghouses and freed from housekeeping duties, the women made social calls. The congressmen worked from late morning until three in the afternoon, dining at four o'clock in their boardinghouses. At seven or eight in the evening, Washingtonians ventured out, "taking tea" with one another in local homes, passing the evening "at cards or in company."[19] Popular pastimes included Mrs. Madison's Wednesday evening "drawing rooms" and the seasonal Jockey Club races.

The Department of War's far-reaching responsibilities encompassed all the country's interior as well as foreign concerns. Eustis became accountable for the vast unknown interior including the new Louisiana Territory, and kept an eye on the two Spanish-owned Floridas: West Florida, and East, or Spanish, Florida on the peninsula, both with uncertain boundaries. Then there was that northwest corner of America beyond the new Louisiana Territory around the Columbia and Snake Rivers, where ownership was equally vague. Trading outposts at the mouth of the Columbia River became the destination of large expeditions both by land and by sea. Jefferson's embargo did not affect trade with newly-opened China, and merchants discovered that otter, seal, and beaver furs commanded substantial prices. With the stimulus of trade in the Pacific, Boston reactivated its shipyards, building merchant ships to sail around Cape Horn to China. In turn, Chinese goods began to appear in American markets.

As the situation in Europe grew steadily worse, the long undefended northern border with Canada, a British colony, worried many Americans. Rumors circulated that the United Kingdom might try to regain her American colonies by staging an invasion from Canada as well as from the sea. As undersecretary, Eustis tackled preparations for defense, searching for suitable locations and land at reasonable prices, and began planning construction or repairs for forts along the Atlantic coast.

The most nagging question facing Eustis and Dearborn was the cost required to develop these military installations. How many fortifications would be enough? What were the best locations? And, indeed, where was the money? For years, Henry Dearborn had tried to balance the requirements for military defense with the congressional limitations on his department's budget. Congress never could see the point of wasting money on military preparations. It held to republican values and favored the use of economic sanctions. Most politicians chose to wear blinders, ignore any potential conflict, and believe they could always call up the militia. Unfortunately, this was not the time to practice Yankee frugality in either the War Department or in Congress.

28

The War Office

Leadership from the president quietly faded. Jefferson had extended executive power to an unparalleled degree, but now he appeared to lose interest and abdicated his responsibility.[1] In a kind of grief-stricken malaise, likely due to the death of Maria, his last remaining child, Jefferson ceased making most decisions and began moving furniture back to Monticello. He did repeal the two-year-old embargo just a few days before officially vacating his office and allowed American ships to resume limited trading across the Atlantic. The costly embargo had changed nothing. Great Britain's wide-ranging navy still stopped American ships while looking for sailors.

Instead of attending the March 1809 inauguration for James Madison, Eustis went to Boston, surveying defensive works along the way. He knew his boss, Secretary of War Henry Dearborn, planned to resign, and he preferred being engaged in the business of the War Department to appearing to wait for Madison to make cabinet appointments. In Boston, he hurried to attend to his friend Henry Jackson, dying from a blood clot in his heart. Arriving just in time, Eustis referenced their old days in the Hudson Highlands to Bill North. "Our friend is no longer among the few of us who are left to recollect the companionship on which it is my pride to reflect

190

and my consolation to dwell."[2] Jackson, unmarried with no direct heirs, left his real estate to his sister and the rest of his property to Hepzibah Swan with whom he lived. Swan had a large tomb built for him in her Tremont Street backyard so she could visit him daily.

James Madison, virtually handpicked by Jefferson, had already assumed much of the presidency. Small at five feet, four inches tall and weighing just a little over a hundred pounds, the former secretary of state's introverted appearance could be misleading. He was a thinker, understood complex subjects, and wrote well. Although not considered charismatic, Madison could be charming in small groups in which he was known for mischievous allusions and off-color jokes.[3] His victory was largely based on his wife's politicking and the decline of the Federalist Party. Campaigning for office had changed. Social contacts and families had become critical, and Dolley Madison played an essential role while entertaining fifteen to twenty guests for dinner each night.[4]

Unlike Jefferson's ceremony, Madison's inauguration had a military flair. The "first couple" arrived at the Capitol by carriage exactly at noon escorted by cavalry. Dolley dressed for the occasion in an elaborate bonnet of purple velvet and white satin ornamented with white plumes. Margaret Bayard Smith, social doyenne and diligent reporter of the Washington social scene, thought Jefferson looked like he was laying down an "irksome burden" and that Dolley "looked like a queen."[5] Madison, dressed in his usual elegantly tailored black coat and breeches, had added a fancy ivory-colored silk vest. After delivering a ten-minute speech in a very low voice, he was sworn in by Chief Justice John Marshall. After leaving the hall to the sound of booming cannon, they passed along the militia-lined route back to their residence on F Street where they held an open house, commonly called a "squeeze." Throngs of people attended; the street surrounding the house filled with carriages.[6] Dolley began shaping the social scene that evening by holding the nation's first inaugural ball for four hundred invited guests at Long's

Hotel.

Eustis, in Boston, commented to Bill North that Napoleon had conquered Spain. "Skirmishing on the ocean . . . will be a good thing because it will serve gradually to increase [the American] navy without which so long as other nations have bulldogs on the ocean our seamen our rights our flag never will be respected." It was a short letter. "Breakfast is ready, and the coffee came over me again."[7]

He watched the mail. As expected, Henry Dearborn, after nearly twenty years on the job, resigned, creating an opening for secretary of war. President Madison decided to keep the position in the hands of a New Englander, hoping to maintain a balance in his cabinet with southern and northern representation. To lead the Departments of War and Navy, he reviewed well-connected Republicans, with geographic considerations taking precedence over military experience. He decided to appoint William Eustis, already serving as the undersecretary, to secretary of war.

Eustis, now fifty-six, accepted, modestly acknowledging the high responsibility of the position and his sense of honor in being given the assignment. Beyond "the inadequacy of my own powers," his greatest concerns involved the equatorial summer weather in Washington and the potential ill effect on his health.[8] It seemed there were no guarantees that, unlike the president, he could get away in the summer. He indicated to Madison that he would inspect the defenses in New York on the way back to Washington City as planned.

Eustis shared the news with Bill North. "On my return to town [from Portsmouth] I found a very obliging gentlemanly letter from the President accompanied with the Secretary's Commission." Eustis had earlier been told he might be appointed secretary of the navy. Although "not desirous of the bed of thorns [included in] an honor of this kind," he accepted the War Department appointment after thinking it over for three days. He hoped North would be available for counsel. "The worst of all is the place of residence – too hot in summer."[9] The *Boston Patriot* gushed its approval, calling the appointment "highly auspicious" and adding, "the crisis of our foreign relations and the state of the public mind at home, particularly in this section of the Union, requires . . . a man possessing the talents and virtues which have so eminently distinguished this early and long tried patriot. To an undeviating adherence to republican principles . . . he adds that candor and urbanity which disarms even party rancor of its enmity."[10]

Eustis became responsible for the safety of the entire nation in April 1809 without a general staff, deputies, aides, or sub-departments. He had eleven clerks with which to cover all national security matters, including the West's rampant expansion, the Native American tribes, all foreign defense activity, and relationships with Europe and beyond. Also serving as the army's acting quartermaster, Eustis personally handled accounts, issued orders, and maintained records. Jefferson wrote praising his appointment, noting his efforts to combat the Federalists' maneuvers to separate the New England states from the Union during the embargo.[11] Even now, a few years before a second war with Great Britain, Jefferson anticipated that New England's regional attitude would not change.

Madison discontinued Jefferson's informal dinners with members of Congress and passed all social responsibilities to Dolley, seventeen years younger and taller than her husband when she was wearing a turban and ostrich plumes. She created a social season, presiding over the throngs with grace and finesse. The turban became her trademark, its plumes adding height and making it easier to locate her in the crowd.

Fashionable ladies copied the neoclassical look of the new French Empire. Every woman adopted the look of a Greek goddess with high waistlines, and low-cut bodices. Thin white fabric fell in column-like flutes to the floor. Dolley usually donned four necklaces; two chokers and two somewhat longer, perhaps emphasizing her low neckline. Rouged cheeks and lips completed the high-style look. Men considered altering their conservative dress of silk stockings and breeches to the French style of long trousers and tapered top hats.

With the help of architect Benjamin Latrobe, the "Lady Presidentress" dove into decorating the nearly empty President's House, using Latrobe-designed chairs and sofas in the fashionable Greek style. These beautiful furnishings had a short life, destroyed by fire when the British burned Washington in 1814. The resourceful Dolley managed to save her favorite crimson velvet draperies and the full-length portrait of George Washington when she fled the house just before the British arrived.

Just three months after the inauguration, the newly-decorated President's House was opened to the public for Dolley's Wednesday evenings. Carriages rumbled up the torch-lit drive to the mansion, and the sound of music wafted from the door. Everyone who was anyone, male and female, foreign and domestic, came to see and be seen in the new splendor of the President's House. Card games were introduced. Dolley's favorite game of chance was loo, somewhat similar to bridge, in which players bet on their ability to win tricks.[12] When ladies lost, they exclaimed they had been "looed."

Newly-elected, unsophisticated men came to Washington with their families during the Madison presidency. New Englanders and people from the South and West viewed each other with suspicion, believing that environment and climate influenced morals and personalities. Mrs. Madison's Wednesday gatherings provided the ideal opportunity for new members of Congress to become acquainted on a level playing field. New access and connections helped form core relationships and enabled business to proceed more smoothly.[13]

Eustis was a good deal more sophisticated than some of the capital city's newcomers. His friendship with Dolley and James

Madison deepened, and with cultivated grace and congressional experience, he easily adjusted to his new surroundings in the executive branch.[14.]

* * *

As governor of the Louisiana Territory, Meriwether Lewis had two goals: develop the territorial fur trade and get Mandan Indian Chief Big White back to his tribe after his two-year absence with the Corps of Discovery.[15] In February 1809, he awarded the job of escorting Chief Big White to the St. Louis Missouri River Fur Company. In exchange, the fur company could control the fur trade along the Missouri River and, once the chief was safely home in today's North Dakota, the United States would pay the company $7,000. Lewis believed he continued to have authorization for expenses related to the Corps of Discovery's expedition. Territorial secretary Frederick Bates, a former Indian agent who hated and undermined Lewis whenever he could, questioned these costs, protesting to President Madison that this agreement would give a total monopoly on the fur trade to the fur company.

Madison examined the receipts submitted by Lewis with Eustis, who wrote to Lewis saying that several of the accounts claimed for the unauthorized military expedition and the $7,000 expense of returning Big White were reluctantly approved, but he must stop charging expenses to the government. "It has been usual to advise the Government of the United States when expenditures to a considerable amount are contemplated in the Territorial Governments." Lewis must operate within War Department regulations rather than the former Corps of Discovery's. Eustis continued: "As the object & destination of this Force [after delivering Big White] is unknown, and more especially as it combines Commercial purposes, it cannot be considered as having the sanction of the Government of the United States, or that they are responsible for the consequences."[16]

Word quickly got around St. Louis, probably thanks to Frederick

Bates, that the government had cut off Lewis's credit. Lewis protested that "he never received a penny of public Money" and demanded a full investigation of any charges against him.[17] He wrote back to Eustis that his credit was "sunk" and all of his private debts had been called in. The government, by not extending credit, had reduced him to poverty. Lewis packed all his belongings, vouchers, and supporting paperwork and headed for Washington in September to meet with William Eustis and defend his position.

Lewis's journey was interrupted by bouts of illness and drunkenness. While underway, he changed his mind about traveling by boat down the Mississippi and decided to go overland on horseback through Tennessee. On October 10, Lewis and his two servants asked for overnight accommodations at Grinder's Stand, two log cabins and a barn in the hill country of south-central Tennessee. During the night Lewis died—likely by suicide. He shot himself first in the head then, with his second pistol, in his side.[18] Mrs. Grinder found him at dawn trying to cut himself with a razor. His last words were, in effect, that he'd killed himself to deprive his enemies of the pleasure.

William Clark went to Washington in December to meet with Eustis. It seemed there had been no particular animosity between Lewis and Eustis, just a misunderstanding over bureaucratic regulations. Clark wrote in his journal that Eustis assured him Lewis had not lost the confidence of the government, and he had planned to ask for Lewis's expertise about the Osage Indians.[19]

29

Secretary of War

William Eustis juggled one crisis after another, dealing with the country's lack of war preparedness as well as Congress's lack of purpose and general confusion. As secretary of war, he was responsible for everything—from the constant turmoil of the British-encouraged Indians fighting in the American West, to the continuing Napoleonic Wars in Europe, to all interior affairs including Spanish spy General James Wilkinson. The eastern states were upset over British blockades and attack on the *Chesapeake*, and the western states worried about settlements and trade on the rivers.

Madison's administration got off to a bad start. Although a superb political theoretician and legislator, the president was not a leader. His refusal to even consider the possibility of another war with the United Kingdom hampered any preparations.[1] For twelve years, the Democratic-Republicans, as the party in power, had championed a policy of minimalism in the armed services, and the results were shockingly evident.[2] All necessities—weapons, uniforms, and provisions—were in short supply. Mountains of requisitions, appointments, promotions, orders, and warrants buried the small clerical staffs of the War and Navy Departments.

Meanwhile, the British navy blockaded New York Harbor and stepped up attacks against American ships at sea.

Both Presidents Jefferson and Madison believed that a neutral United States should only protect its own shores. They refused to build seagoing frigates, planning to defend American harbors with gunboats designed solely for use in protected waters. This navy of one hundred eighty-eight vessels appealed to Jefferson because it aligned with his cherished notion of a citizen militia.[3]

The fifty-foot-long gunboats were rigged with one or two masts and could be sailed or rowed by a crew of twenty to thirty men.[4] The Federalists regarded them as pathetic substitutes for frigates, but they offered a perfect solution to longstanding republican fears of a standing navy. Gunboats were, in practice, ridiculous.[5] The cannon could not be aimed except in a flat calm, and recoil from firing a cannon on either side caused them to capsize. In moderate seas, the guns had to be stowed below decks to keep the top-heavy boats from keeling over. They offered no protection against musket fire, and a well-placed cannonball could reduce them to splinters.

Eustis worked diligently but ineffectually to reorganize the army. Congress often seemed to be of two or more minds, leaving him to figure out contradictory directives. Based on one directive, he pared down the army in May 1809, disbanding a detachment of six thousand sixty-three militia.[6] Six months later, Congress talked of preparing for war but then cut the military budget and further reduced the army and navy.[7] Then, in an about face a month later, Madison asked that the size of the army be increased.

Reporting to Congress in December and again in January 1810 while it discussed preparations for war, Eustis proposed a publicly-funded national force of fifty thousand volunteers, specifically asking that six thousand artillerymen and sharpshooting riflemen be included among the new troops. Hoping to reorganize the War Department, he called for the addition of a superintendent of ordnance and a Quartermaster Generals Department. Congress would not approve these changes for two more years and then independently added a commissary general, overlapping the new Department of Quartermaster General.

Madison needed to defend New Orleans, so he sent notorious Major General James Wilkinson, chief witness during the trial of Aaron Burr. Covered up at that trial was the general's treasonous behavior as longtime Spanish secret agent 13. Outgoing President Jefferson, possibly knowing more than he acknowledged, had ensured that Wilkinson would no longer be the army's only general by creating two new brigadier general positions.

Arriving in New Orleans, Wilkinson took charge of the troops billeted across the Mississippi River in tents and temporary wooden barracks. A month later, in March, nearly a third of the men were unfit for duty and almost a quarter were on the sick list.[8]

Building on his savage criticisms of the War Department's ineptitude during the Burr trial, Wilkinson sent an excuse-filled report to Eustis. "You will observe, sir, we have an army without a general staff; and an hospital without surgeon, purveyor, matron, or nurse... The troops are without bunks or births to repose on, or musquitoe nets to protect them against the pestiferous insect with which this country abounds."[9]

His letter was in the mail at the same time as Eustis's April directive to Wilkinson regarding the health of those same troops. Eustis understood camp hospitals, and, reading the statistics on disease in New Orleans, he ordered Wilkinson to move all troops to higher and drier ground away from malarial swamps.[10] Claiming the men were too sick to move, Wilkinson disregarded the order but moved the troops to a place called Terre aux Boeufs, seven miles downriver from New Orleans and three feet *below* sea level behind a levee.

Reporting back, he assured Eustis that it was perfectly dry and a good defensive position. The rains came, the river rose, and the camp at Terre aux Boeufs became a sinking, stinking swamp with clouds of mosquitoes and miserable sanitation. Wilkinson,

199

comfortable in New Orleans, ultimately lost half of the two thousand men. Eight hundred sixteen died and the rest deserted. Eustis, nearly apoplectic, issued a direct order "immediately to embark all the troops...and proceed to the high ground."[11] It took another six months before the survivors were moved per Eustis's directive to Fort Adams and Natchez.

Conferring with Eustis, Madison finally acknowledged the general's ineptitude and that he could no longer countenance Jefferson's whitewash. Working together, they would force Wilkinson out of the army. Eustis summoned the general to Washington in August 1809.[12] By September, they received acknowledgment from the general who waited in Natchez for the arrival of his replacement, Brigadier General Wade Hampton. The president suspended Wilkinson from command in the United States Army in December pending a congressional investigation. Unlike their predecessors, Madison and Eustis had no intention of letting the general off. Even so, investigations by two congressional committees delayed his court-martial for another two years.

In February 1810, the disaster at Terre aux Boeufs was revealed in the *Boston Gazette* as part of a letter to the editor wondering how "out of an army of 2253 officers and privates there should in the short space of six months, and in time of peace, be found only 414 fit for duty? Oh! Jefferson and Wilkinson, what an account have you got to render Somewhere!"[13]

Madison and Eustis rapidly found out who they were up against. Just before he left Washington for a summer break with personal plans in mind, Eustis received a letter from Wilkinson regarding his court–martial, stating in the "interest of the vindication of his character and conduct" he had the right as commanding general to call selected officers to Washington as his witnesses. Furthermore, he wrote, "I will thank you to give directions to the paymaster general" to pay his salary.[14]

Eustis wrote immediately to Madison, who was summering as

usual at Montpelier, stating his doubts about ordering officers to leave their military posts for the inquiry. Because the officers were on duty, the government would become part of the defense instead of the prosecution. It should present separate testimony from that of the accused. Wilkinson had argued that he had the right to "exercise his own authority in his own case and that he considered himself as being still in command."[15] Eustis firmly advised Madison that Wilkinson had no authority because the army had been turned over to Brigadier General Hampton when Wilkinson was recalled.

Wilkinson's court-martial finally convened in June 1811 with fifteen charges against him including aiding the Burr conspiracy, accepting a pension from the Spanish government, and being responsible for the disaster at Terre aux Boeufs. The verdict would not be known for yet another year.

* * *

Americans' right to navigate rivers for trade continued to be a problem for Eustis. The Creek Nation had been happy to play the game of signing treaties with the British followed by toasts of rum. More and more settlers were coming into their territory, and both the Creeks and Choctaws found this increasing intrusion threatening. When Eustis asked the tribes to permit settlers in Tennessee to bring their goods to market by sailing down the Coosa River to Mobile, Alabama, the Creeks refused. Earlier, Shawnee Chief Tecumseh had paid a visit south, urging a united native nation to halt American encroachment in the Ohio Valley. He wanted to create a confederacy called Thirteen Fires that would rival Mexico as an empire. His speeches agitated groups of Creeks enough to start a Creek civil war, making the Alabama Territory dangerous for settlers.

Madison followed Jefferson's strategy regarding Native American tribes. Jefferson believed that if he could break down the tribal cultures, dismiss tribal allegiances and identities, and convert them from warriors and nomadic hunters into farmers by providing

201

them with farm tools, the United States would obtain more tribal land for its own settlers. On Jefferson's instructions, territorial governors pressured tribes to cede millions of acres for mere pennies per acre.[16]

Other problems involving tribal land rights arose in the Indiana Territory. Appointed its governor, William Henry Harrison, an experienced Indian fighter, established a capital in Vincennes, then spent the next decade acquiring land from the local tribes for white settlement. The British had been conniving with these same tribes for years. Recent history gave Harrison no reason to expect any loyalty to the United States, and if the tribes ever did form a federation, the British could provoke them into war against the Americans. Consequently, he watched Tecumseh, an organizational genius, and his brother, Tenskatawa, a one-eyed mystic called The Prophet, as they rallied the tribes.[17]

William Eustis had complied with Harrison's request for extra troops but ordered that they be used only for defense. This was not a problem for Harrison. He could easily transform any clash into an attack that called for defensive measures. With information on Indian affairs coming directly from Harrison, Eustis had no idea about his intent to subdue the local tribes. When Harrison asked for authorization to purchase Indian lands for settlement or, as he later phrased it, an extinguishment of Indian title, Madison authorized him to negotiate for the land west of the Wabash River.

That September, Harrison met with some tribal representatives at Fort Wayne in the Indiana Territory. In the resulting treaty, various tribes gave up nearly three million acres, essentially the western part of central Indiana. The transaction cost the United States about a third of a penny per acre, and that land would soon be sold to farmers for two dollars an acre. Harrison thought it was the best deal he had ever made.[18]

Although Harrison had earlier reported that the Indians in his jurisdiction were not likely to commence any hostilities, in August

Eustis forwarded Madison's guidance "that peace may, if possible, be preserved with the Indians."[19] Harrison continued reporting on Tecumseh's travels in a large area from Michigan to Mississippi. Despite presidential instructions to maintain the peace, he planned to crush Tecumseh before he could unify all of the tribes. He summoned Tecumseh to a council at Vincennes in August. Tecumseh, arriving with three hundred armed warriors, made a three-hour speech opposing any resolutions. The meeting ended with brandished tomahawks and drawn swords.

Rumblings from the two Spanish Floridas also occupied Eustis's attention that summer. His Excellency Maximilian de St. Maxent, governor of Florida, wrote that Spain suspected a plot to attack Mobile and Pensacola, both in West Florida. Richard Sparks, the local United States representative, had reassured him that the states would cooperate to prevent any uprising against the Spanish government.[20] After consulting with Madison, Eustis instructed that all American forts in the area should be reinforced just in case.[21]

Then, not knowing that Harrison was meeting with Tecumseh, Eustis grabbed the chance to escape Washington's heat and boarded a coach for New England. Throughout August, he kept in constant contact with Madison—writing of his stop to inspect the new military academy at West Point and later reporting from Portsmouth, New Hampshire, about the upcoming elections and the situation with West Florida. He wryly noted that New Hampshire's Governor Langdon said that if the government "does not manage things better he must come himself."[22]

Eustis was on a completely different mission in Portsmouth, proposing marriage to a longtime friend. Although Eustis did not allude to it in his correspondence, Madison knew why he was there, writing that he and Dolley were looking forward to welcoming him with his new wife to "our abode" on their return to Washington.[23]

PART III: FULFILLMENT

1810 ~ 1825

*Years roll away, and soon we shall be numbered among those
who have been atoms upon this atom of a globe and very soon
after, it will be forgotten that we had here any existence. But this
ought not in the least degree to cloud any of our present
enjoyments, it being a condition of our nature.*
—Henry Knox, 1806. Cited by Mark Puls, *Henry Knox; Visionary General
of the American Revolution.*

*... the most trying and critical [time]in our history fastens
forever the chain of respect and friendship by which I have been
invariably bound to the best of men.*
—William Eustis to James Madison, June 6, 1823.
Madison Papers, Library of Congress.

Tamsen Evans George

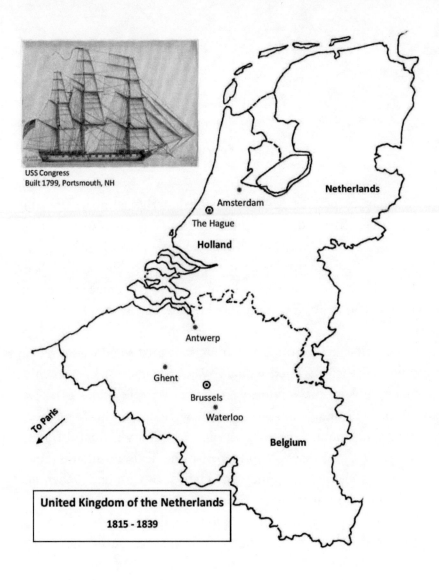

USS Congress
Built 1799, Portsmouth, NH

Netherlands

Amsterdam

The Hague

Holland

Antwerp

Ghent

Brussels

Waterloo

To Paris

Belgium

United Kingdom of the Netherlands
1815 - 1839

205

30

A Sensible Woman

On Monday, September 24, 1810, Presbyterian minister Joseph Buckminster officiated at the marriage of William Eustis, fifty-seven, to Caroline Langdon, thirty-one, in the bride's home in Portsmouth, New Hampshire.[1] The Langdon and Eustis families had known each other for more than eighteen years, ever since William's sister Anne had married Caroline's older brother, Henry Sherburne Langdon.

Having first met Caroline as a youngster, Eustis had watched her grow into an accomplished woman. With his interest in women's education, Eustis likely played an avuncular role while offering advice on her education. He often visited Caroline's father, Woodbury Langdon, especially during Woodbury's final difficult years of illness. At that time, other than medical consultation and party politics, the two men may have talked of Caroline. When an actual proposal of marriage took place is unknown.

In 1896, *New England Magazine* printed a story that Caroline Langdon had refused many suitors. It seems that during an angry exchange between Caroline, then in her early twenties, and her father regarding a shunned beau, he asked for whom she was waiting. Caroline is said to have indicated Eustis, then visiting with her father.

Eustis and Caroline had corresponded at least from the time she was twenty. Having known him most of her life, she signed her letters to him "yours affectionately" rather than the customary "your obedient servant." She asked his advice in 1803 about a procedure for her father recommended by a Philadelphia surgeon. Langdon's illness had been diagnosed, perhaps cancer, and Caroline wanted to know if the dangerous surgery was realistic and if further treatment would help.[2] The *Portsmouth Oracle* reported that Woodbury Langdon died on January 15, 1805, "after a long and distressing illness."

Eustis and Caroline exchanged their vows five years later. The Langdon and Eustis families were pleased with the marriage. Eustis's nephew, Abraham Eustis, offered his congratulations, writing that the family had long expected their marriage and that his wife, Rebecca, was quite delighted for Caroline. Rebecca had always insisted Caroline was in love with the doctor. "If Caroline puts on airs, Rebecca will be revenged by calling her aunt,"[3] Abraham teased.

Weddings were often held in the midafternoon at the home of the bride. Following the ceremony, refreshments would be served to the guests. Later, after the bride and groom had left, the remaining guests and family could have a more substantial meal with celebratory toddy, brandy, and cordials.[4] These ceremonies were not seen as romantic events and a honeymoon trip was not expected.[5] This newlywed couple, however, immediately boarded a coach for the journey of a week or more to Washington City.

Having been away for more than six weeks, driven by his responsibilities, and concerned about weather conditions, Eustis desperately needed to get back before the opening of Congress. He hurried Caroline away instead of making calls on friends and relatives. In a letter to Caroline's uncle, Governor Langdon, he apologized "that we did not allow ourselves time to pay our respects to your family with a few other of our particular friends and particularly that we had not asked the favor of you to be present at the ceremony which has introduced me to so much happiness. The badness of the weather, the uncertainty until it actually arrived of the time when I might be able to commence the journey, a consciousness that my time was exhausted & the haste in which I came away will I hope have been considered and admitted as an apology. To me the omission occurred and was as sensibly felt by my dear Caroline before we had measured the length of a mile." [6]

Perhaps leaving Portsmouth so abruptly was not entirely about getting back to Eustis's work at the War Office but also the anticipation of showing off his bride in Washington City. Newspapers as far south as Charleston, South Carolina, printed the news of the Eustis marriage. William Lee of Massachusetts, an agent and merchant trading in French wine, described Caroline as "a fine, handsome, sensible woman." [7]

Secretary Eustis and his bride became a prominent part of the Washington City social scene. Mrs. Eustis was noted for her "beauty, accomplishments, amiable characteristics and conversational powers." [8] Caroline soon became fast friends with Dolley Madison. And, as was proper, Eustis never mentioned Caroline's name in correspondence unless to a close family member. Instead, it was "Mrs. E" who joined him in wishing well to friends such as James Madison and "Mrs. M."

Why had this aging gentleman decided to marry? From a practical point of view, a politically-savvy William Eustis gained a youthful wife and an enhanced image, increased economic and social connections, and, politically, an excellent Republican alliance with New Hampshire's Governor Langdon.

May-December marriages were not unusual. When a wife died in childbirth, she was usually replaced quickly, often by someone younger, in order to provide proper care for surviving children. Although single men were accepted in the social milieu of Washington City, by the last quarter of the eighteenth century, the general public lacked sympathy for those they called "old bachelors." A man's duty in the civilized world of the United States was to become a responsible part of society by marrying, becoming head of a household, and having children. None of which Eustis had done.

Criticisms about unmarried men focused in part on procreation. Bachelorhood was considered irresponsible and frivolous. There could even be the risk of inevitable questions about sexual proclivities as well as possible social and economic consequences. Essays in Massachusetts newspapers urged compliance with the church-supported norm and warned of a man's wasted potential. A bachelor would end up physically weakened, spiritually bankrupt, and full of regret.[9] There were even rumors of establishing a tax on bachelors. The author of an article in the *Boston Gazette* on February 23, 1784, poked fun at the notion, claiming ". . . an old churl [may] stifle all the dictates of nature and passion; but the annual sum of twenty pounds will frighten him into the arms of Venus, and make him a good member of society."[10]

Alexis de Tocqueville, during his 1830 visit to America, observed a contradiction for woman of independence and domesticity. "In America the independence of women is irrecoverably lost in the bonds of matrimony, . . . which require much abnegation on the part of the woman and a constant sacrifice of her pleasures to her duties."[11] Some educated and ambitious women resisted submission to marriage until there was no other choice. Eventually, upper-class women had to marry. They had no way to support themselves unless a family member took them in. Women of lower status could open a tavern, a boarding house, or perhaps a millinery shop. Marriage determined the course of a woman's life. They were the property of their husbands, unable to own property or conduct any significant cash transactions. Caroline Langdon possessed her father's independent nature and may not have married earlier because she knew she would lose all of her rights when she did. Her future with her mother, now in her seventies, may have looked grim. The proposal of marriage from an old friend of her father's might have seemed ideal.

By the end of the eighteenth century, republican theory cast marriage in a positive light as the "companionate ideal." Couples should be friends as well as lovers, each respecting their partner's distinctive but important part in the household. In the new republic, a husband was the responsible head of the family, and the wife, in a supporting role, managed the home. Men were to be inspired by women to go forth and create the new world, or at least make it better.

Caroline had an impeccable family background. She was born in December 1781, the daughter of Woodbury and Sarah Sherburne Langdon, both from established New Hampshire gentry. Her handsome father was Henry Sherburne, an apprentice in the counting room of a wealthy merchant. Langdon married Sarah, the boss's daughter, in 1765 when she was sixteen and he was twenty-six.

The eighth of fourteen children, Caroline grew up in a dynamic, wealthy, and politically-connected household. In 1781, when Caroline was two, the original family home was destroyed by fire and rebuilt by her father as a Federalist-style brick mansion, prominent as the costliest house in Portsmouth. There are no known portraits of Caroline. Her mother's portrait, done by John Singleton Copley in 1767, reveals a pretty, brown-haired young woman of eighteen with dark, prominent eyebrows.[12] Sarah holds a spray of white and orange lilies referencing the bloom of her youth and offering a clue to her interest in gardens. Her daughter Caroline carried on these horticultural interests and many years later would be a founding member of the Massachusetts Horticultural Society.

The money in the Langdon family came from the sea. During the Revolutionary War, Woodbury Langdon amassed his fortune by outfitting and owning seven privateers including the *Ranger,* captained by John Paul Jones. Various investment interests called

Langdon to London in 1775, just at the start of the war. After two years abroad, and with no financial success, Langdon returned in 1777, sailing into New York only to discover it was under British control. General Howe restricted him to the city, but Langdon slipped out before the end of the year and made his way back to New Hampshire. A contemporary, William Plumer, described Langdon as "a man of great independence and decision, bold, keen and sarcastic. He spoke his mind of men and measures with great freedom."[13] Suspicions of his loyalty to the crown soon dissipated, and Langdon became a delegate to the Continental Congress.

John Langdon, Caroline's uncle and New Hampshire's governor, was the primary politician in the family. He served three terms as governor, 1805-1810, when Caroline and William were married. When George Washington toured the northern colonies in October 1789, he stayed in Portsmouth and visited at John Langdon's home, going for tea and then two days later for dinner. Washington commented in his diary on Woodbury Langdon's spectacular new brick house (parts of which are today incorporated into a hotel on the site). Eight-year-old Caroline was likely presented to the great man at one of those family events.

William Eustis's lengthy bachelorhood, followed by his surprise decision to marry late in life, provides fodder for speculation. How much his finances entered into the decision, how much he realized he needed a female companion to achieve all that he desired, and how strongly he was attracted to the opposite sex are difficult to determine. He had enjoyed the social company of women, but not enough to marry. His deepest friendships were with men. Most of his colleagues, as was expected, did enter into traditional marriages as young men.

The question of his sexual orientation arises when reading some of the letters he and his friends had exchanged during the previous two decades. Men bonded in close friendships, but some male friendships were closer than acknowledged and kept secret, later to

211

be subsumed by conventional marriages. Americans chose to believe that homosexuality did not exist in the New World; instead being left behind in Europe. If homosexuals were identified in the Old World, they would be persecuted or prosecuted, with the death penalty imposed for sodomy. There was no possibility of a future for openly bisexual or homosexual men.

Archivist and author William Benemann at the University of California, Berkeley, studied the sexual interests of the young officers in the Hudson Highlands where Eustis was stationed. He posits that several homosexuals were attached to Baron von Steuben's military family.[14] According to Benemann, von Steuben's questionable sexual practices in Germany may have prompted his flight from Europe. William Eustis's lifelong friend, Captain William North, and Captain Benjamin Walker were aides de camp for von Steuben. The French-speaking Walker served as the baron's translator and remained with him as secretary and property manager for the rest of von Steuben's life, becoming a beneficiary of his estate.[15]

Von Steuben's headquarters were certainly more to Walker's liking. During the last year of the war, after being transferred to General Washington's headquarters in Newburgh, New York, Walker complained to von Steuben that His Excellency's headquarters was a mirthless "Center of dullness" with his only amusement being teaching chess to Mrs. Washington.[16]

Both Walker and North married within several years after mustering out of the service; North to Mary Duane, daughter of one of New York's eminent citizens; and Walker to a Quaker woman. North's portrait by Charles Willson Peale reveals a fair-haired, slender fellow with refined, elegant features. He proved unsuccessful as a farmer and found his calling as a member of the New York State Assembly, then as a senator in Washington City. The two men kept in touch with visits and letters after they were married. Two years after his marriage, North acknowledged to

Walker that taking wives had been the only option for them. "Which of us has the most courage [in marrying] I won't say – our heads had more to do in our marriages than our hearts."[17] Both wives became reclusive during their later lives.

William Eustis knew these men well at West Point, spending his free time with them while waiting for a definite resolution to end the war. Years later, in 1792, he was mentioned in a letter from North to Walker, reminiscing about "the whole squad, & even Eustis."[18] North named his first son William for Eustis. His later sons were named Frederick for the Baron and James for his wife's father. North and Eustis maintained an affectionate correspondence throughout their lives, and Eustis undertook the care of North's mother in Boston. In 1801, he wrote to North that "three commendable friends are two more than one man in three thousand has a right to expect."[19] Perhaps he referred to the close relationship between North, Walker, and himself.

In 1803, when William was a congressman, he invited Bill North to visit him in Washington City: "if you would consent to come here nothing would rejoice me – not on your own account but for a better reason which I will not give on paper. You might do good – you & I might do more and this you would not think was saying too much if I had you by my side in my snug room." He signed off with an "affectionate thought for you and your wife and your children."[20]

31

Miscalculations

James and Dolley Madison left Washington's heat for Montpelier, extending an invitation for Eustis and Caroline to join them. By 1811, Eustis was still juggling congressional indecision, angry settlers in the western territories, the growing, British-supported Indian confederacy, and the lack of army preparedness. There was no stability anywhere. A massive slave revolt had occurred thirty miles upriver from New Orleans the previous January. It was viciously suppressed by General Wade Hampton.

The increasingly volatile international situation made it impossible for Eustis to get away in mid-August. He apologized to Madison. He and "Mrs. E" would visit "your peaceful mansion" another time. Even their time together was influenced by war preparations. For a day's outing, they inspected the arsenal at Harpers Ferry.[1]

* * *

General James Wilkinson had stacked the cards in his favor during the two years of his trial preparation. He met with Eustis in May, writing about it in the first of his several autobiographies, this one entitled: *"Burr's Conspiracy exposed and General Wilkinson vindicated against the Slanders of his Enemies."* It gave an early version of the case that he would present at his court-martial. He related an effusive welcome when Eustis "pressed my hand until it almost ached." Eustis reportedly said that he and Madison were satisfied that Wilkinson had not acted in concert with Aaron Burr, although the business of the general's spying and the army's loss of life remained pesky problems. Wilkinson characterized Eustis's request that he should clear up the spying accusation as a "mere suggestion." It seemed no one was too concerned.[2]

Staging the court-martial fell to Eustis and his advocate general, William Jones. Jones sought a better and larger location than the unfit courthouse in Fredericktown, Maryland, for a reasonable fee. Although the proper place would be Mrs. Rieball's ballroom, at ten dollars for a single day, Jones was pleased to find a large empty house for seven dollars for an entire week. Eustis would not be attending.

Two brilliant lawyers, convinced of Wilkinson's innocence, volunteered to defend him without a fee. As at the Burr trial, the general arrived in the courtroom arrayed in his uniform and sword. The drama began when Brigadier General Peter Gansevoort, the presiding officer, said that, as a prisoner, Wilkinson could not wear his sword. After a week, the trial advanced to the reading of charges and preliminary questions.

The most serious of the fifteen charges were the debacle at Terre aux Boeufs and the general's refusal to obey Eustis's direct order to move the army to a healthier location. Reports of each day's proceedings were sent to Eustis, including the difficulties and challenges from General "W." Accustomed to command and having things go the way he wanted, Wilkinson took control. He "strongly" insisted that Secretary Eustis advise the court on proper trial procedures—what was to be done if some charges were thrown out and if some witnesses were indisposed.[4] Within days, Wilkinson had challenged three colonels for the jury, and they had been replaced by three majors. He increased the number of his friends at court, molded the cause to his liking, and manipulated both the court and its observers. The trial concluded after the general took six days to read his personal statement.

Wilkinson refuted the charges of outrageously neglecting his men by insisting that it was all the fault of the penny-pinching Department of War under Dearborn and Eustis. They had kept the army so badly equipped, without hospitals or mosquito nets, that it was impossible to defend against disease. Wilkinson's military defense team delighted in criticizing the government and the War Department as it deflected all focus from their client.

Madison and Eustis realized they were losing.[5] Wilkinson had successfully turned the tables on them and would likely get an *honorable* acquittal of every charge. Eustis wrote: "In my life I do not recollect an instance of greater embarrassment . . . Confidentially I have consulted with [Alexander] Hamilton who sees the stratagem but is of the opinion that the safest course is to comply" with the court's wishes.[6] The final verdict was determined at the end of December and, as Eustis dreaded, went against them. The military jury, all Wilkinson's friends, hated Congress's financial limitations and misunderstanding of military needs. The decision publicly validated their opinions and exposed the deplorable conditions under which the army operated. Madison, hating to declare Wilkinson not guilty, stalled before announcing the verdict. Once it was over, and Wilkinson had won, his future still remained in the hands of his adversaries. After a momentary gloat, he sent obsequious letters to Madison about resuming his military career, explaining that his diatribes were not directed at Madison, as might have been thought, but really were aimed at Burr and the House of Representatives.

As it happened, the impending war with Great Britain saved Wilkinson from total erasure. The army needed officers, so Madison sent him back to defend New Orleans. Posing as a cringing penitent, Wilkinson meekly asked Eustis to clarify his goals and instructions. When he returned to New Orleans and took over his command from

General Wade Hampton, he could have blamed Hampton for the neglected defenses. But he held back, knowing that Hampton had been Madison's appointee.

Congressional allowances for only the barest necessities for the military mushroomed into substantial problems. The lack of preparedness for any kind of war, with Great Britain or with Native Americans, kept Eustis hustling. Army records and customs complicated his efforts. Responding to a request for arms from the Ohio governor, Eustis offered him cannon that, it was believed, were in Pittsburgh. Unfortunately, the two brass six-pounders were not found there. They were finally located at Fort Independence in Boston, but the cannon could not be moved because the appropriate field carriages were in Baltimore. General Henry Dearborn had instructed that the carriages for the light artillery were to be precisely constructed for uniformity, and Eustis had to forward a plan and dimensions so the correct carriages could be built in Boston before the cannon were transported to Ohio.[7]

Congress relied on selling former Indian lands for income, but Great Britain wanted Indian-controlled borderlands to prevent competition from American traders and fur hunters. They had kept their border forts after the Revolutionary War and armed the local tribes in Ohio. Eustis sent a letter to the Indian nations in the Ohio River Valley on October 8, 1811, adopting a Jeffersonian tone. He addressed them as "my children," writing that their "Great Father, the President, takes you by the hand," urging them to become farmers and prosper like their white brothers. Eustis warned against associating with Tecumseh's brother Tenskatawa, "The Prophet". He wrote "Beware of the man. He is not good," adding that all who follow him would be destroyed.[8]

Despite Eustis's instructions not to initiate a fight, William Henry Harrison watched for an opportunity to gain land for the government.[9] When Chief Tecumseh headed south in September to enroll the Creeks and Osage in his tribal confederacy, Harrison

217

marched north accompanied by about nine hundred militia, looking to stir up trouble. Arriving near the Shawnee village called Prophetstown, (near today's Battle Ground, Indiana) Harrison set up camp at the confluence of the Wabash and the Tippecanoe Rivers but posted no lookouts.[10] Against Tecumseh's instructions, The Prophet's warriors, well-equipped by their British allies, attacked Harrison's camp at dawn. The fighting continued into nightfall. The next morning, Harrison found Prophetstown abandoned. The Prophet and his people had slipped away in the darkness.

Harrison rushed a report of his great victory to the secretary of war, asserting that the Indians had attacked him. Madison reported Harrison's triumph to Congress, claiming it had brought peace to the frontier. Actually, The Prophet and Tecumseh were still active and now openly allied with the British. Congress added the daylong fight, later called the Battle of Tippecanoe, to its list of grievances against Great Britain, the source of the natives' weapons. When later reports contradicted Harrison's account, Eustis demanded to know why Harrison had not taken adequate precautions to fortify his camp. Harrison replied that his units were strong enough and it was unnecessary. Eustis and Madison conferred and decided that it would be bad for military morale if this so-called great victory was investigated or modified. Neither ever trusted Harrison again, but the legend of Tippecanoe propelled Harrison into the presidency in 1840.

* * *

A new congressman arrived in Washington that fall of 1811. The aggressive and articulate Kentuckian, Henry Clay, thirty-five, was elected Speaker of the House on the first day. He became the leader of a group of rabid Republicans from the western states called the War Hawks. They proudly affirmed adding the word "democratic" to their party affiliation, becoming the Democratic-Republicans. The War Hawks held a vision of a decidedly larger United States, adding Canada, Florida, and Texas. Under their plan, all European nations would be expelled from the North American continent.

Before the news of Harrison's self-proclaimed triumph at the Battle at Tippecanoe, Madison had sent a message to Congress asking that the United States be put into "armor and attitude demanded by the growing crisis" with Great Britain and asked Eustis to raise ten thousand regular troops, instigating a congressional conflict over plans regarding Canada. The western states wanted the territory beyond the Great Lakes and an end to Indian unrest. In opposition, the business-oriented New England states, focused on Atlantic trade, sympathized with Canada. They altered their Federalist enthusiasm for a strong central government and began to champion states' rights, threatening secession if there was any attempt to annex or conquer Canada.[11]

Clay and his War Hawks thought the country's first response should be with volunteers and state militia, embracing the idyllic mythology of the American Revolution.[12] If the United States did not go to war, it meant submission to British domination, tantamount to giving up independence, and betrayed the sacrifices of the patriots of 1776. With a secret fear of a military dictator such as Napoleon, the Democratic-Republicans were convinced that a standing army would pose a threat to the country.

Congress had strengthened the army but now questioned if those increases were necessary. Since the country was not actually at war, there seemed to be no need for the expense of a standing army. Congress chose to believe that the volunteer militia could be depended on if the time came. Congressmen in 1810 had voted to reduce the army and navy but not completely eliminate them.[13] It seemed that the ship of state was sailing whichever way the wind was blowing, and Madison waited to see what would happen.

Congress again reversed its position in January 1812. Influenced by the War Hawks and their underlying desire to invade Canada, it passed a bill giving Secretary of War Eustis a year to raise twenty-five thousand troops but voted against building a proposed twelve battleships and twenty frigates.[14] Most northeastern representatives voted to build the naval ships, but the southern and western factions opposed that as a waste of money. Instead of waging a war at sea, they would conduct a land war.

Canada was not the sole reason for going to war, of course, but it was an effective reason for waging a war against Great Britain on land rather than at sea. England's land forces were primarily occupied with battling Napoleon, so Canada was largely unprotected. Thomas Jefferson, who vastly overestimated America's interest and vastly underestimated Canadian loyalties, believed that all Canadians would naturally rally to the American cause.

While Congress debated troop levels in December 1811, Eustis had sent a secret agent, Benjamin Stickley, to scout Canadian defenses.[15] In February 1812, Stickley confirmed dreams of an easy victory. The whole matter might be handled by volunteer militia—a vindication of Jeffersonian theory and Democratic-Republican principles.

Although it was against his better judgement, Madison realized that the years of dispute with Great Britain would have to be settled by a war. He stayed behind the scenes and let Henry Clay take the lead in the House, deferring to Congress' constitutional authority to actually declare war.

To Madison, Eustis, and the Democratic-Republicans, the Canadians seemed sympathetic to the United States.[16] With close to five hundred families a year lured by the British gift of free land, Upper Canada (today's Ontario Province) had grown to seventy-five thousand people by 1812. About two-thirds of the people in Lower Canada (today's Quebec) were of French descent and, therefore, Americans believed, were hardly loyal to the British crown. The country's total population amounted to only about a half-million white people compared to eight million in the United States. No one counted the native peoples.

In March, Henry Clay met with Secretary of State James Monroe and President Madison, convincing them to ask Congress for a thirty-day trade embargo on British goods to give American ships time to return home. Congress expanded the embargo to ninety days, then it expected Madison to ask Congress for a declaration of war in June. In April, after deciding that taxes to pay for the war need not be imposed until the war actually started, Congress authorized President Madison to direct Secretary of War Eustis to call up a hundred thousand volunteers to serve for six months in the militia. Having killed off Alexander Hamilton's Bank of the United States, Congress had no money to conduct a war or pay troops, giving another reason to cling to the illusion that the populace would rise up together and annex Canada. The best idea seemed to be to first declare war on Great Britain, then take it from there.

Despite all of Eustis's efforts, it was clear that the preparations for war had overwhelmed the small number of clerks in his tiny department. Madison asked for help, but Congress denied it on the grounds that an annual salary of $3,000 apiece for two assistant secretaries was a needless expense. Eustis tried a different tack. He asked Madison if "the business of the Indian Department could be transferred to another department." He needed this "alteration" of the War Department because of its additional duties in "prosecution of military operations."[17] But that was also deemed an unnecessary expense, and the western conflict remained Eustis's to resolve.

As instructed, Eustis wrote to the state governors requiring them to call up their reserves, hold their militia in readiness, and, in reference to the Revolutionary War, be prepared to march at a moment's notice. He directed Brigadier General Joseph Bloomfield in Trenton, New Jersey, "that the fortifications on the seaboard be put in the best state of defense, particularly those in the harbour of New York."[18] Eustis needed to establish a Quartermasters Corps, as approved by Congress, and submitted a list of nominees to Congress for deputy quartermasters, including his brother Jacob.[19]

The small War Department could not keep up; it was scrambling but falling behind. No matter what Eustis did, congressmen were annoyed with him. Abner Lacock, the Democratic-Republican senator from Pennsylvania, stated in a note that he had tried to see Eustis three times to talk about the "perilous" situation of his frontier constituents who needed federal protection from local Indians. Lacock acknowledged he was "aware that the important nature of your duties renders it still uncertain when I might find you at leisure to be seen."[20] He pleaded for arms for his local militia or a detachment of the Pennsylvania militia. Desperate, the senator said he would meet with Eustis anytime, anyplace.

32

Rally Round Our Standard

The War of 1812 is arguably the least known and strangest war in American history. While it was a war in its own right, it became part of the larger conflict between Britain and France that had been going on since 1793. It even contained aspects of a civil war within the United States. Not a war of conquest or defense, it became about the honor of a democratic government.

* * *

President Madison asked Congress to declare war against Great Britain on June 1, 1812, citing impressment of American sailors, British blockades preventing safe departure from American ports, safe arrival at other ports, confiscation of neutral ships and cargo, and Indian hostilities in the West. The maritime complaints were not new, and animosity by Native American nations was as much due to the increasing numbers of encroaching settlers as to British incitement. For Americans, British impositions had surpassed the tipping point.

Congress voted for war on June 12, two days after Parliament repealed its restrictions on neutral trade, one of the main issues of contention. The British thought their repeal was a major concession, but it made no difference to Americans; they just wanted an end to British bullying. So they went to war—with little planning or preparation save for a presidential concern about the constitutionally correct way to proceed. The president's role was to conduct the war after Congress made the declaration.

Those same Democratic-Republicans who had opposed all preparation efforts now voted in favor of a war. And why not? The unattainable had occurred before. This was a generation of change and revolutions. Stalwart American rebels had defeated the mighty British lion, and French revolutionaries had done away with their monarchy. The decision to go to war, like belling the cat, seemed a grand idea until it came to carrying it out.

Democratic-Republicans believed that Federalists would come around to their point of view. They did not. To be fair, Democratic-Republicans had not explained how a land war in Canada could resolve British blockades and impressment of sailors on the high seas. Every single Federalist in Congress and 20 percent of the Democratic-Republicans voted no.[1] With their strong New England mercantile interests, Federalists not only voted against war, they denounced it. In New England, it was heresy *not* to oppose the war. Sermons preached in New England pulpits added religious censure; Madison was called a murderer, and anyone who helped him was labeled wicked in the sight of God.

No one seemed more surprised about the declaration than the British ambassador, Augustus J. Foster. Henry Clay explained to Foster that it was an issue of honor, similar to a young officer challenging an opponent to a duel because of bullying or public humiliation. After having tea with Secretary of State James Monroe following the congressional vote, a puzzled Foster reported the "extraordinary measure seems to have been unexpected by nearly the whole nation; and to have been carried in opposition to the declared sentiments of many of those who voted for it."[2] The Madison administration thought that the declaration alone might convince Great Britain to yield on the issue of impressments, that there might not be a need for actual fighting. Meanwhile, at the very least, Canada would join the union.

Once the vote was in, Madison left for Montpelier, giving Secretary of War Eustis the responsibility for conducting the war. Miscalculations and misunderstandings were just beginning. A legally-trained mind and a medically-trained mind would try to conduct a war by letters that enclosed other reports, all taking at least four days to go from Washington to Montpelier and back. The chain of command went from Madison to Eustis and then out to individual officers in the field. Eustis may have based his actions, while assiduously waiting for Madison's directions, on those he had observed by Washington who carefully deferred to the Continental Congress.

Thomas Jefferson predicted that taking Canada would be a "mere matter of marching" across the border.[3] Eustis chose to believe Jefferson's observations, and the report of his spy, and promised a quick and overwhelming victory. "We can take Canada without soldiers," he declared; "we have only to send officers into the province and the people . . . will rally round our standard."[4]

An army of twenty-five thousand men had been created on paper. But when war was declared, fewer than seven thousand troops were scattered across the nation in twenty-three forts.[5] Recruitment had not generated the anticipated numbers. Not all state governors had called up their militias. Whereas New York and Pennsylvania had cooperated, the New England states refused.

Before the war declaration had gone to Congress, Madison, in conference with Henry Clay and James Monroe, devised a grand battle plan championed by General Henry Dearborn, Eustis's old boss, for a three-pronged attack against Canada. They had no misgivings about invading Canada and expected no resistance. The eastern prong of the attack would be aimed at Montreal; the middle would target the heart of Upper Canada [Ontario] through the Niagara Falls area between Lakes Ontario and Erie; and the western prong would be based in Detroit. Dearborn, sixty-one and collector of customs for the port of Boston, was recruited to capture Montreal based on his experience of forty-years earlier when he and Benedict Arnold had invaded Canada.

Eustis had conferred with Dearborn in Washington before the general went to Boston to recruit troops and prepare the attack against Montreal. Despite taking part in the initial planning, Dearborn seemed unsure of the campaign's timing and dallied in Boston. His recruiting did not go well. Very few New Englanders volunteered. Finally, Eustis sent a direct order for Dearborn to proceed to Albany and organize his recruits there.

Madison selected Revolutionary War veteran William Hull to lead the western prong of the invasion. Eustis knew Hull, fifty-nine, from their mutual adventure of quelling Shays' Rebellion. Hull was to attack east from Detroit into Upper Canada. He tried to decline his assignment but could not argue his age because the seven other generals being commissioned also were Revolutionary War veterans, all between fifty-eight and sixty-three years old.[6] When Hull at last agreed to serve, he certainly did not realize he would have to subdue all of Upper Canada with only fifteen hundred men.

Eustis had no experience in conducting a war. He communicated orders directly to his generals by mail. Roundtrip correspondence could take a month or more and usually included going to Montpelier and back. He spent his time doing what he knew and, having passed on Madison's instructions, assumed that his veteran commanders knew what to do. Correspondence on his desk piled up with everything from supply reports to military advice to petitions for appointments. Difficulties with coordination across a sprawling nation demanded all his time and attention. Serving as the quartermaster general, and with concern for the welfare of the men, he spent much of his time ordering and moving supplies besides coercing states into providing volunteers.

Even before war had officially been declared, General Hull set out for Fort Detroit with about twelve hundred militia and three hundred regular troops to get in position for the western campaign. They hacked their way through two hundred miles of wilderness. On June 27, Hull received a letter from Eustis written on June 18, a week *after* the declaration, stating: "Circumstances have recently occurred which render it necessary you should pursue your march to Detroit with all possible expedition."[7] Eustis wrote to Hull later that day, clarifying that Congress had indeed declared war and suggesting Hull should be on his guard. Unfortunately, that second letter traveled by public mail rather than private courier and did not reach Hull until three days after the neighboring British had learned of the American declaration of war.

When Hull reached Fort Detroit on July 5, he discovered another fort rising across the river. The British had started building immediately. The Americans began recovering from the month-long march, and Hull awaited instructions from Eustis. That packet contained Madison's proclamation of war and directed Hull to take possession of British Fort Malden and "extend your conquests." Hull wrote back that he did not have sufficient troops to drive the British from their new fort at Detroit, much less capture the fort at Malden. "The British command the water and the savages,"[8]

With the invasion of Canada, the realities of twelve years of limited congressional funding and military inexperience became painfully apparent. No chief of staff or any command structure had been created. Secretary Eustis had neither defined the lines of responsibility nor created an effective military bureaucracy.[9] There were no rules about seniority in the regular army or with the militia officers. No one seemed to know who ranked whom or when or where they had authority. While Hull was slogging west through the wilderness, General Dearborn asked Eustis: "Who is to have command of the operations in Upper Canada [where Hull was headed]? I take it for granted that my command does not extend that far."[10] Eustis' efforts to manage communications, ineffective to begin with, disintegrated further.

Getting supplies to the right places proved hugely difficult. Supply lines were attacked, and some materials were delivered to the wrong places. The Samuel B. Young Commissary of the Vermont Military Stores, in Bennington, reported that forty-five tons of cannon balls were lying exposed and undefended in the eastern part of town. It was "daily diminishing" and soon would be gone. Young was sure the ordnance would be needed in the north, and he wanted orders from Eustis. Should he secure it or remove it?[11] Eustis forwarded the letter to General Dearborn.

Hull reported to Eustis from Fort Detroit in August.[12.] He expected between two thousand and three thousand Indians and British troops to attack, so he was building up his defenses. Although Hull did not say so, he had a growing obsession with an assault by crazed hordes of bloodthirsty savages, and he was running out of supplies. British ships dominated Lake Erie, so food, uniforms, and boots were not arriving, and the army was unable to keep an overland supply line open to the south. Tecumseh had led an ambush against Major Thomas Van Horn who was sent out with two hundred men to meet some expected volunteers. One hundred soldiers and seven officers were killed, and a delighted Tecumseh captured the army mailbag with a letter from Hull to Secretary Eustis expressing his worry about attacks from Indians and pleading for provisions.[13]

Hull was in a bad situation. As he was preparing for a siege, Eustis sent discouraging news to not expect reinforcements since "the Governor of Massachusetts with the opinion of the Judges of the Supreme Judicial Court, and the Governor of Connecticut" had both informed him they would not order militia into the service of the United States.[14] New Englanders were boycotting "Mr. Madison's War."

Meanwhile, British Major General Isaac Brock, acting lieutenant governor of Upper Canada and commander-in-chief of its forces, joined Tecumseh's native forces. They knew of Hull's fears from the letter to Eustis discovered in the captured mailbag. After circulating rumors that thousands of Indians would attack the fort, a hoax devised by Brock that caused Hull to collapse with terror, the British and Indians marched to Fort Detroit. On arrival, Tecumseh paraded his six hundred Indians three times to give an illusion of a larger force.[15] Brock dressed his militia in castoff British uniforms. When Brock pounded the fort with cannon fire, Hull's son, Abraham, emerged with a white flag.[16] Without firing a shot, Hull surrendered and was taken to Montreal as a prisoner.

Eustis relayed a message to Madison from a frantic General Dearborn who had heard that Tecumseh threatened to put more Indians on the warpath. According to Dearborn, Tecumseh had said to General Brock, "you have done as you pleased at Detroit, let me have my way at Fort Wayne [Indiana]." Eustis informed Madison that General Dearborn "contemplates only the conquest of the *south* side of the St. Lawrence" River. He pleaded for "my directions by as early a mail as possible."[17]

Eustis appealed daily for Madison to come back to Washington. The president had been sick most of the summer, diagnosed with a bilious fever, so he was not eager to return. Writing privately, Eustis vented to Dearborn about the fall of Fort Detroit. He thought the western country was in an "unusual state of alarm." To his knowledge, there was no want of provisions, ammunition, or men. He was baffled that the Americans had not fired a shot. "Colonel Cass brought a Gen'l Order with the capitulation! Without a drop of British blood!" He had heard "not a word from the general."[18]

Hull finally wrote to Eustis explaining the difficulties he had faced; being reduced to eight hundred men, some two hundred of whom were sick and wounded, and the lack of medicine or "comforts necessary for their situation."[19] He cited the vulnerable people who had come into the fort for safety and that his troops could not defend against the massive strength of the Native Americans and the forces of Upper Canada. If they had been provided with reinforcements as requested, provisions, military

229

stores, clothing, pack horses for transport, and comforts for the sick and wounded, they might have prevailed.

For everyone, especially for Hull and for Eustis, a great deal was at stake politically in the assignment of blame. Stories circulated of a nonfunctioning general cringing in the corner, covering his head as the first British shots were heard. Rumors suggested he might be a traitor or that, despite having plenty of provisions, he had denied sufficient rations to the troops. Once hailed as a war hero of the Revolution, Hull, in disgrace, faced a court-martial.

Secretary Eustis was not perceived kindly either, considering the disaster had occurred on his watch. Henry Clay lost respect for him, declaring to James Monroe on August 12, 1812, that "the sec. of War (in whom already there unfortunately exists no sort of confidence) cannot possibly shield Mr. Madison from the odium which will attend" Hull's defeat.[20]

The Canadian campaign failed on all fronts. Hull's surrender was just the first disaster. General Henry Dearborn, in ill health, did not even make it from Albany to the Canadian border. He further confused everyone by arranging for an unauthorized armistice with the governor of Lower Canada to buy time to pull his army together.[21] The puzzled British thought that America might be calling off the war. Madison canceled the armistice and told Dearborn to get on with the invasion. The disgusted militia declared it was illegal for them to cross into Canada and left for home. Then in October, the British defeated General Stephen van Rensselaer at Queenstown Heights above Niagara.

Democratic-Republicans tried to understand what had gone wrong. Their plans had seemed perfect; to capture Canada before Great Britain could reinforce its troops or deploy the fleet. Canada could then be used as a bargaining chip to extract concessions. The Canadians proved the greatest surprise. They did not want to become part of the United States.

As it turned out, no part of Canada was taken. Instead, Canada captured the entire Michigan Territory.

33

'Difficulties Peculiarly Arduous'

Within three months, even government officials began to lose confidence in the war's designated leaders. Eustis wrote to reassure Ohio Governor Return J. Meigs Jr. that the president would persevere and regain lost ground. Surely with the cooperation of the well-known Indian fighter, General William Henry Harrison, he said, everything would improve.[1]

Washington socialites, unsure about wartime conduct, attended few social events other than Dolley Madison's Wednesday evenings. Dolley recounted to her sister, Anna Cutts, that she "Went to Eustis on Sunday evening.[2] Mrs. [Alexander] Hamilton and Mrs. Eustis have had parties – no one else." Mrs. Madison found the Eustis party "dull." The women, including Caroline Eustis, supported the military forces as best they could, organizing "fringe parties" where they braided white cotton trim for epaulets.[3]

As during the Revolution, the army's welfare came down to a lack of money; a throwback to army units desperate for everything—food, winter clothing, arms, wood, and even stationery. The War Department's limited appropriations for clothing and supplies ran out, and Eustis asked the president to redirect funds of $500,000 originally meant for the army's payroll to supplies.[4] Eustis's own experience with Hudson Highland winters taught him that the army could not function without adequate uniforms and shoes. Letters from officers begging for money deluged his office.[5]

Transporting supplies collapsed. Suppliers wrote excuse-filled letters to Eustis about the difficulty of getting goods and materials to the army in Michigan from its nearest source in Ohio. They could not locate wagon drivers willing to risk the possibility of ambush, unpredictable rivers, and weather while traveling through nearly two hundred miles of wilderness to reach Detroit.

Lieutenant H. Johnson, the assistant deputy quartermaster, related yet another fiasco in a letter from Fort Fayette, an army supply depot on the Ohio River. "Five wagons have been here several days with an hundred & fifty three barrels of Navy powder & could find no one authorized to receive it. They were about to sell it. I have paid the transportation & put it in store. It was sent by a Mr. Ewall from Washington. Be pleased to tell me what I shall do with it?"[6]

Lack of supplies and transportation were not the only problems. Eustis received reports that Indian tribes—the Miami, Kickapoo, Chippewa, and Winnebago—were growing more dangerous and increasing their attacks. Territorial governors were alarmed by British Major General Brock's attempts to unite the tribes under his control.

By October, Eustis was a target for everyone. Where were the promised victories? An article in the Federalist-leaning *Whig Chronicle*, a Philadelphia newspaper, declared that Eustis was totally unfit. "An old woman would do as well for secretary of war as granny Eustis." The 1812 elections were approaching. Claiming the Democratic-Republicans were no better than the Federalists, the article urged the electorate to start fresh by getting rid of President Madison and both Secretary of the Treasury Gallatin and Secretary of War Eustis.[7]

The lack of military communications encouraged independent activity by various officers. Planning ahead for the spring campaign,

Colonel Zebulon Pike wrote to Eustis from his post in Plattsburgh, New York, asking for funds for new medieval-like armaments he had designed: pikes [eight-foot-long spears with hatchet tops] for his third rank, and casques [helmets] for the whole regiment as well as special twenty-six-inch short swords made for his pike bearers. He argued that the casques with hanging chains would completely defend the head and shoulders of his men from the strikes of a saber. In a final note, Pike added an update that it "yet remains undecided whether we enter Canada this season."[8] Colonel Pike was killed about four months later during the April 1813 assault on York in Canada by an explosion of the powder magazine in its fort.

While disastrous attempts to invade Canada continued, President Madison took heart from news of surprising victories at sea during this last naval war fought entirely under sail. The Royal Navy had one hundred ninety-one battleships of sixty to eighty guns each. America had none. The Royal Navy had two hundred forty-five frigates with thirty to fifty guns each. America had seven.[9] One, the *Constellation,* in Norfolk for repairs and bottled up by the British blockade, saw no action. Had Thomas Jefferson had his way, the United States would have had no frigates at all. Sea battles proved him wrong

The *Constitution*, captained by Isaac Hull, escaped a British squadron then famously captured the British ship *Guerrière* in August 1812. The *Constitution* got its nickname "Old Ironsides" from that battle when a sailor observing British shot bouncing off the ship cried out: "Her sides are made of iron." They were actually made from extremely dense live oak timbers grown in the Carolinas. Captain Hull's success offset the failure of his uncle, General William Hull, on land. A New York newspaper reported: "Captain Hull, who has immortalized himself in the capture of the *Guerrière*, is a relative of General Hull who has been sacrificed by an imbecile administration on the borders of Canada."[10]

That American sea forces succeeded and land forces failed might be attributed to the youth of the captains at sea, who were under forty, and the age of the generals on land, who were over sixty. The generals found excuses for not fighting, while the captains rushed to sea and into battle. As soon as war was declared, the *United States,* captained by Stephen Decatur, and the *President,* captained by John Rodgers, immediately sailed from New York Harbor.[11]

The sea battles redeemed the war effort and got Madison reelected. When he returned to Washington in the fall of 1812, the president waited until after congressional confirmation of his reelection to belatedly reorganize his cabinet and military establishment, beginning with removal of the habitually intoxicated secretary of the navy, Paul Hamilton.[12] The situation also demanded replacing the secretary of war with a farsighted military leader who had a talent for organization. William Eustis was described as "an amiable man and an efficient politician."[13] Despite the War Department's meager budget and shortage of equipment, after six months of war, everyone joined together in denouncing Eustis as incompetent. It was easier to blame than explain.

By then, House Speaker Henry Clay had little to no regard for Eustis. In Clay's opinion, Eustis was adequate in his position in peacetime but inept as a wartime manager. Impatient over the slow communications between the capital and the West and the evident incompetence in Washington, Clay led a chorus seeking Eustis's removal. Clay thought military operations had been wretchedly planned and that President Madison was "unfit for the storms of war."[14]

Fully aware of the increasing criticism, Eustis wrote his letter of resignation in December 1812, suggesting that "some other citizen might be selected, possessing greater military knowledge, and commanding in a higher degree the public confidence." Although the secretary's ineptness in military affairs was generally acknowledged, Madison praised him two days later for the "zeal and constancy" of his "exertion for the public good, under difficulties peculiarly arduous & trying."[16] Congressman Jonathan Roberts wrote that "Dr. Eustis gave ground at once & however he might have failed to fill his office with success he quit it with a magnanimity that has enabled him to [carry] away a very general respect."[17]

Replacing his secretary of war was a complex matter for Madison who unsuccessfully sought a New Englander to balance his cabinet. He offered the post to James Monroe as the only cabinet officer with military experience. Finding he had little to do in the State Department, Monroe still hesitated about taking on the whole war effort and agreed to serve only as interim secretary. He believed that if he was identified with an unpopular war, his chances of becoming the next president would be damaged.[18]

* * *

Eustis and Caroline packed up their belongings, shipped some by packet to Boston, then sold or gave at least two chairs to Albert and Hannah Gallatin. As 1813 dawned, they boarded a coach heading north.[19] Eustis may have left Washington, but, being so well-known, he could not escape the rumor mill.

On January 4, 1813, an unsigned letter from Philadelphia sent to Anna Cutts, Dolley Madison's sister, revealed Eustis had arrived after some difficulty on the road, including a day's illness in Wilmington, Delaware. The nameless writer passed along the gossip that William Duane's criticism of the former secretary of war was welcome at the White House, and the writer had this information from Dolley Madison herself. Dolley had supposedly urged Duane, editor of the radical Democratic-Republican newspaper the *Philadelphia Aurora*, to continue writing his salacious material. Undeterred, Eustis responded that he knew it was "false and a base calumny."[20] His friend Mrs. Madison would never plot against him.

Eustis arrived in New York after a short stay in Philadelphia and headed upriver to Albany to testify at General William Hull's court-martial on charges of treason, cowardice, negligence of duty, and conduct unbecoming an officer during the Detroit campaign. The prosecution's focus was more emotional than factual. Hull deplored the admission of hearsay and officers' opinions as evidence instead of facts. Furthermore, testifying officers were rewarded with promotions from colonel to general. Hull thought that much of the blame for mismanagement of the overall campaign should be placed on General Dearborn's incompetence. But, as it happened, Dearborn presided at the trial. Hull had little chance.

Testifying on January 23, Eustis was asked to verify letters issued through himself that proved General Hull had been operating under orders from Madison.[21] Despite all evidence, whether fact or fiction, Hull was not going to be let off, and Eustis would not contradict Dearborn. Someone had to be blamed for the debacle. Although there may have been mitigating circumstances, Hull became the national scapegoat. He faced censure on all sides—from Federalists who denounced the entire venture to Madison loyalists who blamed Hull instead of administrative failures.[22] General Dearborn sentenced Hull to death for cowardice, but the court recommended that the sentence be commuted.[23] William Hull, now infamous and publicly shamed, lived the rest of his life in disgrace.

And Dr. and Mrs. Eustis went home to Boston.

34

Washington Burning

In Boston, Eustis and Caroline moved in with William's brother Jacob and his family. Eustis quickly set about finding other accommodations and purchased the mortgage for a square, hipped-roofed house and barn (today near 1715 Massachusetts Avenue) in Cambridge from Ebenezer Wells, his sister Catherine's husband.[1] Once this relatively new house, built in 1802, was made ready, the Eustises moved to Cambridge.

They had returned to a somewhat hostile home state where most residents spoke out against the war. Eustis, sixty, had a wife to support in an appropriate manner and very little in the way of financial resources, so he renewed his political contacts with the local Democratic-Republican Party and sought another government appointment.

There did not seem to be good news anywhere. In May, Caroline called his attention to a newspaper announcement that William North's wife had died. "Mrs. E joins me in all the sentiments which oppressed us when she pointed to the paragraph in the newspaper," he wrote to North and enclosed a sentimental poem.[2]

The *Boston Gazette* grimly reflected on the national situation. "We went to war, it was said, for the conquest of Canada and the liberty of the seas. Instead of taking Canada, we have lost three

238

armies, Forts Detroit, Michilimackinac, and the Michigan Territory. As to the <u>Liberty of the Seas</u> we have not now left the <u>liberty of our own rivers and bays</u>."[3.]

Great Britain's ships had blockaded Chesapeake Bay and the Delaware River throughout 1813 but left New England alone. Supplies continued to be smuggled into Canada as New England brazenly ignored Mr. Madison's War, selling grain to anyone willing to pay for it.

Overseas, after Napoleon's defeat and exile on Elba, thousands of British soldiers became available for service in America, and the British promptly extended their blockade along the entire East Coast. Although some towns in New England supported the war, the governors of Massachusetts, Connecticut, and Rhode Island continued to refuse to detach any militia for federal service. In response to British coastal raids, they independently equipped and organized their militia for their state's defense. Nantucket declared neutrality.[4]

Infuriated by New England's smuggling, President Madison declared another trade embargo on December 21, 1813. It prevented American ships and cargoes from leaving their harbors, outlawed the import of certain British goods, and banned foreign ships from American ports unless they could prove that three-quarters of their crew came from the country the ship represented. Earlier embargos had backfired, and this one did as well. With their economy dependent on maritime trade, New England's ships and trading vessels were kept idle in ports, and businesses supplying the shipping trade closed. New England took it personally, interpreting the embargo as Madison's declaration of war against that region.

The increase in British coastal activity made Bostonians uneasy. Their own defenses, the fifteen cannon on Governor's Island and the ten at Charlestown Point, might not be enough. Paul Revere, now seventy-nine and a lieutenant colonel in the militia, took the lead to protect Boston.[5] He directed that old ships be sunk at the entrances to the harbor and that additional defenses be constructed. Fort Strong, named for Massachusetts Governor Caleb Strong, was built in East Boston, and a battery was positioned on Dorchester Heights. The commonwealth blamed the federal government for not occupying its forts and defending it, even though Massachusetts had refused to participate or contribute militia to any federal effort.

Governor Strong sought federal funding for the state's defense, maintaining that the state had to defend itself and the federal government should cover local militia expenses. Secretary of State James Monroe responded by reiterating the administration's longstanding position that if the United States Army was provided state militia forces as requested, the cost would be covered. Otherwise, the state would operate as a separate entity at its own expense. Governor Strong compromised and allowed a militia detachment to join federal troops at Fort Warren in Boston Harbor.

William Eustis, persistently seeking employment, drew President Madison's attention to General Dearborn who, besides commanding troops in the war, still served as collector of taxes for the Port of Boston. Eustis offered to fill the post himself since Dearborn had come into some money and could now retire comfortably.[6] His hopes were dashed when Madison wrote back that the appointment was impossible but offered no explanation.[7] Not to be put off, Eustis responded immediately. He was sorry the position would not work out but that the war would continue and would need the exertions of all friends loyal to the country. He was available for any assignment Madison cared to give him, perhaps something more extensive in some other area.[8]

Eustis diligently wrote letters throughout 1813. He followed the war news, reading his newspapers daily. Understanding that Madison was fully engaged in the business of the country, he tried not to nag. By the first of January 1814, however, he could not resist taking note, as a former maligned secretary of war, of the mess caused by his and Madison's common nemesis, General James

Wilkinson, during his inept St. Lawrence campaign to invade Canada.[9] Eustis commented that "our army is made up of old men, boys and other non-effectives." He assured Madison that he was "holding myself ready for any service at home or abroad."[10]

On July 4, 1814, Eustis was a special guest for the national holiday in Lexington where his mother had spent her final days. The town's daylong celebration began with a parade followed by church services. A spacious marquee, erected on the famed Green, hosted a tea party for the ladies, and in the evening there was a "splendid" ball. Many notable Democratic-Republicans were there including Dearborn and Madison's new vice president from Massachusetts, Elbridge Gerry.[11] The day was a purely patriotic escape from the realities of the war. No one was aware that a large British fleet had entered Chesapeake Bay.

British Admiral Sir Alexander Cochrane had assigned Admiral George Cockburn to join forces with General Robert Ross and create a diversion in retaliation for the American's success in invading and burning York (now Toronto), the capital of Upper Canada. Transports carrying General Ross's army brigade sailed into Chesapeake Bay and rendezvoused with Admiral Cockburn's warships.

Washingtonians did not think their city would be a target. President Madison chose to believe his new secretary of war, John Armstrong, who claimed the capital was safe, needed no further defenses, and could not be reached by the British. That August, as the capital dozed in the heat, British ships put troops ashore in Maryland to march overland toward their objective—Washington City. The only enemy they encountered was the summer's steamy temperatures. Rumors reached Washington that the British were headed that way, and the militia gathered at the Navy Yard expecting the attack to come up the Potomac. Panicked, and fearful that their gunboats would fall into British hands, the militia blew them up as well as the two bridges across the east branch of the river.

Confirmation that the British were advancing overland threw the War Department into disarray. No attempt was made to impede their march through Maryland toward Bladensburg where a bridge remained intact. Instead, President Madison, Secretary of State Monroe, and Secretary of War Armstrong rode out to survey the front lines. Upon their arrival, furious at Armstrong's incompetence and lack of preparation, Madison sent him home on the spot. Monroe took charge, ordered gunners to make a fast deployment toward the north, and changed the disposition of the lines. This was the only time that a sitting American president, as commander-in-chief, appeared on an actual battlefield. Armstrong resigned the next day, and Monroe became the acting secretary of war.

Meanwhile Dolley Madison, on her own back at the President's House, determined to do her best for her husband. She had turned Jefferson's office into the State Dining Room featuring her favorite red velvet draperies. She saved those draperies, packed up official governmental papers, and had the huge portrait of George Washington removed from its frame, sending everything away in commandeered wagons. She departed about a half hour before the British arrived.

The British burned Washington on August 24, 1814.[12] Barely twenty-four hours after arriving in their enemy's capital, the troops marched back to waiting ships. They had burned the Capitol, the President's House, and the Library of Congress. Retreating Americans had burned their own Navy Yard. There had not been much of a capital city to begin with, and now most of it was charred ruins.

About a year and a half later, Dolley Madison, still mourning the loss of the President's House and her beautiful furnishings, cast about for replacements. She wrote to Hannah Gallatin in Philadelphia, knowing Hannah and her husband, Albert, were packing to leave for Europe. Dolley asked if they intended to sell the furniture in their Washington house. She specifically asked about beds and "the two Eustis chairs." Those Eustis chairs likely wound up in the White House.

Eustis wrote to Bill North about British progress in the war. "The British are advancing gradually – they have taken & will make a fixed post in Penobscot." He described his homey surroundings: "my wife & Anne [his sister] . . . are sitting by me with the light of a pair of candles which are old or make me so . . ." He had been pondering the war and joked "my evil genius rises in calamity – the piping times of peace are too insipid for my disordered imagination." Reporting an interruption by Caroline, he confided, "Is your letter almost done asks Mrs. E – 'I interrupted you to hear the sound of your voice – Tell him [North] I wish I could hear the sound of his voice' – I have." Eustis signed off with "Amen."[13]

Eustis still received petitions from people pleading for his help for a variety of reasons. A letter arrived from John Greaton, a young officer aboard the *Guerrière*, the former British frigate captured by the *Constitution*. "My aunt Lucretia Greaton had waited on you at my request," he wrote. Greaton could not rise above his rank as chief mate without a warrant, a coveted appointment by the secretary of the navy. Warrant officers, as opposed to commissioned officers, held specialized positions. After serving with Commodore John Rodgers on the *Guerrière,* Greaton wanted to move with him to his next ship, the *President*, hoping to be master's mate.

Aware of how the patronage system worked, Greaton reminded Eustis that his uncle was Sylvanus Bourne, the American consul in Amsterdam. (Neither knew at the time that Bourne and Eustis would later work together in the Netherlands.) He complained: "<u>Merit</u> without powerful friends cannot procure what inexperience can get with <u>powerful friends</u>."[14.] Fortunately for young Greaton, Eustis still had his connections and obtained the warrant for him in December.

Petitions asking for an end to the war arrived from Massachusetts towns at the state legislature in Boston. When 1815 dawned, and the legislature convened, Governor Strong attributed all of the state's economic suffering to the unreasonable conflict with England. Despite the mounting risks, the commonwealth held firm to its antiwar position. New England banks refused to lend money to the war effort. And Governor Strong mulled over the idea of following Nantucket's example—seeking a separate peace with England. In the end, Nantucket declared itself neutral.

35

O Say Can You See ...

Americans thought differently about themselves following the fiery destruction of their capital. They had been more concerned with personal advancement than national pride and unity during the previous decades, and few had believed in the war. Now they were offended. Eustis reflected that personal sense of insult. "To destroy our navy – the bee which has stung their pride must be their object – the capital taken!!!!!!!"[1] It was a question of honor. By targeting Washington City, the British unwittingly gave Americans a single focus verging on a noble quest.[2] Americans responded as if challenged to a duel.

In Massachusetts, antiwar sentiment persisted despite British occupation of the upper third of Maine, a district in the commonwealth. The concept of states' rights began to appeal to New England Federalists in direct contradiction to their long-held belief in the strong central government of early Federalists including Washington, Adams, and Hamilton. Lengthy peace negotiations, and fear of the onerous terms England might impose, inspired thoughts about leaving the Union. Governor Strong called a special session of the legislature to consider what to do and made a secret overture to the British in Halifax to see what kind of separate peace might be arranged.

Eustis had a growing leadership role in the local Democratic-Republican Party. That October 1814, he presided over its monthly meeting in Boston and voiced his alarm that the legislature would consider establishing a sovereign New England or rejoining Great Britain. "Look around you, and see what your fathers have acquired for you, what you now enjoy, and what you are to expect by submitting to your former masters! Your civil and religious rights are enjoyed by no other people on earth, and will you yield them? Will you give up the ship?"[3] Clearly, any attempt at secession by New England would lead to civil war. Readers of newspaper reports about his speech responded with approval for what he had said.[4]

A legislative committee called together by Harrison Gray Otis pondered the situation for three days, then, echoing Samuel Adams and Joseph Warren in 1775, issued a call for a regional conference to weigh New England's options.[5] Connecticut offered to host the gathering and invited delegates to convene in Hartford in December.

Massachusetts' Federalist base sent a twelve-member delegation led by Otis and George Cabot. Repelled by the prospect of secession, New Hampshire and Vermont refused to attend. Angry local Democratic-Republicans tolled church bells and flew flags at half-staff. In Hartford, the solemn delegation marched into the Connecticut state house to a funeral dirge. Secrecy surrounded the proceedings, creating widespread belief that the delegates were talking treason and rebellion. Otis presided but delayed the final vote on secession until the conference reconvened in June 1815.

Just as the Hartford convention was called to order, a letter from Dolley Madison's brother-in-law, Richard Cutts, alerted Eustis that the peace commissioners in Ghent expected to conclude a treaty. If everything worked out, he wrote, Madison intended to nominate William Eustis as minister to the Netherlands and John Adams would be brought home. Cutts asked mischievously: "How will these appointments suit the Federal Gentlemen of Boston?"[6]

After defeating Napoleon, representatives of the four allied powers—Russia, Prussia, Britain, and Austria—had gathered in Vienna to redraw boundaries and establish a new balance of power in Europe. They rearranged most of Europe's geography.[7] By grouping Holland, Belgium, and the Duchy of Luxembourg together, the Congress of Vienna created the United Kingdom of the Netherlands. During the fifteen years the countries remained united, Brussels, as the financial center of the kingdom, and The Hague, the largest city on the North Sea, would share capital status, and the royal court moved between the two. It was this newly-created country that had asked for an ambassador from the United States.

A ministerial position was one of the few important appointments Madison could make. He knew Eustis followed the international news, was adept at managing a variety of living and social conditions, and could gracefully handle the political and court duties. He may also have wanted to compensate Eustis for taking the hit for administrative mishandling of the war. The president offered him the post with the breathtaking title of Envoy Extraordinary and Minister Plenipotentiary of the United States to the Court of His Royal Highness, Prince William II, Sovereign Prince of the United Provinces of the Netherlands.[8]

Eustis sent a modest reply. "Without having contemplated such an appointment I should not decline attempting to execute the duties required by it in case it should be confirmed."[9] Congress approved his nomination within days, and official confirmation followed.[10] Eustis accepted a week later. He seemed more confident, offering his appreciation and the assurance that he could leave for Europe in four to five weeks if necessary.[11]

This new presidential appointment presented a fascinating opportunity, and it paid $12,000 a year. For Eustis, it was a longtime dream come true. He had written to Bill North in 1799 that he wanted to go abroad. "If I had two thousand dollars in my pocket I would spend this winter in Europe – my curiosity – my heart's desire is there, and I never shall die content without a peep at the old world."[12]

The war between Great Britain and the United States, however, was not over. Neither Congress nor the president had seen the treaty. And before any notification arrived, General Andrew Jackson defeated invading British troops in New Orleans on February 4, 1815. In celebration, residents marched through the streets carrying candles and torches. Ten days later, Henry Carroll, the secretary to the Ghent peace delegation, arrived in Washington with a draft of the treaty signed in Ghent six weeks earlier on Christmas Eve.

Unanimously ratified on February 18, 1815, two weeks after the Battle of New Orleans, the Treaty of Ghent did not offer much beyond an end to fighting and the return to the *status quo ante bellum*. There was nothing about the rights of American sailors, but the British would abandon their forts and Native American allies along the Mississippi at Henry Clay's insistence and give up their positions along the coast of Maine. Thanks to John Quincy Adams, New England would keep its fishing rights. Great Britain agreed to return all the slaves it had taken; but later decided to pay reparations instead. Native Americans were the primary losers. The winners were the Canadians, who realized they were a country unto themselves.

President Madison skyrocketed from a popularity rating of zero to a national hero. Before the Senate confirmed the treaty, William Eustis, having avidly followed the news, sent Madison congratulations. His "heart was elated with joy" at "the great, the auspicious event."[13]

The news of peace spread rapidly through the country. America had triumphed; David had defeated Goliath. Cannon fired and bells rang throughout the night when Hartford heard the news. A general holiday was proclaimed in Boston; shops and schools were closed, and citizens paraded through the streets. Everyone in New England celebrated getting back to business, and sailors hauled sails and supplies out to forlorn ships as traders prepared to go back to sea.

The convention in Hartford had adjourned after appointing three delegates to go to Washington with a list of their grievances. Arriving in the midst of the celebrations, they had a brief meeting with President Madison, found that no one was interested in their complaints, and quietly rode home. The Federalist Party never regained its lost prestige. The Hartford Convention became synonymous with treason, and Harrison Gray Otis and the other Federalists would spend the rest of their lives explaining away their actions. Not many years later, the convention played a role in William Eustis's campaign for governor of Massachusetts.

A wave of patriotic fervor combined with national amnesia set in, and the Democratic-Republicans declared this second war of independence an American triumph. True, there had been economic chaos, poor military leadership, inept administration in Washington, and dangerous dissension in New England. But all of that made the country's survival even more spectacular. There was a new freedom in its relationships with Europe. Americans gained respect abroad and began to think of themselves as a country rather than a group of allied states. They had freedom to sail the seas, to trade where they wished, and to develop the western lands. Most importantly, there was a new national pride. The country entered the "Era of Good Feelings."

36

A New Europe

Once appointed, William Eustis began to establish the new American embassy in Holland. He assembled his "family," the entourage associated with an officer or leader, and forwarded to President Madison his recommendation for a possible secretary.[1] In March, the newly-hired Alexander Hill Everett went to Washington City for instructions, special directions, and any documents the mission would need.

It was a strategic posting. Holland, part of the United Netherlands, was a critical trading partner and a source of loans for the United States. Eustis needed to maintain a cordial relationship with the new king and the Dutch people, encourage business and trade relationships between the United States and other European countries, and keep Madison informed about all of that activity.

John Adams had purchased a house in The Hague for the United States in 1782. Eustis heard it was run down and "in a state not respectable to its owner."[2] He wondered if the expense of putting the house in good order could be authorized by the president or Congress. He would use limited personal funds to support his family and the mission until he was reimbursed by overseas banking contracts.

Then Napoleon escaped his exile on Elba.

In Boston, Eustis researched the best arrangements for passage to Europe.[3] By May, news arrived that Napoleon had raised an army in France and begun an offensive to break up the coalition of British and Prussian forces in Belgium. Crossing the Atlantic immediately after enactment of the Treaty of Ghent could be dangerous. British warships still at sea might not know the conflict had ended, Eustis could be traveling into a warzone, and the Congress of Vienna would offer no protection. An American warship would be the safest transport.

Three months after accepting Madison's assignment, Eustis secured passage on the *Congress,* one of the original six frigates commissioned by George Washington. After being repaired and refitted in Boston, the ship was to return to service in the Mediterranean for the Second Barbary War, joining a four-ship squadron commanded by Admiral William Bainbridge, famous for captaining the *Constitution* during the significant defeat of the British warship *Java.*

Eustis discussed the Algerian pirate situation with Madison while waiting to sail. Knowing that four ships would sail to the Mediterranean, and indoctrinated in government frugality, he suggested that only two were really needed. After a year, the blockading squadron could be relieved by the other two ships. Thus a "succession of ships and officers could be trained with half the expense of the present squadron." The public and Congress might more readily support the growth of the navy if it were less expensive, and they could save "a million or two."[4] He passed on Admiral Bainbridge's recommendation to capture the Dey of Algiers and throw him in jail for eighteen months. When crew members arrived, he wrote, the *Congress* would sail, and the Eustis party would be ready to embark unless "the late change," the return of Napoleon, in France called for modifications to the mission. "Bonaparte," Eustis predicted, [will] "be ultimately felt in every quarter of the globe."[5]

251

Issues of social propriety arose when Madame Elizabeth Bonaparte wrote to Caroline Eustis asking to join them for the voyage. She wanted respectable traveling companions, a necessity for a woman traveling alone. She also wrote to Dolley Madison, hoping Dolley would convince the Eustis party to let her accompany them. A Baltimore girl, Elizabeth Patterson Bonaparte was considered a bit scandalous. She married Jerome Bonaparte, the emperor's youngest brother, in 1803 and visited Washington City. Dressed in the French style, Mme. Bonaparte's revealing, nearly transparent outfits created a stir among the ladies at Jefferson's dinner parties.

Infuriated by his brother's unapproved marriage, Napoleon had demanded that Jerome renounce his by-then pregnant American wife and return to great reward. The couple sailed to France to talk with the emperor. Jerome accepted his brother's bribe to become the King of Westphalia. By Napoleon's order, Elizabeth was not allowed to enter France. She fled to England, gave birth to a son, and returned to her parents in Baltimore. Napoleon annulled his brother's marriage himself because the Pope would not support that effort. Years later, officially divorced by a special decree of the Maryland Assembly, Elizabeth decided to go to France and sought the company of the Eustis party.

Caroline sent Dolley Madison an update "as respects our poor little friend, Madame Bonaparte (for we find she has not yet relinquished the name so unfortunate when in disgrace)."[6] Mme. Bonaparte hoped to join the Eustis party in Boston, but Caroline suggested she stay in New York, citing the uncertain state of politics in France. William Eustis also asked Madison to help discourage Mme. Bonaparte from traveling with them. Eustis feared that her appearance "as one of my family under the circumstances" might prove embarrassing.[7] Consequently, the determined Mme. Bonaparte did not travel with the Eustis party on the *Congress* but still managed to get to France.

When the ship's departure was delayed for another six to seven weeks, Caroline forwarded local gossip to Dolley regarding their difficulties in leaving Boston. Rumors had it that Captain Charles Morris had recently married the beautiful Harriet Bowen and did not want to leave. The true reason, Caroline believed, was the inability to get sufficient crew members.[8] There were two ships, the *Congress* and Bainbridge's own new command, the *Independence.* They were being refitted at the same time at the Boston shipyard, and both were vying for crewmembers.

While the Eustis party waited, the latest news, already several weeks old, revealed that Napoleon had been declared an outlaw by the Congress of Vienna and, after retaking Paris, intended to reclaim his former lands beginning with Belgium.

A cloud of uncertainty hovered over the Eustis party, including Caroline, Alexander H. Everett as legation secretary, and William's nephew and private secretary George Eustis, when it departed for Europe eight days *before* the Battle of Waterloo. Sailing into an unknown situation, Eustis sent a final farewell note to Bill North. "We embarked this day on board the frigate *Congress* about one mile from Fort Independence in Boston Road, June 10, 1815 at 2 o'clock. Wind is in the south and expect to go out this evening. High-ho!"[9]

Not knowing what the political situation would be when they arrived must have been exciting, worrisome, and frightening. Surely there was a mixture of emotions for the passengers as the ship rose to meet those first swells of the gray-green expanse of the North Atlantic. Eustis and Caroline would gradually adjust to the ship's constant movement for the three thousand miles across the ocean. The frigate's passenger quarters, tiny cramped cabins in the officers' area below decks, offered only basic essentials. Walking on deck would be possible, although reaching it by the steep stairway could be daunting for a proper woman in bonnet and long skirts.

Eustis occupied some of his time noting daily happenings in his diary including the wind direction and position of longitude based on the navigator's noon reckonings. Taking advantage of currents on the northern route across the Atlantic, the ship passed porpoises one day and an "island of ice" on another. Most disturbing, they sighted a dismasted American brig floundering toward home under jury-rigged sails.[10] Captain Morris thought the voyage was pleasant thanks to good weather and interactions with his passengers.[11]

Eustis had hours to ponder his assignment. This voyage of a month or more, sailing toward an unknown horizon, was not unlike the time in 1776 when, as a young man, he had joined other boys marching toward New York after the British had evacuated Boston. Eustis and his brother Benjamin, both with Knox's artillery regiment, had hiked along with the fledgling Continental Army. Nearly all of the soldiers had never been farther than twenty miles from their homes.

But now it was 1815, and Eustis was at sea. He had to establish an embassy rather than a hospital. He was an ambassador from the New World sailing toward the Old World where he would present his credentials to the new king in The Hague, presumably where Napoleon was headed.

On June 15, while the Eustis party and the *Congress* were still on the high seas, the commander of the Anglo-Allied forces, Arthur Wellesley, Duke of Wellington and his staff attended a ball given by Charlotte, Duchess of Richmond, in Brussels. Shortly after midnight, a message was brought to the "Iron Duke" that Napoleon's army was approaching. The Battle of Quatre Bras, a strategic crossroads, began early the next afternoon, and the decisive battle at Waterloo, a village twenty-five miles south of Brussels, soon followed.

The huge allied armies, about one hundred fifty thousand men in all, continued marching south to retake Paris. A week later, the winning forces led by Tsar Alexander marched down the Champs Élysées. But squabbling among the allies delayed any treaty until the end of November. It seemed more important to sort out the spoils of war and how France was to be ruled.

Shortly after that triumphant march into Paris, the *Congress* approached the English Channel and briefly stopped for news. The ship most likely sent a boat ashore at Le Havre, the port of Paris at the mouth of the Seine River. Eustis had sufficient time to go ashore where, as he reported to Madison, he discovered that the world had changed, that Napoleon, having lost at Waterloo, had surrendered July 15.

The *Congress* put the Eustis party ashore in the Netherlands at Flushing a few days later. Escorted by Captain Charles Morris, the Eustis party sailed on a small vessel provided by the Netherlands government up the coast to Rotterdam, then to The Hague, disembarking in late July 1815.[13] Ambassador Eustis had to make sense of it all: the international moves and countermoves among London, St. Petersburg, Vienna, and Berlin.

37

Life on the Edge of Royalty

Other than accounts of Parisienne fashions and European politics they had read, neither Eustis nor Caroline knew what to expect. Eustis had hoped he might see Albert Gallatin who was expected in Paris as the new ambassador to France. Bravely stepping forward, they undertook their new posting amid the international turmoil following the allied victory at Waterloo. The Hague was not a typical Dutch city hemmed in by canals and walls. This seaport had wide, tree-lined cobblestone streets and stately homes built for diplomats and affluent Dutch families. Prosperous and immaculate, it fairly hummed with its worldwide trade economy.

Reporting about their situation to Madison in mid-August, Eustis gave Caroline credit: "on account of Mrs. E my opportunities of forming an opinion of the state of affairs was somewhat enlarged." John Adams had described their home when hc purchased it in 1782 as a house "fit for the Hotel des Etats Unis"—the first American-owned legation building in Europe. Forty years later, Eustis confirmed reports of its sorry condition. "The American house at The Hague should be repaired or sold. The old arms of the United States put up by Mr. Adams will tumble in the street in another year." The house needed fixing, and so did Europe.

As far as the Congress of Vienna was concerned, France was without any head of state—emperor, king, or president. After the upheavals created by the French Revolution and Napoleon's collapsed empire, the Congress of Vienna had to sort out rulers and boundaries of most European countries and was considering many possibilities for France before the likely reestablishment of the Bourbon monarchy. Louis XVIII was waiting in the wings after returning to Paris.

The potential for instability and chaos during this fluid interval with no French government concerned Eustis. "It is a common sentiment agreed on all sides that the present state of things in France cannot be of long duration," he wrote. The French were considering all options; talking about the Dutch Prince William of Orange, or the King of Rome, or Prince Bernadotte of Sweden. "They appeared willing to take any king from a reputable stock."[2] Europe remained in this state of flux well into the fall of 1815 when many of the exiled kings, including Louis XVIII of France, were given back their thrones with the understanding that they agree to constitutions.

News arriving from America was constantly out of date. Although it was generally a quicker passage west to east, the winds were not always favorable. In August, Eustis responded to a letter from Madison sent in mid-May. It somehow had traveled to The Hague via London. Eustis sent Madison any European news that might interest him. "Lafayette retired on his farm waits patiently for a better state of things. The best informed will have it that France is arming . . . For the first time in my life I accord to the sentiment of Mr. Jefferson that ours is in all essentials, the strongest government on earth." Madison would remain president until March 1817, and Eustis was not sure he would see his old comrade again. He wanted Madison to know of his affection and good wishes. "The best account we receive in Mrs. M's letters to Mrs. E is of your confirmed health of more value to its proprietor than The Floridas, Louisiana or all the honors the earth will yield."[3]

This was William Eustis's first and last journey to Europe, and he approached the opportunity with considerable diligence, writing family members of his excitement to see the elegance of the court and his desire to travel to France. After a few weeks of residency, however, he grew tired of merely being a presence at court activities. Serving as a diplomat did not feel very effective or efficient to the former secretary of war. Most of the day-to-day business involved merchant affairs, all ably handled by the two consuls general: Sylvanus Bourne in Amsterdam, whose nephew Eustis had helped become a warrant officer, and Samuel Hazard in Antwerp. Eustis attended to the social scene as a liaison between Washington City and the Dutch court, the consuls, and the other ministers in Europe. Eustis complained to his brother Jacob just a few months after his arrival that an ambassador's primary duty was to master the art of sitting in a chamber biding one's time and trying not to look impatient while awaiting his turn to see some royal personage.[4]

The establishment of a newly combined Netherlands meant that the Dutch royal court moved from The Hague to Brussels for half of every year, and each ambassador needed to move as well and arrange his own lodging. Eustis found it remarkably costly and logged every expense in his diary. Within two months, Eustis and Caroline were in the midst of court society and the anticipated coronation of William I as the first king of the United Netherlands. Thrilled to have a relative mixing with royalty, Jacob urged them to write regularly to the American newspapers about their reception at court and all of the glamorous European personalities.

Caroline supervised their permanent residence in The Hague as well as a rented house in Brussels. Their nine-room home required an appropriate staff of cook, housemaid, coachman, and a jack-of-all-trades servant listed as "boy." They also kept carriage horses and a cow for milk and cream.[5] When the court moved, the Eustis household dutifully followed. Staff and clothing had to be transported from The Hague to a rented establishment, not always the same one, in Brussels, and vice versa. Travel each way required about six hours. Living in two households was not particularly to Eustis's liking.

He wrote to Madison offering to return to the United States "if [his return] could be accompanied by some appointment at home which added to my humble means [so he could] go on with comfort for a few years." He hoped the suggestion was "not indelicate but it arises out of my actual circumstances."[6] Other men in the service of their country had run through their limited savings as well, but there was another problem. Eustis could not express himself well in French, the language of diplomacy, and it caused him to speak cautiously, and often not at all. His studies of Latin and Greek at Harvard did not help very much.

Caroline sent news of their royal activities to Dolley Madison. We "received an invitation from his majesty to attend the coronation at Bruxelles which will take place on the 18 [of September 1815]. The invitation is considered an order for the foreigners, many of whom are already on the road."[7] William, King of Holland, would be crowned William I, king of the United Netherlands. Only three months before, his son, Prince William II, had fought with the allied forces under the Duke of Wellington at Waterloo. After the coronation, the prince would go to Russia to marry the Grand Duchess Anna Pavlovna in St. Petersburg. The Eustises arrived in Brussels in time for the coronation.

Eustis sent his impressions: "The inauguration of the king in Brussels was marked with splendor but appeared to want the cordiality which a welcome chief might expect to receive. The Belgians, who appear to have no national character complain 1st that with a superior population they have only an equal role with the Hollanders and 2nd that they are married to the Dutch debt." Eustis was uneasy about how long the king would remain in power because the unsettled situation in France threatened the Netherlands' stability. "How long this will last God only knows."[8]

Eustis and Caroline, thrilled with her new title as Madame Eustis, found friends primarily among English-speaking aristocrats. They rubbed shoulders with the Duke of Wellington, the future Czar Nicholas I of Russia, and Edward, Duke of Kent, son of King George III. As an old lady, Madame Eustis would reminisce about dancing with King William I of the United Netherlands. They sent back the latest European gossip regarding various neighboring rulers, among them Russian Emperor Alexander I and King Frederick William III of Prussia. Both were attempting, wrote Eustis, to recover further parts of their territories previously claimed by Napoleon. "The astonishing events which have taken place in [France] during the past year teach us to be astonished at nothing in the future and I am prepared accordingly."[9]

As the couple settled in for their first winter, Eustis continued working on trade agreements for the United States. These negotiations and securing commercial treaties had to be carefully arranged so as not to show any overt favoritism to France. America's highest priority was to secure favorable arrangements with the Dutch that would remove the tariffs and taxes imposed on trade shipments from the United States. Making the best of his situation, Eustis wrote to his friend, Bill North: "We are here in the dull weather of a Dutch winter – I have time to read, to reflect, to write."[10]

There had been other difficult winters, some a great deal colder than the dismal damp of the Netherlands, particularly during the early Revolutionary War years. The winter of 1779-80, known as the "Hard Winter," was one of the most severe of the eighteenth century and possibly the coldest on record, even worse in terms of temperature and snowfall than the Valley Forge winter of 1777-78. Now some forty years later, William Eustis found the dampness and constant winter grayness of the Netherlands equally daunting. Sickness seemed to be everywhere. His consul, Sylvanus Bourne, wrote from Amsterdam asking for time to get away in the spring, complaining of constant coughing. He hoped for a cure in Aix la Chappelle, where he intended to partake of sulphur waters, cold baths, and different air to help him get rid of phlegm.[11]

Personally paying for the delegation's voyage across the Atlantic had diminished Eustis' available funds. In January, for the third time, he wrote to Secretary of State James Monroe requesting reimbursement of expenses and authorization to draw on the United States Bankers at Amsterdam.[12] He reminded Monroe of his earlier requests in August and September. It took until April, nearly ten months after they left the United States, before he could withdraw 4,380 florins (about $60,000 today) from the Amsterdam bankers, cover his debts, and pay his staff.[13]

Eustis and Caroline anticipated the possibility of seeing Paris. They would go "if our finances & other circumstances permit it – there is no certainty in this life."[14] In May, Madison cheered Eustis with news of congressional improvements at home: a national bank had been reestablished, there was a "gradual augmentation" of the navy, and Eustis's friend Albert Gallatin would soon be leaving for Paris to serve as ambassador.[15]

Dolley Madison wrote to Caroline in her typical breathy way, with a considerable number of dashes, noting it was only the second time she had written since the Eustis "debarkion." The gift of portrait engravings of Caroline and William, sent by Jacob Eustis, had arrived and "are of high value coming from you and bring fine likenesses . . . I may say in truth all here – who knew you, love you – Mrs. Gallatin sails in a few days for France – perhaps you will meet in that country, for surely your dear & amiable husband will see Paris before he returns to America . . . My dearest hope is that Mr. Eustis and you will visit us [at Montpelier] whenever you return."[16]

The prospect of visiting Paris kept them going.

38

A Pilgrimage to Paris

A passport arrived in Brussels for Eustis, likely including Caroline, in May 1816.[1] They began their monthlong adventure to fabled and resplendent Paris by traveling in their own coach, changing horses at roadside stops. After passing through areas damaged by war and neglect, they finally reached the outskirts of Paris, joining a line of assorted haycarts, carriages, and wine wagons waiting to pass through the *barriére*, one of sixty gates in the city walls. Vibrant and filthy, Paris, the second-largest city in the known world with seven hundred thousand inhabitants, sprawled in stark contrast to the compact Dutch cities.

Paris contained a jumble of neighborhoods jammed with crooked gabled houses standing shoulder-to-shoulder with elegant, eighteenth-century townhouses built of beige sandstone that was darkened with grime. Wrought-iron balconies ornamented buildings, and shuttered windows overlooked the daily street theater of barrowmen wheeling their wares, carts, carriages, and every type of person imaginable: fashionable ladies and war-weary or crippled veterans, beggars, prostitutes, dandies, students, musicians, and some with dancing dogs. Abigail Adams had thought the city's sanitation and soot-covered buildings left much to be desired and much to be scrubbed.[2] Despite its disheveled appearance, Paris seemed the most fascinating place on earth.

Arriving at the Hôtel de la Paix, Eustis and Caroline disliked the third-floor location of their rooms accessed by a steep, dirty stairway, so they moved to a "superb" location and quarters in the Hôtel Dator on the rue Bonaparte for £10 per week.[3] Rue Bonaparte, in the St. Germaine des Prés district, the sixth arrondissement, ran south through the heart of the Left Bank.

Paris was a medical Mecca in the early nineteenth century with enviable hospitals and celebrated schools. Of its twelve hospitals, the largest and oldest was the Hôtel Dieu, an immense, five-story complex near Notre Dame Cathedral on Île de la Cité. It held fourteen hundred beds and served more than fifteen thousand patients each year. It was overwhelming to this visiting Bostonian whose two hometown hospitals cared for fewer than eight hundred patients in a year. Nothing could compare to the École de Médecine with twenty-six faculty members. Its impressive library had thirty thousand books compared to Harvard Medical School's one thousand volumes. Guidebooks listed lectures and hospitals for visiting doctors to attend.[4] Hospitals specialized in different medical practices and procedure. One featured a school for anatomy and dissection. Another offered *les operations plastique* as corrective surgery. As a practical matter, cadavers were supplied for students to dissect. Shockingly, male students could examine female patients. In America, most women would rather die before she let a man examine her—and they often did. There were even a few female medical students.

William and Caroline were inexhaustible tourists. He enthused about their adventure to Bill North: "We have spent a month in Paris – have seen from the King down to the animals – the creeping things & flying fowl – the works of art – paintings, canals, [and] museums, libraries, the catacombs said to be eight centuries [old with the] appearance of the bones arranged in perfect order as is said of two million skeletons . . . but the Abbé Sicard's institution [for mental patients] transcends description – interests and astonishes."[5]

Caroline kept a list of their daily sightseeing ventures, noting that construction continued on Napoleon's Arc de Triomphe.[6] She wrote to Dolley: "We have seen everything in this wonderful City and environs but we do not see our friends, [the Gallatins] and we depart half satisfied."[7] Eustis wrote affectionately about his indefatigable wife: "Mrs. E is more ardent of course [than he] and when we arrived at the wood & castle of Vincennes her disappointment was extreme – not having taken the precaution to get tickets of admission we could not see the apartment of the Iron Mask . . . The fortress is still the prison for state offenders & is said to contain hundreds."[8] French fashions appealed to Caroline and they bought her a stylish hat. "Finally," both saw the not-yet-official King Louis XVIII and his family. The gouty, corpulent king was barely able to walk, they reported, but displayed nobility and dignity.[9]

Sir Thomas Charles Morgan, an English physician, and his second wife, Lady Sydney Morgan, an Irish novelist and travel writer, became new friends. Eustis likely talked with Dr. Morgan about his studies on smallpox and his connection with Dr. Edward Jenner who developed the cowpox vaccination. Eustis had been involved with the introduction of that vaccine to Boston.[10]

The expatriate community welcomed them into the fashionable Parisian salon society with its dinners and soirees. Within this social milieu, the Eustises encountered Elizabeth Bonaparte, who had wished to sail with them. She had arrived in Paris and quickly became Lady Sydney's special friend.

When Eustis left "to visit the Marquis de Lafayette in Brie," Caroline stayed behind to go to the flower market.[11] There is no explanation why Eustis, who had maintained contact with Lafayette for years, did not take Caroline on his overnight visit. Perhaps he thought it a question of propriety, or that Caroline was indifferent to reminiscing about the war or might be happier shopping in Paris. For Eustis, dinner and an overnight stay at La Grange with

Lafayette, idolized by most Americans, seemed well worth the grueling, six-hour ride. Lafayette lived in the Brie region, east of Paris, in a walled estate, Château de La Grange-Bléneau, surrounded by his children, grandchildren, relatives, and in-laws. The château, a rather romantic-looking, Romanesque structure, featured five fifteenth-century round stone towers with conical roofs.

Eustis reported to Bill North that he "spent a night with the Marquis Lafayette. It was an interesting interview. He is plump, healthy & younger both in appearance and reality more than you or I. He cultivates 500 acres much in our style – has five flocks of sheep & cows – lives in a castle of ancient date formed into a commodious dwelling house with courtyard . . . loves America – speaks of the country & his old comrades with great affection."[12]

It was the custom at the château for about thirty people to dine each evening at six o'clock in its huge dining room. Lafayette hosted such events by himself; his wife Adrienne having died. At the table with him would be about twelve children and grandchildren and however many guests had arrived, including Americans for whom a visit to La Grange was a patriotic pilgrimage.[13]

Eustis made the long ride back to Paris the next morning and with Caroline began preparations to leave for Brussels; repaying visits to friends and repairing their carriage, at a cost of £12, for their journey.[14] Shortly after their coach rattled out of Paris for the one hundred sixty-two-mile journey back to Brussels, the French cheered the return of King Louis XVIII, finally sanctioned by the Congress of Vienna.

In September 1816, Secretary of State James Monroe, destined to become president in March 1817, sent unwelcome tidings. Although he expressed concern for Eustis's health, and recommended a visit to Ballston Springs in New York after he returned, Eustis must remain in Europe. Congress had ended the ineffective trade negotiations with the Netherlands, and the ambassador now needed to renegotiate a most-favored nation treaty.

As a former ambassador to France, Monroe speculated about how much Paris had changed since the French Revolution. When in Paris, his wife Elizabeth had gone to the Bastille and rescued Lafayette's wife Adrienne from imprisonment and impending execution in 1795. Considering his long connection with Lafayette, Monroe wanted a full report.[15]

Caroline and Eustis made a quick trip to The Hague from Brussels in October to check on their house before renting it out by November 1, 1816. They returned to Brussels to a different leased residence. A Mrs. Palmer of the diplomatic community wrote to Caroline about staffing this new household. Mrs. Palmer was preparing to leave Brussels for Paris and recommended her own housemaid. She also reported that the proprietor of the Eustises' "new" house had found a good male cook for them. Mrs. Palmer thought it was most prudent to board men cooks, probably to supervise their dependability, but negotiations for wages would be left to the Eustises.[16]

Taking up her pen, Caroline confided to Dolley Madison: "We have received the formal communication that the King and Queen depart for Bruxelles the present week. It is left to the convenience of the corps diplomatique when to follow – they generally depart the next week."[17] Once there, Eustis wrote to Secretary of State Monroe about his late arrival. "The house prepared for me at Brussels could not be made ready until the first of November which occasions my delay."[18]

Eustis attended the celebration of Prince William's return with his Russian bride, Princess Pavlovna. The royal couple would live in Brussels so that the new prince or princess would be born in its father's country. While the mother-to-be was in "confinement" in Brussels, the diplomatic corps had to be in attendance. Caroline wrote to Dolley: "The new princess, her imperial highness, is not handsome, but very much admired, resembling her mother, the Queen of Holland, in her amiable affability which never fails to charme everyone who is presented . . .. Her Brother the emperor of Russia has presented a rich marriage present ... the most costly jewels & plate and the most splendid furniture which could be found in India, France and England for <u>40 rooms</u>."[19] The prince and princess would have at least three residences: a palace in The Hague, a country palace in Guilderland, and another in Brussels to be built to the left of the royal palace.

For the six months through April 1817, Eustis and Caroline would await the birth of the royal baby with the rest of the diplomatic community. Caroline had not been well when they arrived and missed the royal couple's wedding reception. That worried Eustis's sister, Anne Eustis Langdon, who believed the Dutch climate was adversely affecting Caroline.[20] All of their relatives knew that both wanted to return to the United States and hoped they could be back by the following spring.

Suspicious about hazardous health for those living in the Netherlands' damp climate, Eustis recollected General Wilkinson's army dying in the swamps of Louisiana and the resulting embarrassment. John Adams had become seriously ill while in Holland, and now others of Eustis's acquaintance were not faring well. Eustis wrote to the perpetually sick Sylvanus Bourne, concerned that his own secretary, Alexander Everett, should be under a physician's care, "bled & blistered for a complaint in his breast which he says (and I think probable) he received in this country – with fever, etc. he talks of resigning – in the meantime I am without a secretary."[21] Everett soon left for Boston.

In December 1816, Lafayette expressed his appreciation in writing for Eustis's gifts of military memorabilia—an engraving of a naval battle and several newspaper accounts. He was disturbed by the political parties in the United States and the vitriolic rhetoric leading up to the presidential elections. He believed each party had abandoned the original principles fought for in the Revolution. Despite his concern, he assured Eustis of their personal friendship and that he was "forever your constant old friend."[22]

Cold weather came on, and the Eustises settled into their Brussels home for their second winter. As Eustis wrote to North, "Holland is a good country to travel through but not to live in . . . we knew it all before we came."[23]

39

Frustrations, Furniture, and France

Expatriates and others eddied around both capitals of the United Netherlands while waiting for news about the royal birth from Brussels. Gossip and card games helped pass the time. Talk included the activities of royalty in Europe as well as across the English Channel, with scandalous tales about the British royal family. The "old" King George III was now considered hopelessly mad, and, until his death, his son George, a shrewd but lazy playboy, served as prince regent. George's brother, Frederick, Duke of York, was the nominal military commander-in-chief whose mistress peddled army commissions. Taken together, the seven royal sons were described by the Duke of Wellington as "the damndest millstones about the neck of any government that can be imagined."[1] And one of them came to live in Brussels.

Caroline and Eustis became acquainted with Edward Augustus, the Duke of Kent, fourth son of George III, and future father of Queen Victoria.[2] The duke had arranged in 1816 for part of his royal salary to go toward paying off his debts, and he moved to more affordable Brussels and into one of the city's most exclusive neighborhoods. He lived in a morganatic marriage, not recognized by the king for royal succession, with his mistress of twenty-seven years, Mme. Julie de St. Laurent.

Eustis dealt with a variety of frustrating situations while waiting for news from the palace. He worked on trade negotiations between the United States and the United Netherlands, including questions about how much armament was legally allowed on each country's trading ships. An American ship captain wanted permission to carry two cannon because his vessel was bound for the volatile Dutch East Indies.[3] Then there was a missing shipment of sugar maples imported at the request of Comte de Thiennes de Lombise and destined for gardens in Mons, Belgium.[3] Finally, the Netherlands' long-awaited baby, Willem Alexander, the future King William III, arrived on February 17, 1817. Sending the news to the United States, Eustis wrote of his great pleasure that the Princess of Orange was "happily and safely in bed with a prince."[4]

Knowing of Eustis's eagerness to return, Madison had checked with Monroe and wrote that "it was understood that your stay in Holland would prolong until next fall if not next spring." Trying to be encouraging, Madison wrote that once the trade treaty was secure, Eustis and Caroline could come home and, referencing his own approaching departure for Montpelier, "Mrs. M will write to Mrs. E but she is intensely occupied with packing."[5] There would be no Washington farewells for the Eustises. Experiencing American events vicariously through long-delayed letters, they followed reports of the presidential inauguration of James Monroe.

Sworn in on March 4, 1817, Monroe continued Madison's "Era of Good Feelings." A few months later, wearing the classic Continental Army uniform, he made a national tour, much as President Washington had done, that raised his reputation as an appealing leader. Monroe toured through New England despite his intense disgust with its Federalists for trying to secede from the Union in 1815. However, he was unexpectedly welcomed as a conquering hero in Boston on July 3-7, possibly because he was not Madison. A friend reported to Eustis: "You have no doubt seen in the newspapers the manner in which the president was welcomed in

Boston. The only conflict was between the political parties on who offered the most respect."[6]

Eustis also dealt with the irritating lack of mail security. In one instance, a man entrusted to carry the diplomatic mail had been pickpocketed in London and lost a "considerable" sum of money as well as the packet containing Eustis's letters.[7] He wrote to Colonel Thomas Aspinwall, the American consul in London, asking if the best way to send dispatches was through Liverpool. Not recommended, answered Aspinwall. The weather was a problem; only one vessel had sailed from Liverpool in seven weeks that past winter because the winds had been so bad. An American vessel loaded with a cargo of flour had recently wrecked.[8] There seemed to be no good solution.

Then, Sylvanus Bourne, Eustis's righthand man in Amsterdam, died suddenly in April of an "apoplectick fit."[9] Bourne had handled much of the work for the trade negotiations. It would be three months before Joshua Clebborn arrived in Antwerp to succeed Bourne and manage America's trade affairs.[10]

Albert Gallatin and his family finally arrived in France in July 1817. Hearing that Gallatin would be traveling in their direction, Eustis had invited them to stay in Brussels. Gallatin declined, explaining he was traveling with his wife and three children as well as his servants. They would first visit Ghent where he had served as a peace commissioner in 1814 and stay at a hotel.[11] Later they would come to Brussels to see their friends. He asked if Eustis could locate an apartment for them there.

The Eustises and the Gallatin family enjoyed their visit which provided plenty of time to talk. After he returned to Paris, Gallatin wrote to Eustis about a conference he had attended with the Dutch. Knowing of Eustis's frustrations with the ongoing trade negotiations, he passed on Dutch complaints about receiving less favorable treatment than the British in American ports. Gallatin suggested a compromise could be achieved if the Netherlands offered some benefit or advantage to the United States and a repeal of their own discriminating duties. Perhaps the tea and products of China transported by the Dutch could be given some favored status by the United States.[12] Despite Gallatin's suggestions, the impasse went on.

Eustis tried devising a personally happy solution, urging that final negotiations be held in Washington City, thus enabling him to return to the States. It did not work. All negotiations remained in the Netherlands. After seven conferences, and despite the mutual goal of promoting commerce, by September 1817 the parties were stalemated, and further discussions seemed fruitless. Eustis believed that extending the earlier treaty of 1782 would be the best they could do, meaning another damp and gloomy winter in the Netherlands.[13] The Eustises would not be able leave until spring.

Instead, they would escape. Eustis was worried about his health, particularly about a pain in his chest, and decided to spend the winter in the warm South of France. Anticipating a springtime departure for home, they packed their belongings, decided what furniture they would sell and what they would keep. Caroline listed all of their belongings and where they would be stored until their later transport to the States. They had clearly been doing a great deal of shopping, especially Caroline.

Her lists of furnishings included boxes and bundles going to Amsterdam for later shipment to Boston.[14] Two carriages—a chariot and a barouche—were being held at a coachmaker. Two baskets of wine were stored in the cellar of Baron Friedrich von Binder with the Austrian legation in the Netherlands, formerly at the Congress of Vienna. Caroline listed all of their silver, including flatware, candlesticks, tea and coffee pots, creamers, and ladles. Another account was the furniture to be sent separately to Boston from Brussels via Antwerp in the care of Mr. Clebborn at the consulate.[15]

Although moving the contents of a household was a complex undertaking, they preferred European décor, and it seemed sensible to ship everything. The mirrors and marble tabletops could not easily be obtained in the United States and, as everyone knew, the finest mirrors came from France. In November, with packing done, the Eustises boarded a coach, left the legation in charge of J.J. Appleton, its new secretary, and hurried south. Their timing was exquisite. The new secretary of state, John Quincy Adams, confirmed their release from duty shortly after their departure. Eustis's former legation secretary, Alexander H. Everett, would return to succeed him. Adams asked Eustis to let him know when they planned to leave. The mail caught up to them in Lyons.[16]

Friends were concerned, and letters followed the traveling couple across France. Appleton, left alone in charge of their personal business as well as the legation, attempted to dispose of their unwanted furniture. "Chevalier Rainer has . . . expressed the desire of having a dozen chairs. Be so good as to let me know the price you ask in case you consent." In a later letter, Appleton reported that he had offered chairs, sideboard, and card tables to the Chevalier but that he declined them because the sofas in the set were not included. Appleton would sell them through an auction.[17] Albert Gallatin kept track of the couple and sent a note to Lyons expressing his hope that their journey to Marseilles would be pleasant.[18]

Eustis and Caroline were settled in Marseilles by mid-December 1817. Feeling somewhat better, Eustis sent a note to Secretary of State Adams observing that "our national character is less generally understood on the continent of Europe than is generally imagined." In a later letter, having fled Holland as if from the plague, Eustis remembered to let Adams know that he had left Appleton in charge for the winter.[19]

Four months later, after stopping at the Hotel D'Angleterre in Bordeaux on the way back, the Eustises arrived in Antwerp ready to leave for the United States. Eustis again asked the advice of Consul Thomas Aspinwall in London about booking passage from Liverpool in early to mid-May.[20] He remained the ambassador to the

Netherlands for another three weeks until May 5, 1818. Farewells included an audience with King William I, whose coronation he had witnessed and to whom he cited his continuing ill health as his reason for departing. He met with Prince Frederic, the king's second son, while Madame Eustis was received by the Dowager Duchess of Orange.[21] It is not clear whether Eustis felt that his time in the Netherlands was a success or a fruitless and uncomfortable three years on his country's behalf. He had developed mild hypochondria and had not achieved the commercial treaties that were his mission's objective.[22.]

Just before their departure, the Eustises received tragic news.[23] William's youngest sister, Nancy "Anne" Eustis Langdon, was dead. Their nephew, William Eustis Langdon, wrote that his mother, forty-seven, had died of childbirth fever on March 23, 1818. She had been married to Henry Sherburne Langdon, Caroline's brother. Their union had initiated the long association between the Eustis and Langdon families. Anne, already the mother of thirteen children, had suffered a bilious colic and delivered her fourteenth child, a girl, prematurely. They thought her difficulties were over, her son wrote, but his mother died three weeks later. Devastated, Eustis would remember how he had gone to his sister Anne for solace after he had been unable to save their younger sister Prudence, who also died in childbirth in 1794.

The saddened couple left Europe, traveling first to London where they stayed for three weeks with Consul Aspinwall while waiting to board the ship that would carry them and all their bundles and boxes back to the United States.[24] Writing to Eustis nearly a year later, Aspinwall relayed that his wife missed "Mrs. E . . . It seems that Mrs. A's regret at losing the society of your lady will never abate." He noted that his wife had been "violently ill during most of the [London] season," but the illness was resolved when "On the evening of the 10th [January] she gave birth to a little boy whose name I am glad to inform you is William."[25]

40

Shirley Place

The Eustises sailed into New York Harbor on the packet ship *Pacific* forty-four days after leaving Liverpool and took the steamboat *Connecticut* up the coast, arriving in Boston on July 25, 1818. Newspapers announced their return from their three-year sojourn in The Hague.[1]

Eustis and Caroline moved into Congress Street's Exchange Coffee House, at seven stories tall the largest building and first proper hotel in Boston. It was huge, combining a hotel, a coffeehouse, a place of business, a reading room, a post office, and a dining salon with green walls and scarlet hangings. The *pièce de résistance* was the ballroom described as having yellow satin curtains, festoons of purple silk, and five crystal chandeliers. It had been President Monroe's choice for lodging during his presidential tour a year earlier.

Pleased to be back, the couple renewed Boston acquaintances. Eustis checked on his wharf tenants[2] and planned to visit with John Adams, but bereaved relatives in Portsmouth, New Hampshire, required their attention. William sent a note of apology to Adams: "Among the first objects of my intention on arrival in this country was that of paying my respects to you. From causes not under my control I have been disappointed, and now I am called to make a melancholy visit to New Hampshire."[3]

A month later, on September 17, 1818, Eustis's widowed and last surviving sister, Catherine Eustis Wells, fifty-seven, died of consumption. Two of the original nine siblings were left—Jacob and William. Catherine, interred in the Granary Burying Ground, had brought eleven children into the world in sixteen years. Several of her daughters would live with Caroline Eustis in her old age. After the round of family visits and Catherine's funeral, the Eustises boarded a coach and headed south. Newspapers noted their arrival in Baltimore during the first week of November.

While in Washington, they stayed at William O'Neal's Franklin House, one of the leading hotels in the city, at the corner of Pennsylvania Avenue and I Street. Looking like a row of tall brick residences with several entrances, the Franklin House had not changed in appearance from its early days as a boardinghouse. On Eustis's request, O'Neal had sent him the hotel rates.[4] After completing their business in the capital, they hurried on to Montpelier and James and Dolley Madison.

Montpelier was a wonderful place to spend time with dear friends. Slaves maintained the large plantation as was the way for any estate or household in the South. Caroline and Eustis had experienced various lifestyles, from the trappings of English estates to southern plantation slavery. Within a short time, Eustis would speak out against the institution during congressional debates about the Territory of Missouri.

Madison and Eustis decided to check on the health of Thomas Jefferson. He was slowly recovering from a staph infection. Their wives "equipped" Madison and Eustis for their December 3 excursion to Monticello.[5] The men were relieved to find Jefferson "restored from his indisposition, with good appetite, and in the daily practice of taking exercise on horseback."[6]

Eustis wrote to Madison several weeks later. "Since leaving your hospitable roof, which was truly a home to us, we have been coursing the roads, country and inns without much comfort. That we are cheating a New England winter of its main force is our consolation." They had left Montpelier to meet "fellow traveler" General William King in Richmond. He was an old friend from the Massachusetts legislature, a War of 1812 veteran, and he had visited Monticello in December. Communications went awry, however, and by the time the Eustises arrived in Richmond, the Kings had left for Norfolk.

Eustis relayed the saga of constantly missing each other to Madison. Ultimately, everyone managed to get together back in Richmond. Two weeks later, Caroline and Eustis returned to Williamsburg for a longer stay. He reported to Madison: "The state of the roads & a winter premature at this season preclude the idea of going further south, at least for the present."[7]

All this moving about did not make sense to Madison. He chastised them for so much traveling, saying that they should have just stayed at Montpelier. "I find by Mrs. E's letter to Mrs. M that you had taken up your winter quarters in Wmsbg. Why did you not take a Western instead of an Eastern direction from Richmond? We should have been truly glad to have had you with us during the sequel of your visit to this Country. It is not too late yet to give us part of that pleasure. After taking a quantum sufficit of the air of Williamsbg come breathe a little more of ours."[8]

Eustis and Caroline left Virginia when the green mist of spring appeared over the trees in late March. They had spent four months pondering what they might do and, once back in Boston, they began hunting for a house that might be similar to the large estates they had visited. Although Eustis owned a house in Cambridge, the two wanted something else, and they scoured the Boston area for their hearts' desire. By June, they were negotiating the purchase of property in nearby Roxbury from Margaret Magee, the wife of Captain James Magee, a merchant captain in the China trade. Eustis offered some cash along with his property in Cambridge. In preparation, he had, with difficulty, gotten his tenant moved out of the house so it was ready to trade or sell.[9] Without waiting for an answer from Magee, and perhaps feeling confident that their proposal would be accepted, the Eustises left for Portsmouth, New Hampshire.[10]

On July 1, 1819, Mrs. Magee wrote to them rejecting their offer. "I have this day advertised the house and 14 acres of land at auction on [July] 14th if not sold before at private sale. I shall not alter from the price named to you . . . that if you are disposed to give $11,000 for the house and 14 acres of land . . . [it] is yours – I am not disposed to [accept] in part payment the estate in Cambridge." She thought that Eustis could sell his Cambridge property separately for more money.[11]

Eustis decided to buy the house. Designed by architect Peter Harrison in 1747 for British Royal Governor William Shirley, the last of the royal governors, and modeled as an English Georgian manor, Shirley Place looked right to them, presiding on a hill overlooking the South Bay side of Boston Harbor.[12]

A carriage could approach Shirley Place up a long, lilac-bordered drive flanked by two stone lions left by the royal governor and stop in a circular driveway in front of the house. The Eustises' yellow coach, used for trips into Boston, would be housed in the stable and coach house to the left of the main house. To the right, or east, stood another outbuilding that may have been used for tenants, servants, or guests. The estate's country setting featured a brook on the east side and a small pond on the west.

Eustis had been a visitor, a lodger, or had lived with his brother for most of his life. Caroline and he had lived in Cambridge for less than two years. The two had constantly moved from one rented place to another during the nine years of their marriage. As a self-made man, Eustis yearned to have the right personal setting because, "It was once objected to me when a candidate that I did not live in a splendid house like the other gentlemen."[13]

In July, Eustis contacted Tristram Barnard, part of a Nantucket trans-Atlantic merchant family, who had transported and stored most of their belongings. "I have committed the last extravagance of my life in purchasing the Magee place, of which we expect to take possession tomorrow week where there will be a bed for you with as much room as you wish and if you could make yourself conversant with the humble or rather the plain style of living which we shall adopt, both Mrs. Eustis and myself shall be gratified by your society."[14]

Barnard wrote informally back to Eustis with the goal of clearing out his warehouse. "Say to Mrs. E if she does not send for the things according to my request I shall not come to see her. God bless her (Mrs. E) she is a good soul – make much of her – you'll never get another such a one –." He also sent his good wishes: "I hope you may continue to grow better and enjoy your new home many years, – adieu – Kiss Mrs. E for me. Am with much good feelings for you both."[15] Barnard yearned to get back to sea, being described as "sighing for the moment when he can inhale ocean breezes."[16]

Eustis and Caroline moved into the Magee property in August 1819. By September, he could report: "We are in our new abode, fixing & furnishing, and planning & arranging for how long a time God only knows. One good at least has been derived whether from the change, the additional exercise or both, my health has improved. Mrs. Eustis continues to enjoy good health and if constant occupation implying great exercise will confirm it, she will not fall off."[17]

The Eustises began planning for the winter—a well-justified concern in New England—as soon as they moved in. With all heat provided by fireplaces or stoves, people consolidated their living space into fewer rooms. Eustis reported at length to Barnard: "We [are] ready to go into the southern and eastern apartments for the winter. These rooms, the largest and best of which we shall sleep in

280

and keep in a great part of the time, mornings at least, are said to be and must from their situation be warm."

Based on his experience, Eustis was nervous about extremes in climate. "My health is so much improved as to determine me to try at least a winter in this climate," he wrote. "Our establishment is very economical, our number, of course, small – we shall make the experiment . . . I have made a bedroom of the best parlor because it is said to be the warmest and if it is the most elegant, we shall not [be disturbed by] its elegance – comfort is the object. William Heath [former General] has been with us for a few days. We missed you [Barnard] and your tool chest – fixing doors & windows and locks and hinges & blinds & carpets."[18]

By December, they were "as comfortable as good fires in large rooms can make us. We consist of Miss Mary Ann L[angdon] sister of Mrs. E, one of the Miss Wells [a niece], one man and one woman servant and no more." As usual, Eustis was monitoring his health, reporting to Barnard that he was feeling restored, breathing well if not better than at Williamsburg. Huddled around their fireplace, they looked forward to spring and planned a garden. "Garden seeds we have in plenty – a box of Cobbetts (seeds from Cobbett's farm in Kensington, outside of London) in addition to those we have gathered and saved on the place."[19]

41

Congressman Redux

Early in 1819, Henry Clay had presented a "memorial" in Congress for admitting the Territory of Missouri into the Union as a slave state. The issue of slavery combined with the admission of new states to the Union dominated debate for the next two years. It was not a simple issue. Two influential writings seemed to support slavery: Leviticus 25:44-46 in the Bible and our own Constitution.

It revolved around the interpretation of the Constitution. The document recognized slaves as "three fifths of all other Persons" to determine congressional representation based on population, as stated in Article I, Section 2). In Article IV, Section 2, dealing with states and citizens, all persons "held to service or labor in one state, under Laws thereof, escaping to another," must be returned to their owners. That seemed to apply to runaway slaves. In order to do anything about slavery, the federal government would have to change this sacred document. It would take forty-five years.

Clay raised no objection when the district of Maine, a part of Massachusetts, requested admission as a separate state. But he planned to use Maine's admission as leverage.[1] He proposed to first admit Missouri as a slave state. Southern senators followed his lead.

The northern states feared that admitting Missouri would alter the slave-to-free representation of the states, eleven to eleven, in the

Senate. With Missouri's admission, the South had a chance to gain a one-state and a two-vote majority to compensate for its minority status in the House of Representatives. In the House, the free states' larger population of one hundred five congressmen dominated the slave states' eighty-one. When Congress adjourned, Massachusetts had not yet worked out the details of Maine's separation, and Missouri's statehood was undecided.

Then, because it could affect the admission of Maine as a separate state, the Massachusetts legislature decided to do its own research on the key question—if the federal government could control the spread of slavery. The legislature invited the prominent Democratic-Republican William Eustis to chair an inquiry into the prohibition of "involuntary servitude" in future states.[2]

Eustis and his committee began deliberating at the end of November 1819 in Boston just as the Sixteenth Congress convened in Washington to discuss, for the second year, what to do about Missouri.[3] Clay, reelected Speaker of the House, insisted that Maine's application should be a *quid pro quo*. Clay would not object to Maine's admission as a free state if Missouri was admitted unconditionally as a slave state.

Eustis found it a simple matter to go from Roxbury into Boston for meetings. By early December, his committee resolved that the United States Congress had the power to make the prohibition of slavery a condition of admission to statehood and sent their report to Washington. But as the year ended, nothing had changed in Congress, and Missouri continued to insist that it be admitted to the union as a slave state.

That winter after congressional speeches and politicking, Illinois Senator Jesse B. Thomas proposed the unrestricted admission of both states as well as establishing an imaginary line through the remaining Louisiana Territory to include the southern border of Missouri.[4] All states north of this extended Mason-Dixon Line, except for Missouri, would be free states, and states south of the line could opt for slavery. Despite the South and the North finding different parts of this compromise objectionable, Senator Thomas's proposal for this arbitrary line passed the Senate as the Missouri Compromise in March 1820. Clay's victory was bringing Missouri into the union as a slave state, not the Compromise.

But the question was not yet resolved.

* * *

In Massachusetts, William Eustis had enjoyed working with his committee on the Missouri Question. The old dog had again caught the scent. After his committee completed its work, he threw his hat into the ring in February 1820 as the Democratic-Republican candidate for governor of Massachusetts.

Spring found Eustis and Caroline pleased that their winter had gone well. Caroline could plan their gardens, and Eustis was running for office. Eustis sent traveling directions to their friend Tristram Barnard in May 1820. Take the coach from Boston to Roxbury, he advised, "the best is to get out . . . at Mayo's Tavern and he will either send you up in one of his chaises or he will send up a boy and we will send down for you – or walk a short mile and we will send down for your baggage."[5]

Eustis lost his campaign for governor that fall, decisively beaten 31,072 to 21,927 by another Revolutionary War veteran, Federalist John Brooks. Gubernatorial loss aside, Eustis almost immediately wound up back in politics. The Massachusetts legislature appointed him to fill a year-long vacancy in the United States House of Representatives.[6] Eustis, sixty-seven, and Caroline, thirty-nine, packed their trunks and headed for Washington City.

Arriving in early November, Eustis found the nation's capital greatly altered. The President's House, now called the White House for its gleaming white paint, was restored after being burned by the British, but reconstruction continued at the dome-less Capitol. The federal government's entire workforce had doubled to about six hundred people during the twenty years since Eustis had been a first-time congressman. Impressively, thirty-four employees now labored at the War Department, Eustis's old stomping grounds.[7]

Eustis answered the noon rollcall when Congress convened on November 17. The unresolved issue of Missouri's statehood arose for the third year. Congress had conditionally admitted Maine as a free state and Missouri as a slave state because of the Compromise and directed them to submit their constitutions for approval. When Congress read Missouri's constitution and its ban on free Blacks entering the state, the decision of the previous year unraveled, the question of statehood was reopened, and the Democratic-Republican Party divided along sectional lines. The northern majority in the House insisted that Missouri must change its constitution as a condition of admission. Southerners threatened to walk out which would mean that Congress could not function.

The balcony overlooking the House Chamber was filled with ladies each morning as debate continued. A month after Eustis had taken his seat, and with the background of his committee's studies, he rose to speak about the citizenship rights of "black men and mulattoes." He called attention to Massachusetts, where "at least, [Blacks] are citizens, having civil and political rights, in common with the whites."

One of his fundamental points rested on the service of "many blacks, and other people of color" during the Revolutionary War. Eustis asked, "Who could have said to them, on their return to civil life, after having shed their blood in common with the whites in the defense of the liberties of the country, you are not to participate in the rights secured by the struggle, or in the liberty for which you have been fighting? Certainly no white man in Massachusetts."

He particularly called out a fellow representative who had spoken just before him. "The gentleman from Virginia says he must not be told that the term, we the people, in the preamble to the Constitution, means, or includes, Indians, free negroes, mulattoes. . . .To justify the inference of the gentleman, the preamble ought to read, we the white people." Then, "By whom, and for whose use and benefit, was the Constitution formed? By the people, and for the people, inhabiting the several States. Did the Convention who formed it go into the consideration of the character or complexion of the citizens included in the compact? No sir."[8]

Eustis believed that Missouri's constitution violated the United States Constitution, citing the laws for the interactions of citizens and states in Article IV, Section 2 which states "citizens of each state shall be entitled to all Privileges and Immunities of citizens of the several states." Eustis offered a compromise resolution to the House proposing that Missouri be granted admission into the Union if it agreed to remove from its constitution the clause excluding free Blacks and mulattoes.[9] His proposal was defeated.

Accepting its failure, Eustis wrote: "We are in a bad way here. Missouri is the order for tomorrow. My proposal for her prospective admission had as you see but six votes. It was more it seems than our friends were willing to give & less than others would take. It is now said [that] this vote proves that there was something besides the objectionable clause in her constitution which influenced the majority & that is neither more or less than the whole slave question."[10]

Eustis threw up his hands. He had made his argument based on the Constitution and about being the right thing to do. If others chose to delay a solution, it was not his problem. "The decision on my proposal . . . relieves me from all future trouble & responsibility, of which I have great cause to rejoice."[11] When the vote was called to admit Missouri on December 18, the ninety-three nays, including Eustis, defeated the seventy-nine yeas.[12]

President Monroe was running for election to his second term. Grasping at the distraction, Congress shifted its attention to campaign politics, and Missouri believed it had become a state despite the controversy over its constitution. But the question arose, could Missouri's electors vote in the presidential election?

Both houses of Congress gathered early in February 1821 to count the electoral votes. The states' names were called. When it came to Missouri, a New Hampshire congressman leaped up to object that Missouri was not yet a state and its votes could not be included. The response was volcanic. Members shouted objections. Senators walked out and the House was left to clean up the mess. Finally, the Senate returned, and in a compromise of sorts two totals were recorded—one with Missouri's votes and one without. In the end, it did not matter as Monroe had run for president unopposed.

Monroe was sworn in for his second term inside the newly-restored House Chamber on Monday, March 5, 1821, as heavy rain verged on snow outside. This time Eustis attended the ceremony. Exasperated about his ineffective five months in Washington, he wrote to Tristram Barnard: "At midnight on Saturday died the 16th Congress and if anyone can boast that he was a member of that Congress I am not that one. The inauguration has taken place and we shall leave tomorrow. What time we shall be at home depends on the roads and the weather."[13]

The Eustises were eager to return to Roxbury. They planted apple trees—the Roxbury Russet, probably the oldest American cultivar, and the Baldwin, a Massachusetts native since 1700s, and consulted with their neighbor, Enoch Bartlett, developer of the Bartlett pear.

Eustis campaigned again for the annually-elected governorship. This time he partnered with Levi Lincoln Jr., formerly Thomas Jefferson's attorney general, as lieutenant governor. The *Village Register* in Dedham presented its reasons why Eustis should be elected for the coming year: his recent satisfactory stint in Congress, his service to his country at home and abroad, his friendship with the present Democratic-Republican administration, and his support for manufacturing and finance.

Later that summer, Missouri rewrote its constitution to remove the laws that infringed on the rights of citizens of other states including free Blacks. It made the required pledge and became a state on August 10, 1821. The resolution was not particularly different from Eustis's original proposal, but because Missourians had written it themselves and it had not been imposed by a northern outsider, it seemed more acceptable.

The Democratic-Republicans lost to the Federalists once again in the commonwealth's gubernatorial election. After losing this second time, Eustis was nominated to be the Democratic-Republican Party's candidate for Congress. The only question raised about his qualifications during the party's convention concerned his support for the intended 1823 nomination of Secretary of State John Quincy Adams for president. Finding that Eustis was pro-Adams, despite being defeated by Adams in 1805, the party backed him, and he was elected to the Seventeenth Congress to serve until March 1823.

In a familiar routine, the congressman traveled south with his wife in November. When he and Caroline stopped in New York along the way, Eustis wrote up a brief business summary for Tristram Barnard. "The wharf and store on Mill Creek, the store at No 2 Union Street, and the old stable . . . are rented. The tenants paying all taxes." Having received complaints from his undertaker tenant, he was dealing with the soggy problem of waterproofing the cellars of his rental properties. He had insurance amounting to $7,000 on Shirley Place.[14]

Once in Washington, Caroline and William Eustis moved into temporary quarters with Mrs. Myers. Her house was conveniently located near the Central Market along Pennsylvania Avenue, between 7th and 9th Streets.[15] Three other congressmen from Pennsylvania boarded there. By now Eustis knew it was important to arrive early as desks were claimed on a first-come basis.

The Seventeenth Congress opened on December 3, 1821, with one hundred fifty-nine Democratic-Republicans and twenty-four Federalists in the House of Representatives; a total of one hundred eighty-three men. Six seats were reapportioned from Massachusetts to Maine, and Arkansas and Michigan Territories sent nonvoting representatives. As a former secretary of war, Eustis became chairman of the Committee on Military Affairs.

Without a strong opposition party, the Democratic-Republican Party began to lose focus during Monroe's second administration. The secretaries of state, treasury, and war all decided to run for president, and party members fragmented into warring factions instead of paying attention to legislation. This cabinet of competitors, looking ahead to the 1822 campaign season, rallied support through social activities.[16] Each held salons variously called drawing rooms or assemblies or circles. The candidates' wives and friends rounded up different groups for rival theater parties. Food, games, poetry readings, and chamber music entered into the mix as members of Congress joined a particular candidate's salon. Sixty-eight "parlor partisans," including Eustis, attending Massachusetts man and presidential candidate John Quincy Adams's salon.[17] Campaigning for office had changed, and a great deal more personal and persuasive interaction now seemed critical for gaining congressional and electoral support.

42

Patriot Governor

William Eustis lost his third race for governor, beaten again by Federalist and Revolutionary War veteran General John Brooks, a fellow member of the Society of the Cincinnati. The poll numbers, however, indicated that the political climate in Boston was changing, and longtime colleague Dr. David Townsend urged Eustis to make one more attempt. He had "many friends who are advocates for the genuine Republican character of the state," Townsend advised. They "will not fail as heretofore in placing their candidate in the governmental chair."[1]

At seventy-one, Eustis ran for a fourth time, partnering again with Levi Lincoln Jr. His Federalist opponent would be the well-known Harrison Gray Otis. The local Democratic-Republican Party backed Eustis after being reassured that he supported John Quincy Adams. He was touted as the Revolutionary War veteran who could finally repair the disgraced character of Massachusetts that had been besmirched by the traitorous Hartford Convention of 1814. Otis had led the Massachusetts delegation and had chaired the convention. Eustis's main campaign issue was Otis's disloyalty to the federal government.

The gubernatorial contest warmed up early that year, well before Congress adjourned and before Eustis could get back to Boston.

290

Campaign literature proclaimed that he had never been involved in the traitorous Hartford Convention nor any other subversive plots. Federalists fought back, claiming that he was involved in the Newburgh conspiracy and near revolt of the Continental Army for lack of pay in 1783. Federal reimbursement for the state's wartime expenses became a side issue. By refusing to cooperate with the federal government and Secretary of War Eustis's requests, the commonwealth had gone into debt providing its own defense during the War of 1812.

The *American Advocate & General Advertiser* on February 22, 1823, noted: "A gentleman at Washington says that there is much reason to fear that Massachusetts will not be . . . reimbursed the expenses [incurred] during the late war, in consequence of withholding her militia from the service of the General Government when they were required." President Madison had noted the state's refusal to cooperate and stopped all federal reimbursements. The state's war debt and support of the Hartford Convention were mortifying.

A newspaper clarified the two candidates: "William Eustis, a patriot of the revolution, by the Republicans, and Harrison G. Otis, a patriot of the Hartford Convention, by the Federalists . . . Every man who believes the Hartford Convention to be a patriotic assemblage intended 'to promote the public welfare', will vote for Harrison G. Otis; and every man who does not so believe will vote for William Eustis."[2]

By early April, the congressional session over, Eustis arrived back "at his farm in Roxbury" with only two weeks to garner votes.[3] Organized wards in Boston provided excellent places to campaign, although newspapers were still the most effective way to reach the people. One portrayed Eustis as the right candidate for the times: "Let, then, no man, who is friendly to good laws, correct principles, and just measures, lay his head upon his pillow, on Monday night, without the pleasing reflection, that he has performed the important duty of voting for EUSTIS and LINCOLN."[4]

On April 5, 1823, the *Independent Chronicle & Boston Patriot* expounded on the sacred duty of voting and evaluated the two candidates for governor, promoting Eustis as "a patriot of the revolution; a patriot in times which tried men's souls; a co-patriot with the 'Father of his Country'; and ever since the guardian and protector of those sacred rights his early toils had contributed to gain for you. Ponder well before you decide." The *Essex Register* described Eustis as "The companion of Warren and the friend of Washington, his youth, his manhood, his age have all been spent in a generous devotion to the liberties and interests of his country."[5]

Some comments could be amusing. The *Boston Commercial Gazette* opined "we have no fear of offending the delicate nerves of republican federalists by asserting that Mr. Otis keeps a coach and drives a splendid pair of horses; nor have we any notion that the simplicity of Dr. Eustis, in driving into town in a cart or waggon, will give him an additional vote, or gain for him the belief that his feelings and principles are more humble than the former person." Otis, the newspaper suggested, might arrive with liveried servants and full retinue.[6]

In a significant shift, April voting revealed that the twelve-year domination of the Federalist Party had ended. William Eustis became the governor-elect of Massachusetts with 34,402 votes to 30,171 for Harrison Otis. He carried all of the counties that he had won previously as well as Essex and Hampden. Boston, however, the last remaining Federalist stronghold, gave its votes to Otis. At noon on May 23, William Eustis and Levi Lincoln Jr. stood before the legislature at the State House to be sworn in as governor and lieutenant governor for the coming year.

Eustis immediately wrote to James Madison about the "Triumph of Republican Principles," mentioning the younger people joining the Democratic-Republican cause. This new generation sought a change in politics, and young men had come to him seeking his political wisdom and guidance. "To be the medium thro' which this change has been affected & will be announced, is the last and most consoling circumstance of my life."[7]

Eustis hoped that the election and shift in party control would begin a new era. It appeared he would be conciliatory toward his defeated opponents, but he got off to a rocky start. His enthusiasm got the best of him during his inaugural address. He could not resist firing one final denunciation at the Hartford Convention, provoking a quarrel with Otis whom Eustis never forgave for some of his earlier campaign remarks. After his speech, David Townsend reportedly tapped the new governor on the shoulder and commented: "Now, Bill, you have stuck your foot in it, and it will be hard work for you to recover yourself." Eustis replied, "I was determined to get it out and begin anew."[8] And he did, subsequently treating all Federalists as colleagues.

Newspapers were full of comments and analyses the following day. The *Boston Patriot* called Eustis a "venerable oak of the Revolution" and one of those "that show themselves the true children of those whose heart's blood dyed the turf of Lexington."[9] A joyful *Boston Commercial Gazette* declared: "Massachusetts is at length restored to the American family. Her character is redeemed in the estimation of the patriots of our own country and of every statesman in Europe."[10]

Eustis sent a copy of his "debut" speech to Madison. Rethinking his words, he confided that perhaps he should not have revived the Hartford Convention as it may have reopened old wounds. "You will, my dear sir, bear with me, for there is no one else except my wife to whom I can say it, it was the proudest day of my life."[11]

Madison sent congratulations for both the speech and the election. He called Eustis's speech "the *coup de grace* ... to the fractious ascendancy, so long forming a cloud over the State of Massachusetts." A caring friend, he sent wishes that Eustis would live to enjoy and be nourished by Massachusetts' resuscitated patriotism. Aging himself, and not happy about it, he added: "The excision of life is a painful operation and the more quickly it is performed the better for the patient."[12] He would outlive Eustis by ten years.

Celebrations and commemorations accompanied the new governor's election. Local artist Henry Williams painted his portrait, called "one of Mr. William's happiest efforts."[13] It went on view in the artist's rooms on School Street, and a month later a notice advertised that engravings of the portrait would be available for two dollars.

On view today at the State House in Boston, a well-fed Governor Eustis looks out on the world sporting ruddy cheeks and thick gray hair, seemingly confident in his life's accomplishments. His chin is dimpled, and his eyebrows arch over quizzical, kind eyes. He holds a letter, and there appears to be a map on the table where he sits. The background, perhaps a student's effort, is amateurish.

Hailed as a good likeness, the portrait reinforces one description of Eustis: "Perhaps he measured over six feet; walked well; stood firmly and genteelly, and when in full uniform dress, with fine three-cornered beaver [hat], . . . his whole appearance was venerable. His complexion was clear; but the uncommon redness of his cheeks, even at an advanced age, was the subject of remark, wherever he appeared."

When sitting, he had contracted a habit of inclining his head a little towards one shoulder which consequently affected another habit of raising one eyelid higher than the other and actually gave more interest to his person, and a peculiar sort of archness of expression. The governor's hair . . . was bushy, partially gray, and flowed over the forehead . . . In dress, he was fashionable; generally wore blue, with metal buttons, though not remarkably neat about dust [perhaps dandruff] – though his collar was invariably white and well starched."[14]

Harvard College awarded Governor Eustis an honorary

Doctorate of Laws during its summer commencement ceremonies. He was a member of Harvard's visiting committee in the fall and regularly attended meetings of its board of overseers.

News of Eustis's election prompted a letter from old friend James Swan. Eustis and Caroline had called on Swan several times in 1816 when they were in Paris. A member of the Sons of Liberty, Swan participated in the Tea Party and fought at the Battle of Bunker Hill. In 1798, he left his wife and moved to Paris where he lived until his death in 1830.

In spidery handwriting, Swan congratulated Eustis on his election. "At any rate, it is your due: for I pretend that all old patriots in the Revolution merit the preference to all upstarts since then." He recalled some political advice from decades before. "I shall never forget what old friend Dr. Warren said at one of the evening meetings at Ben Ede's office in Queen Street, namely that the public ought to be played with as one does with a coy woman, who will shun you if you persecute her with importunities; but if you appear to shun her, she'll make advances towards you."[15]

His acceptance speech delivered, the new governor got down to business and signed into law an act to incorporate the Bunker Hill Monument Association. To Eustis, a commemorative monument would celebrate the battle and memorialize his mentor Dr. Joseph Warren and all the others who died there, thus fulfilling his lifelong commitment to Warren's dream for a free republic.

Eustis likely was aware of the activities of his old Hudson Highlands comrade, Dr. James Thacher, by then an eminent physician living in Plymouth. Thacher founded the Plymouth Society in 1820 to celebrate the arrival of the Pilgrims. The society is now based in Pilgrim Hall in Plymouth.

The Massachusetts legislature took up a variety of issues.[16] Representatives voted to cede land on Kutta Hunk (Cuttyhunk) Island to the federal government for a lighthouse. They debated fraud in banks, the regulation of fisheries, jails, hay scales, and the inspection of gunpowder. They decided that justices of the peace were not exempt from service in the militia and that a person could not be considered a pauper and ward of the state if they were between the ages of twelve and sixty years old. Those people should earn their livelihood and work as indentured servants if nothing else. One decision that offered relief to married women, legally designated *femme covert*, stated that, with the help of a guardian, a woman could sell real estate owned by her husband if the husband was deemed a lunatic.

By the end of his first gubernatorial term, Eustis had one remaining goal—federal reparations to the state. He ran for a second year, this time with Marcus Morton as the candidate for lieutenant governor, and appointed Levi Lincoln Jr., the current lieutenant governor, to the Supreme Judicial Court of Massachusetts.

Massachusetts Federalists gave up on Harrison Gray Otis and offered lawyer Samuel Lathrop as their candidate in a last-ditch effort to keep the party alive. Lathrop became the last Federalist candidate for any statewide office. He campaigned on Eustis's neglect of the state's best interests in 1811 when he supported President Madison's embargo that ruined the state's economy. The *Boston Commercial Gazette* thought one of the points in Eustis's favor was that he had quit the War Department before the country was "irretrievably ruined" by Mr. Madison's War.

The campaign focused on aspects of the War of 1812 that no longer seemed relevant. Eustis promised resolution of the still-unsettled claim against the federal government for wartime reimbursement, including the cost of several ships sunk by Paul Revere to defend the main channel of Boston Harbor. Some movement toward reparations had already begun in Congress due to Eustis's first-term efforts.

President Monroe gave the campaign a boost by recommending that Congress "make provision for the settlement of the claim of Mass. for the services rendered in the late war in conformity with the rules which governed settlements for militia of other states."[17] The claim, first filed in 1818, would go forward. Monroe credited the "present Executive of Massachusetts" with the fact that the state was placed on the same ground as the other states. During the past ten years, no previous state administration had succeeded in making so much headway. The financial reparations for Massachusetts would be approved and paid during the next session of Congress.

Eustis supporters pasted up posters wherever a surface could be found. One broadside celebrated the money to be gained by his election and final settlement of the state's claim: "The amount owed [to the state] is $840,000 and with interest this now amounts to $1,700,000 which would relieve you of your entire state tax leaving $25,000 for internal improvements." Playing on stereotypical Federalist tendencies, it trumpeted: "Federal Rulers have mismanaged claims to this money . . . Vote the Republican ticket and ensure repayment of this sum into your state treasury."[18]

One newspaper article reassured Eustis voters: "Of his merits, it cannot be necessary to remind people. A long life devoted to his country; a firmness and integrity of principle which have never been denied, and a constant succession of public services are the claims he holds out to his fellow citizens – claims which they have recognized and allowed, and his exceptionable conduct the last year fully shews that their confidence has not been misplaced."[19]

Eustis won 36,650 - 34,210. On May 31, 1824, speaking to the legislature in the House Chamber, he said: "Our path of duty is plain. The government must be administered on those republican principles which produced our glorious revolution, and conform to those rules and precepts which we have sworn to maintain."[20] Eustis called for several legislative considerations for the coming year— one being his continuing concern about the state judicial system imprisoning people for debt. And by mid-June, pushing another one of his projects, he provided the legislature with documents from a survey for uniting Buzzards Bay and Cape Cod Bay with a canal.

43

Lengthening Shadows

President Monroe, planning the country's fiftieth anniversary celebration in 1825, thought that the presence of the Marquis de Lafayette would put the icing on the cake. Hailed as a national hero, Lafayette was admired for his actions during the decisive Battle of Yorktown and assistance in acquiring the essential French support. Congress sent an invitation to come as the "nation's guest," and the Marquis accepted, saying that he would tour the states.

Lafayette's anniversary visit to Massachusetts would be the grand finale. Governor William Eustis was in charge. The occasion would also mark the culmination of Eustis's political and personal life. This was not the first such celebration that Eustis had organized. There had been the production for Lafayette's first visit to Boston in 1784. And in 1789 he had arranged an extravaganza to welcome President George Washington. The planning for this event initiated a flurry of committee activity within nearly every organization in Boston. Counting the Marquis as a member, The Society of the Cincinnati took a leading role in the welcoming ceremonies. Boston Mayor Josiah Quincy issued a special invitation for Lafayette to come to Boston. Not to be outdone, Harvard College invited him to its commencement.

The celebration frenzy began on August 15, 1824, when

298

Lafayette arrived in New York Harbor where he was greeted by a cheering crowd of thirty thousand. The states he visited honored him in every way imaginable. Cannon fired salutes, bells pealed, and bands played wherever he traveled. After several ceremonial days in New York, Lafayette headed north for Boston, planning to visit with Eustis and then spend September and October touring New England before wintering in Washington City with President Monroe. Hindered by activities and crowds, the normally two-day journey to Boston took four days. Lafayette continued to be gracious about the constant recognition as his carriage crawled along the roads. His arrival in Massachusetts ignited a production worthy of Cecil B. DeMille.

Residents illuminated Dedham at eleven o'clock at night when Lafayette's entourage reached the village. People held torches along the road and lit bonfires. Every house sparkled with candles in the windows. The militia formed up, the fife and drum corps played, and various townsfolk made welcoming speeches. It was after midnight before the procession of coaches, including Eustis's own yellow coach in which Lafayette was riding, finally left Dedham. Lafayette was to spend the night at Shirley Place. In the wee hours of August 28, five years after Eustis had visited Lafayette's chateau in France, the governor embraced his old friend in the foyer of his own home. It was an emotional moment, Eustis reportedly exclaiming: "I am the happiest man that ever lived."[1]

Boston's own weeklong celebration began later that morning with, quite literally, a bang. Booming cannon and martial music below his second-floor window startled Lafayette awake after only a few hours of sleep. Looking out, he saw the Revolutionary War Lafayette Light Infantry in parade dress, complete with distinctive red and black plumed hats. The commander of a local company of riflemen had reproduced the old uniforms and arranged the eye-opening surprise. Society of the Cincinnati members arrived to offer greetings and to prepare for Lafayette's grand entrance into Boston.

There was barely time for a hurried but substantial breakfast for the Marquis—six perch, a canvasback duck, a dish of hominy, and a glass or two of Bordeaux.[2]

Shortly thereafter, a cannon fired the signal, and the proud procession headed for Boston. Lafayette, seated with Governor Eustis in an open barouche drawn by four white horses, was followed by another carriage carrying his two secretaries and his son, George-Washington Lafayette, forty-four. Masses of riders, cheering townsfolk, and running boys followed the carriages. It took two hours to go the two miles to Boston's town line. There, Mayor Josiah Quincy gave a welcoming speech and took Eustis's place in the barouche for the procession into Boston. Eustis hurried by another route to greet the procession when it arrived at the State House.

Boston had built twenty-four triumphal arches, one for each state in the union, covered with canvas that was painted to look like granite blocks.[3] This reflection of the Arc de Triomphe honored Lafayette and France. The carriages and riders proceeded amid jubilant throngs, and ladies waved their handkerchiefs. Lafayette acknowledged the cheers by constantly bowing to the nearly seventy-five thousand people who mobbed both sides of the streets. The procession wound its way through the arches, ending at Boston Common for the first of many official receptions.

More than a thousand schoolchildren greeted him. After a small girl offered a garland of flowers, a military escort conducted Lafayette up the hill to the State House where Governor Eustis, now in his Continental Army uniform, received him in the Senate Chamber. The governor began his official welcoming speech but broke down, too overcome by emotion to finish the first sentence. An aide read his address referring to Lafayette as the "last surviving Major General of the American Revolutionary army." After the ceremony, Lafayette was escorted to a nearby mansion "fitted up in a very rich style" at the corner of Park and Beacon Streets, designated his Boston home. As Guest of the Nation, he would not stay in private houses for the rest of his tour.[4]

The festivities of the first day culminated when Eustis and Lafayette dined at about three o'clock that afternoon in the Exchange Coffee House. Despite a disastrous fire a few years before, the newly-restored hotel offered the most glamorous setting in Boston. Its ballroom was decorated with festoons, flags, and portraits of Revolutionary War heroes. Eustis and the mayor joined others in offering toasts. In response, Lafayette raised his glass: "To the City of Boston, the cradle of liberty—May Faneuil Hall ever stand a monument to teach the world that resistance to oppression is a duty, and will, under true republican institutions, become a blessing." He may well have thought of the difference between the French and the American quests for independence.

Eustis accompanied Lafayette wherever he went that week, including a visit to Bunker Hill to see the pyramid of stones erected on the spot where Joseph Warren fell. On Wednesday, August 30, dragoons, a visiting deputation from New York, and various distinguished citizens escorted Lafayette and Eustis to Cambridge to attend the Harvard College commencement.

Eustis then hosted Lafayette for a midday dinner at Shirley Place.[5] At Caroline's direction, a carpenter had fit together two great curved wooden boards to form a horseshoe-shaped table seating thirty guests. Plates were placed on the outside of the table, and servants served from the inside. The governor sat at the head of the table with Lafayette on his right, General Henry Dearborn on his left, and former Governor John Brooks second on the right.

In the early September evening, just as it got dark, and before Lafayette left for Boston to attend a ball given by Mrs. Sears on Beacon Street, celebratory fireworks erupted on the governor's extensive lawn, an expression of his delight with the visit. At Mrs. Sears's that evening, ladies wore kid gloves with Lafayette's portrait stamped on the back. This left Lafayette the option of kissing his own face when he greeted a lady.[6] A new industry in souvenirs developed because of Lafayette's visit, and hundreds of artists and craftsmen worked to meet the demand for mementos bearing his name and image. A similar fad had developed years earlier in Paris where souvenirs bore the likeness of Benjamin Franklin.

The day before Lafayette departed, he went, without his usual grand escort and procession, to dine with former President John Adams, eighty-nine, at his home in Quincy. Charles Francis Adams, the former president's grandson, wrote in his diary that the dinner party was small with only Lafayette's son, his secretary, and two other guests—Boston Mayor Josiah Quincy and Governor William Eustis. Young Adams was aware of his unique opportunity. "How many people in this country would have been delighted with my situation at this moment, to see three distinguished men dining at the same table, with the reflections all brought up concerning the old days of the revolution, in which they were conspicuous actors and for their exertions in which the country is grateful!"[7]

On the last day of Lafayette's visit, more than six thousand people attended a military pageant on Boston Common. Governor Eustis had ordered a decorated and especially large marquee erected on the higher ground of the Common for another of those "elegant collations" offered to invited guests and officers. Featured as a centerpiece on the long table was a large silver basin filled with fragments of weapons and military buttons collected on Breed's Hill long after the battle. Governor Eustis offered Lafayette his choice of souvenirs. The afternoon featured demonstrations by various regiments of battle formations and systems of attack and defense. It was a spectacular sendoff. The exhausted marquis left the next morning for Portsmouth, New Hampshire, by way of Lexington, Concord, Salem, and Newburyport.

When the toasts ended, the bands stopped playing, the fireworks ceased, and brisk fall weather started turning the leaves, Eustis went back to his gubernatorial duties. He carried on with several of his projects, among them finalizing the state's borders.[8] All fears about the Cape Cod Canal freezing in winter, as did the Erie Canal, had been resolved, and that project would begin in June 1824. Satisfied with his life and the state of the commonwealth, the governor called for a statewide day of thanksgiving and planned for the winter.[9]

As was customary, Eustis rented rooms to avoid his carriage commute, reduce exposure to cold, and be closer to the State House. The state paid rental expenses for its governors' winter lodgings in downtown Boston. For this winter, he arranged for rooms at Mrs. Miles's distinguished four-story residence on Howard Street. Health concerns, including rheumatism, were always on his mind. He thought the pain in his left shoulder had been activated by trips "in my own open wagon into State Street" and believed in sarsaparilla tea for aches and pains.[10]

In his annual message to the Massachusetts legislature on January 6, 1825, Eustis mentioned his satisfaction with the manner in which the commonwealth had hosted Lafayette. Reflecting on the year past, he said, "nothing has occurred to disturb the public tranquility, or to interrupt the enjoyment of those blessings with which we have been indulged by a munificent providence." He was pleased with plans to lay the cornerstone of the battle monument on Breed's Hill (called the Bunker Hill Monument today) the following fall.

Summing up his own philosophy, Eustis referred back to the infamous Hartford Convention as a symbol of all that had led the state astray. "Whatever may have been the professed object of the Convention, it had the certain effect of encouraging the enemy, of discouraging and impairing the means and resources of the country and of alienating the minds of the citizens." He praised the Constitution and republic, "which, in the emphatic language of Washington, constitutes us one people, [and] is the main pillar in the edifice of our real independence, the support of our tranquility at home, our peace abroad, of our safety, of our prosperity, of that very liberty which we so highly prize."[11]

On the first day of February, Eustis took his top hat from the hat stand in the foyer of Shirley Place and left for the Council Chamber in Boston. At the moment of departure, he took a pen, and wrote on a slip of paper "February 1st, '25, when surely I was alive" and gave it with a kiss to a visiting niece.[12]

He remained at his intown residence that night and was suddenly "attacked with a very violent fever fit, accompanied with a sharp pain in the right side of the breast."[13] Learning of William's illness, Caroline hurried into the city the next morning. Dr. John Collins Warren, the son of Eustis's old associate, Dr. John Warren, arrived, and Eustis "was bled very copiously."[14] This remedy seemed to help temporarily. Plans to return to Shirley Place changed when the weather turned stormy and the Eustises remained in the city overnight.

Hearing Eustis was sick, William Sumner, who lived nearby on Beacon Hill, came to visit. "In the ante-room, I met his brother, Jacob Eustis who just then came out of the governor's sick room." When Sumner asked about the governor, Jacob, agitated, replied: "He is as good as dead. They have bled him to death; he never will recover in the world. They have reduced him so low that he will never get up again. I have just seen him, and says I, 'Bill, you are gone.'"[15]

Eustis began to fail that evening, fulfilling his brother's prediction. His heart seemed weak, and pneumonia set in. By Saturday, temporarily regaining his strength, "being supported by cordials," he spoke cheerfully with visiting friends.

The end came at seven o'clock on Sunday morning, February 6, 1825. William Eustis, seventy-three, died with his wife Caroline by his side in Mrs. Miles's boarding house on Howard Street in Boston.

Epilogue

*The verification of my own participation "at a period the
most trying and critical in our history ... fastens forever
the chain of respect and friendship by which I have been
invariably bound to the best of men."*
—William Eustis to James Madison, June 6, 1823

Acting Governor Marcus Morton officially announced the death of
Governor Eustis in the Council Chamber on Monday morning. "At
about seven o'clock yesterday morning His Excellency William
Eustis departed this life at his lodgings in this City after a
confinement by the disease which proved mortal of five days only."[1]
A hearse discretely transported Eustis's body back to Shirley Place
that day.

Three days later, at six o'clock Thursday evening, state officials
gathered with Eustis family members at Shirley Place for a candlelit
prayer service conducted by a family friend, the Reverend Thomas
Gray, minister of the First Congregational Church in Jamaica Plain.
Later, a hearse conveyed the body to the State House where it was
received by the Governor's Guard, the Independent Corps of Cadets,
which stood watch through the night.

On Friday, February 11, a large commemoration conducted by
Boston and Massachusetts, with military honors, honored their chief

executive's life.[2] Artillery batteries posted on Meeting House Hill in Roxbury and on Bunker Hill in Charlestown fired salutes every half hour from the winter sunrise until the funeral cortège began to move from the State House at one o'clock. Pallbearers, the president of the Senate, the chief justice, the Speaker of the House, the president of the Council, the mayor of Boston, and the chaplain led the procession, walking on both sides of the horse-drawn hearse. Eustis's rider-less horse, led by a servant, preceded carriages carrying Caroline Eustis, relatives, and the governor's aides. The acting governor, lawmakers, and state government administrators followed in a long procession. The Society of the Cincinnati, Harvard College, and the Massachusetts Medical Society were among the groups in attendance. Sixteen companies of light infantry, four companies of riflemen, and four artillery batteries were formed into an appropriate regimental escort. Bostonians lined the streets in silence.

The cortège culminated at the Old South Church, the largest church in town and site of Revolutionary War activities. Its galleries and organ loft were draped in black. Eustis's hat, sword, and gloves topped his coffin in the church. A sermon by the chaplain of the Senate was followed by prayers offered by the chaplain of the House.

The entire procession regrouped after the service and marched to the Old Granary Burying Ground where the coffin was temporarily entombed. The naval defense militia, the Sea Fencibles, fired cannon every minute during the procession. The Woburn and Cambridge Companies of Light Infantry fired final volleys before the mourners returned to the State House to disband.[3]

The result of Eustis's autopsy was detailed in the *Columbian Centinel* newspaper the day after the state funeral.[4] His heart was said to be generally sound but his lungs were excessively inflamed and obstructed, probably due to the pneumonia. William Sumner remembered the governor was convinced that his heart was failing.

Eustis had for several years consulted celebrated physicians in Boston as well as in London, Paris, and Holland. Sumner thought "he never had any confidence in what they said" and remained apprehensive that he would die from heart failure.[5]

The governor had hosted weekly card parties at Shirley Place, to play whist, and he served elegant repasts to his guests. Sumner, about twenty-five years younger, remembered the "old-fashioned hot supper" of roast duck and game provided for the cardplayers. Those friends, knowing Eustis enjoyed his food and remembering an acquaintance who had died after eating plum cake, initially attributed his illness to "hot suppers and high living."[6]

The Reverend Thomas Gray, who had earlier conducted the private prayer service at Shirley Place, delivered a special funeral sermon at the nearby First Church of Roxbury, where Governor and Madame Eustis were members, on Sunday, February 13, 1825. The memorial sermon was published at Caroline Eustis's request. Not until the end of his grim homily did Gray offer details of Governor Eustis's life: "He was a man of amiable disposition, and his heart was the repository of social feeling, whilst his hospitable manners rendered his house always pleasant to his friends and visitors."[7]

Lafayette, wintering in Washington, wrote to Caroline as soon as he heard the news. "I hope that amidst your too just and mournful feelings the condolence of an old friend [will be welcome]. Promise me to mingle my own grief with yours, accept the sympathizing respects of my son . . .."[8]

Caroline Eustis ordered a large obelisk from Cary and Dickerson of Boston to mark her husband's grave next to his mother in Lexington. The design was a miniature Bunker Hill Monument—a pyramidal shaft rising over ten feet tall. After it was erected in the Lexington Burying Ground, Eustis's body was transferred and interred the following December.[9]

For years afterwards, Caroline diligently followed the progress of the Bunker Hill Monument's construction. Her husband had shown the intended site to Lafayette during his visit. True to his word, Lafayette returned to Boston in June 1825 to lay its cornerstone and to call on Caroline before he returned to France. Massachusetts Senator Daniel Webster, the featured speaker for the occasion, would watch over Caroline for years.

It took twenty years to build the monument which was completed in 1843. Before construction could begin, a railroad line had to be built to haul the granite from the quarries in Quincy, south of Boston, to barges that floated the huge pieces across the bay to Charlestown. Funds repeatedly ran out, forcing the monument association to sell off most of the ten-acre site for house lots.

Despite his life of patriotic service, his diligent pursuit of the founders' original vision, and his celebrity at the time of his death, William Eustis soon disappeared into the shadows of history. The month after he died, another Revolutionary War general, former Governor John Brooks, who had been at Eustis's dinner for Lafayette, was dead. Eustis's star was eventually and completely eclipsed when two of the Founding Fathers and former presidents, John Adams and Thomas Jefferson, both died on July 4, 1826, exactly fifty years after the Declaration of Independence that they had championed was adopted. Wrote the *Boston Gazette:* "The heroes of the Revolution are falling around us, as the last leaves of the tree in the autumnal blast." [10]

* * *

Eustis died without heirs, and, despite his health concerns, he had surprisingly neglected to write a will. It fell to the Massachusetts probate court and common laws of coverture to determine the dispersal of his estate. Caroline, named as "administratrix," in March 1825 wrote to her nephew, George Eustis, that she was "ignorant of the manner in which our lamented friend ment to dispose of his property. I never heard him mention a will." [11] George had traveled with Eustis and Caroline to the United Netherlands and was now an established lawyer, married and living in New Orleans.

The law of dower rights stipulated that without a will, if there were no children, the widow could inherit half of her husband's estate. Caroline wanted to remain at Shirley Place and could do so if it was acceptable to the other heirs, namely George Eustis. She would have the right of approval for all real estate transactions that affected her occupancy of the house such as sublets by the other owners. It was not until 1833 that widows' rights were expanded. Married women did not write wills until 1842 because they could not own property. In 1825, however, a widow might be asked by the probate court to serve as a personal representative to answer questions about her husband's intentions.

In April 1826, a year after Eustis's death, his brother Jacob accompanied Caroline to probate court in Dedham for the settlement of an administrative allowance and the assignment of her dower for the real estate. Jacob, as the senior surviving male heir, would speak for Caroline in legal proceedings.[12]

An inventory of property owned by William Eustis, other than Shirley Place, included the brick store at 2 Union Street, Boston, and the house and stable in Cambridge that were rented to "good" tenants, relatives of his sister, Catharine Wells. Eustis's old stores and wharf had been sold the year before for $15,000. The stable for boarding horses had gone several years before that for $3,000. Caroline reported that she had paid taxes of $1,900 against Shirley Place—the large house, stable, and offices on fifteen acres in Roxbury—valued at $19,500.[13]

A detailed room-by-room inventory of Shirley Place listed three hundred seventy volumes in Eustis's library. It is startling to read about the number of chairs in each room, reflecting the practice of keeping them against the walls and moving them into the room for the purpose of the moment. For example, Caroline's small morning or breakfast room had eight straight chairs and a lolling chair.

A one hundred fifty-two-piece china dinner set made the list; possibly the same set of china that was especially crafted with the insignia of the Society of the Cincinnati. It is now part of the White House china collection. Eustis's yellow coach, valued at $275, and his barouche, chaise, and wagon were housed in the stables. Among the listing of harnesses, saddles, and garden tools was the forty-four-foot dinner board and benches remaining from Lafayette's visit just months before. All of these assets as well as his shares of stock brought Eustis's total worth to $51,619.52.[14]

Caroline worked out beneficial arrangements with tenants in exchange for accommodations and minimal rent. For instance, she leased "the farm on Eustis Street on the Dorchester line known as the Governor Eustis farm, together with a barn but not the dwelling house," to Eben T. Hitchcock as a tenant farmer.[15] Rental income would be $200 per year to be paid quarterly. Hitchcock would have the milk of the two cows and would furnish the Eustis household with milk, half of the butter he made, and all necessary vegetables. Hitchcock could also live in the former servant rooms on the third floor in the main house without charge.

A senator from a southern state who knew Caroline when she and Eustis lived in Washington came north to court her, later proposing marriage. But she made it clear that she would not entertain the idea of marrying.[16] She continued her friendship with William H. Sumner for whom Boston's Sumner Tunnel is named.

When Sumner founded the Massachusetts Horticultural Society with William's nephew, James Wells Eustis, in 1829, Caroline became one of its early members, exhibiting her own homegrown fruit at the society's annual agricultural and flower shows. She presented large orange and lemon trees and an assortment of flowers in 1834. She sent in Sweetwater grapes and a basket of peaches in 1838. She sent Bartlett pears for the society's fourteenth annual exhibit in 1842.

As Boston became more populated, the rural farms and villages disappeared under the influx of small businesses and the factories that employed thousands of Irish immigrants who were pouring into the country. Waves of workers filled boarding and apartment houses in the expanding village of Roxbury by the 1840s. Street directories continued to list Caroline as Madam Eustis, relict of Governor Eustis.

Remembered as a grand dame and local character, Madam Eustis favored wearing a turban as did Dolley Madison. Stories circulated of her pet toad sporting a blue ribbon on special days and likely living in the orangery attached to the south side of the house. It is possible that she was the Caroline Eustis who submitted poems in the 1850s for publication in Sartain's Union Magazine of Literature and Art, one titled "Blue Flowers."

In 1853, when Caroline was seventy-two, Daniel Webster, who continued to watch out for her, obtained an annual pension of $600 because of her husband's services in the Revolutionary War.[17] By 1860, the value of Shirley Place had fallen to $3,700.[18]

By the final years of Caroline's life, the world had changed considerably in philosophy, politics, and appearance. The Civil War divided the Eustis family. Caroline did her part in the North by knitting socks for the Union soldiers. George Eustis Jr., her nephew in New Orleans, fought for the Confederacy. Initially a congressman from Louisiana, George served during the war and went to France as secretary of the Confederate States Mission to Paris.

Caroline Langdon Eustis died at Shirley Place on October 12, 1865. She was eighty-four, having survived her husband by more than forty years. Retaining her title of Madame, she kept Shirley Place as a shrine to the governor's memory with his hat, cane, and coat in their usual place in the hall. Whenever Madame entertained local children for tea, there was always a place set for the governor at the table. Living frugally by necessity, she invited her Wells nieces to live with her for companionship.

Caroline was buried beside her husband in Lexington, and ownership of Shirley Place was transferred to George Eustis, Jr.[19] He was in France when the Civil War ended and remined there. He had no interest in the estate or returning to America. The contents of the house were sold at auction two years before the house was sold in 1869. George Eustis, Jr. died of tuberculosis in Cannes in 1872.

By the time of the 1903 publication of Mary Crawford's book, *The Romance of Old New England Rooftrees*, the Shirley Place mansion had been moved a short distance to make way for construction of Shirley Street with its accompanying housing. The old Georgian house became tenement housing, its grand rooms partitioned into small apartments. "Laundry dries in the cupola and a 'To Let' sign hangs in the window." [20]

Acknowledgements

During more than eight years of research, pouring through the remaining desiccated bits and pieces of William Eustis's life, and preparation of this biography, I received encouragement, cooperation, and assistance from many, many helpful people. I will always be in their debt.

This odyssey began about twenty years ago when the late Olivia Dworkin brought letters to me as executive director of the Shirley-Eustis House Association and suggested we look into William Eustis. And we began. Rebecca Potter wrote a brief Eustis biography for the association in 2001. Some years later, I began this more extensively researched biography.

My appreciation goes to Posy Evans Parsons for her research at the Massachusetts Archives; to my sister, Dr. Dorinda Evans, for online newspaper research and information about Gilbert Stuart; to Margaret Costello, archivist at the Falmouth Historical Society in Massachusetts; and Thelma Spicer for in-depth genealogical research.

Many people at historic sites were generous with their time. Elyse Goldberg, executive director at Washington's Headquarters State Historic Site in Newburg, New York, enabled my visit to West Point and a conference about military leaders. Melvin Johnson and Aaron Robinson offered advice, information, and troop listings in the Hudson Highlands.

The Dedham Historical Society willingly laid out their Eustis material, and the New York Historical Society Library offered a collection I did not know existed. Hilarie Hicks, senior research manager at Montpelier, put me on to the William Eustis and James Madison expedition to Monticello to see Thomas Jefferson.

My appreciation also to John Fierst, librarian/bibliographer, Clarke Historical Library at Central Michigan University for General William Hull-William Eustis correspondence; to Tara Z. Laver, interim head of Special Collections, Louisiana State

314

University, for a Eustis-Aaron Burr letter; to Duanesburg Historical Society, Duanesburg, New York, for answering my many questions.

My gratitude goes to Christine Hughes at the Naval History and Heritage Command in the Washington Naval Yard for help in locating the log of the *Congress.*

My college roommate, Barbara Nichols Bennett, early on waded through various chapters, offering suggestions and critiques. Christian Di Spigna, author of *Founding Martyr*, a biography of Dr. Joseph Warren, offered support and reviewed several chapters. Thanks to Dr. Robert Allison, professor of history at Suffolk University, for his encouragement. Charles Sullivan, executive director of the Cambridge Historical Commission, informed me about the Eustis house in Cambridge.

My special thanks to Barbara Sillery, Melanie Merriman, Hugh Blair-Smith, and Sandy Macfarlane for nearly three years of diligent critiquing and encouragement for this beginning writer in a nonfiction group of the Cape Cod Writers Center. I am grateful to Marguerite Krupp for her astute suggestions and edits.

Finally, many thanks go to editor Bob Haskell, who tidied up all of my errors and made this a better book by far, and to Stephanie Blackman at Riverhaven Books. This would not have been possible without them.

Any inaccuracies and mistakes are, of course, all mine.

Source Notes

Abbreviations:
BPL Boston Public Library
DHS Dedham Historical Society
LOC Library of Congress
LHS Lexington Historical Society
MHS Massachusetts Historical Society
N-YHS New York Historical Society
WE William Eustis

A number of very informative secondary sources have been written over the past several decades that help us understand the world in which William Eustis lived. Unfortunately, no substantial body of Eustis materials has survived in any one place, and, as Eustis had no heirs, little personal correspondence was saved. There are no surviving letters written before 1776.

I have retained the spelling and punctuation in all quotations.

In regard to British shipping, HMS was not used to distinguish His Majesty's Ships until after the Revolutionary War.

Prologue
1. History of Boston Latin School is found at *www.bls-blsa.org*.
2. Richard Archer, *As If an Enemy's Country*, xvi., xvii. Very helpful in filling in the background on Boston's rebellious activities.
3. Conrad Edick Wright and Edward W. Hanson, eds. *Sibley's Harvard Graduates*, Vol. XVIII, 1772-1774.

PART I: REVOLUTION, 1753 – 1783

Chapter One: Counting Down to Liberty
1. Benjamin Eustis, Account Book, Ms. N-1191, MHS.
2. Archer, xvii
3. Proceedings of Cambridge Historical Society, Vol. 9. Minutes of Thirtieth Meeting.
4. Eustis, Account Book, MHS. Bleeding during pregnancy and delivery was advocated by William Dewees in a book dedicated to Benjamin Rush; *An Essay on the Means of Lessening Pain, and Facilitating Certain Cases of Difficult Parturition* (Philadelphia, 1806). See also Ulrich, Laurel Thatcher. *A Midwife's Tale: The Life of Martha Ballard Based on Her Diary, 1785-1812.*
5. The Rev. Thomas Gray, *Funeral Sermon for His Excellency William Eustis*.
6. Michael M. Greenburg, *The Court-Martial of Paul Revere*, 8.

Chapter Two: Fire and Ice

1. Archer, 191-193.
2. William Tudor, *Life of James Otis of Massachusetts*, Boston, 1832.
3. Samuel Eliot Morison, *Three Centuries of Harvard,* 141.
4. John K. Alexander, *Samuel Adams,* 10.
5. Hutchinson hurried to the Town House, announced that the rule of law would prevail, and sent the mob home. The next day Captain Preston and eight soldiers were indicted for murder and imprisoned. Despite incendiary efforts by the Sons of Liberty and Sam Adams, a volunteer armed watch was created to patrol the town and keep the peace. The trial was postponed until the fall, and when no other attorney could be found for the defense, John Adams and Josiah Quincy represented them. Preston and the soldiers were acquitted and returned to England.
6. Morison, 136. For Harvard life, see also Harlow Giles Unger's *American Tempest,* 23-25.
7. Ibid., 127.
8. Hutchinson, Thomas. History of the Province of Massachusetts Bay, 1749-74, Vol. 1, 18.
9. Morison, 75.
10. Morison, 141.

Chapter Three: Grave Issues

1. Judith W Leavitt and Ronald L. Numbers, eds. *Sickness & Health in America,* 43.
2. The treatment involved a lengthy preparation for the recipient with purging and a milk diet before being inoculated. In that process, after collecting pus on a thread from an infected person, Warren would insert it into a cut on the arm of his patient and then bind up the wound.
3. The Greeks had developed the theory that there were four *humours,* or bodily fluids, in the body: blood, phlegm, yellow bile (or choler), and black bile (or melancholy). If any of these were out of balance, disease (dis-ease) resulted. Expulsion of one kind or another seemed the best remedy to bring the body into balance again. Therapies included bloodletting, sometimes by the application of leeches, and various kinds of purging and blistering. Purges were administered internally by mouth or clyster (enema). Sometimes purging "both upward and downward" was recommended for the wretched patient.
4. Leavitt and Numbers, 47.
5. When the site of Warren's house was excavated in 1835, wired skulls were discovered that gave evidence of apprentice studies.
6. WE to John Warren, John Collins Warren papers, November 17, 1773, MHS.

Chapter Four: Rally Mohawks!

Nathaniel Philbrick's book, *Bunker Hill: A City, a Siege, a Revolution,* is an excellent resource for the full impression of that dangerous though exciting time in William Eustis's young life. For the life of Joseph Warren, see Christian Di Spigna's *Founding Martyr: The Life and Death of Dr. Joseph Warren, the American Revolution's Lost Hero*; Samuel A. Forman's *Dr. Joseph Warren: The Boston Tea Party, Bunker Hill, and the Birth of American History,* and Rhoda Truax. *The Doctors Warren of Boston: First Family of Surgery.*

1. Philbrick, *Bunker Hill*. 33.
2. Nelson, 79-80.
3. Joseph Warren, Account Book, 1774-75, MHS. Also see Forman's biography of Joseph Warren.
4. The seven groups or political associations have been identified as St. Andrew's Lodge, the Loyal Nine, North Caucus, Long Room Club, Tea Party, Boston Committee of Correspondence, London Enemies List. Fischer, David Hackett, *Paul Revere's Ride,* 302-303.

Chapter Five: Oppose, Oppose...

Excellent resources are Nathaniel Philbrick's countdown to the Battle of Bunker Hill as well as James L. Nelson's *With Fire and Sword: The Battle of Bunker Hill and the Beginning of the American Revolution,* and Rick Atkinson's *The British Are Coming.*

1. Philbrick, *BH*, 47.
2. Ibid., 56.
3. Congress was traditionally a word for the meeting of differences or even the collision of opposites. Although used as a common term for sexual intercourse in the eighteenth century, it also described a meeting of people from different countries or states or places. The idea of a Congress was very different from a Parliament, which meant literally a group of people who came together to talk things over. A true congress—a meeting of opposites from different places—occurred in Philadelphia. Discussed by Fischer, *Liberty and Freedom*, 192.
4. Philbrick, *BH*, citing an account by Dawes's granddaughter, 78.
5. Forman, 227.
6. Philbrick, *BH*, 97.
7. *Diary of Dr. Nathanial Ames of Dedham, Massachusetts, 1758 – 1822.* March 30, April 8, 1775. DHS. Also for his discussion, Philbrick, *BH,* Notes on 101, 319.
8. Mercy Scollay Papers, Cambridge Historical Society.

Chapter Six: Listen, My Children ...

1. James L Nelson, *With Fire and Sword: The Battle of Bunker Hill and the Beginning of the American Revolution*: 48. Also cited in Rhoda Truax, *The Doctors Warren of Boston: First Family of Surgery*, 53, and Nathaniel Philbrick. *Bunker Hill: A City, a Siege, a Revolution*, 150.
2. Nathaniel Philbrick, *Bunker Hill,* 110.

3. Christian Di Spigna, *Founding Martyr*, 125.

4. Philbrick, *BH*, 55.

5. Michael M. Greenburg, *The Court-Martial of Paul Revere: A Son of Liberty & America's Forgotten Military Disaster*, 44. See also Philbrick, *BH*, 118.

6. *Yankee Doodle*: A macaroni was a fop or dandy. The term "Yankee" was derogatory and applied to New Englanders as a term of contempt. The song "Yankee Doodle" was written about 1759 to make fun of these supposed country bumpkins. The British played it as an insult while marching through Boston streets. Years earlier, Americans used it to express excellence as in a "yankee" good horse, or "yankee" cider. Now the colonials took it up again and boasted of "yankee" courage. James Thacher, *A Military Journal*, 19. Also Fischer, *Liberty and Freedom*, 216.

7. Philbrick, *BH*, 152. British regulars had no experience with guns other than the Brown Bess muskets issued when they joined the army. Americans had an assortment of firearms, from their father's flintlock muskets, French-made and captured during the French and Indian War, to the latest in Pennsylvania long rifles (so called for the new rifling in the barrels that made them more accurate). Most had been raised with guns and taught to shoot from an early age, to add food to the family's table if for nothing else. And Americans certainly did not succeed in putting dinner on the table by firing in the open. They shot and fought from behind obstacles, houses, walls, or trees. The generally older American militia had more recent fighting experience in the French and Indian War than the young British regulars brought across the Atlantic in troop transports

8. Muster rolls for Lexington town militia, LHS.

Chapter Seven: Death and Defeat

1. Rev. Thomas Gray, *Funeral Sermon*, 1825. Also, Papers, LHS, 104.

2. Philbrick, *BH*, 16.

3. Ibid., 164.

4. Nelson, 154.

5. Philbrick, *BH*, 189.

6. Nelson, 226. Also, Lonergan, *Henry Knox*, 25.

7. For fortification details, see Lockhart, 193, 195.

8. Nelson, 264.

9. Philbrick, *BH*, 216.

10. Lockhart, 261

11. British generals Clinton and Burgoyne watched the action from the battery on Copp's Hill as General Howe led the assault. Pleasure-loving William Howe was an Eton-educated British blueblood with a penchant for vices common to his class. He indulged in gambling and whoring, taking as his American mistress Boston-born Elizabeth Loring, offering her husband, Joshua Loring, the lucrative job as commissary of prisoners. Bawdy street ballads were written about opportunistic Joshua collecting the cash and his wife collecting the general. See Ron Chernow, *Washington, A Life. 239.* See also Philbrick, *BH*, 225, and Nelson, 288.

12. Philbrick, Ibid., 224.
13. Philbrick, BH. 228. See also Di Spigna, *Founding Martyr: The Life and Death of Dr. Joseph Warren, the American Revolution's Lost Hero.*
14. Nelson, 37. Also Commager and Morris, 131.

Chapter Eight: His Excellency and the Yankees

1. Philbrick, 235. For the identification of Warren's body, see Nelson, 314. Also, Philbrick, *BH*, 287-288, and Di Spigna, *Founding Martyr,* 201.
2. Philbrick, *BH*, 110.
3. Chernow, *Washington*, 192.
4. Philbrick, *BH,* 241.
5. Simon Shama, *Rough Crossings,* 7.
6. Philbrick, BH, 242.
7. Randall, 135.
8. Palmer, 142.
9. Commager and Morris, 153, citing French, Allen, *First Year of the American Revolution*, 300-301.
10. Rakove, 123.
11. Philbrick, *BH*, 245.
12. Wilbur, *Revolutionary Medicine, 1700 – 1800*, 4.
13. Thacher, James, *Military Journal, during the American Revolutionary War, from 1775 to 1783*, July 1775, 31.
14. Fenn, *Pox Americana: The Great Smallpox Epidemic of 1775-82*, 27.
15. Chernow, *Washington*, 200.
16. Wilbur, 5.
17. Ibid., 5.
18. Ibid., 6.

Chapter Nine: Liberating Boston: Evacuation Day

1. WE to Henry Knox, Eustis Papers, MHS-P-094, MHS.
2. *Diary of Dr. Nathanial Ames of Dedham, Massachusetts, 1758 – 1822*, 100.
3. Thomas Paine, cited in Rakove, 95.
4. Philbrick, *BH,* 265.
5. Lockhart, 365.
6. Thacher, February 22, 1776.
7. Philbrick, *BH*, 283.
8. Winsor, Justin, ed., *The Memorial History of Boston*, Boston, Tichnor, 1881, vol. 3, 159, cited in *Paul Revere's Boston,* Exhibition Catalog, Museum of Fine Arts, 1975.
9. Richard Brookhiser, *Gentleman Revolutionary: Gouverneur Morris,* 27.
10. Chernow, *Washington*, 23
11. WE to David Townsend, excerpt, New England Historical & Genealogical Register and Antiquarian Journal. Eustis's entire letter to David Townsend was published in Boston in 1869 by David Clapp & Son, with accompanying notes by Rev. Edmund F. Slafter. "The Assassination Plot of 1776" pamphlet is in the collection of the American Athenaeum in Worcester, Mass.

Chapter Ten: A New Constellation
1. Chernow, *Washington*, 237.
2. Ibid., 235.
3. For descriptions of this flight, see Lonergan, 64, and Schecter, 160.
4. WE to John Warren, October 7, 1776, Warren Papers, MHS.
5. Thacher, Journal, September 20, 1776
6. James Thomas Flexner. *Young Hamilton: A Biography*, 33.
7. WE to John Warren, October 7, 1776, Warren Papers, MHS.
8. WE to John Warren, November 22, 1776, Warren Papers, MHS.
9. Commager and Morris, 841.
10. For a good description, see Chernow, *Washington*, 273.
11. Heath Papers, April 3, 1777, MHS.
12. Wilbur, 7.
13. Heath Papers, April 16, 1777, MHS.

Chapter Eleven: Trying Times
1. WE instructions, August 19, 1777, MSS Coll. AHMC Eustis, N-YHS.
2. Flexner, 222
3. Thacher, Journal, July 8, 1778, August 4, 1778.
4. Commager and Morris, 815.
5. Leavitt and Numbers, 5, 133. See also Fenn, 94.
6. Raphael, 140.
7. Ibid., 153.
8. Dr. Nathaniel Ames, Diary, DHS.
9. Mercy Scollay Papers, Cambridge Historical Society.
10. *Diary of Dr. Nathaniel Ames of Dedham, Massachusetts, 1758-1822.* March 30, April 8, 1775. DHS. Also for his discussion, Philbrick, *BH,* Notes on 101, 319.
11. *Diary of Dr. Nathaniel Ames of Dedham, Massachusetts, 1758-1822.* 100.
12. WE to Nathaniel Ames, August 26, 1778, DHS. See also Dr. Nathaniel Ames, Ledger Book, 1765-1822, August 26, 1778, DHS.

Chapter Twelve: Protests and Petitions
1. WE to John Warren, August 26, 1778, Eustis Papers, MHS.
2. For more on the campaign, see Christian M. McBurney, *The Rhode Island Campaign: The First French and American Operation in the Revolutionary War*, 148-169. Also, *The Boston Riot,* The Universal Magazine, vol. LXXIV, February 1784, 87.
3. Thacher, Journal, June 11, 1778.
4. J. Fish to WE, July 21, 1779, MSS Coll. AHMC Eustis, N-YHS.
5. WE to Josiah Bartlett, August 12, 1780, MSS Coll. AHMC Eustis, N-YHS.
6. WE to John Warren, October 5, 1779, MHS.
7. William Heath to WE, December 12, 1779, Heath Papers, MHS.
8. Thacher, Journal, May 1780, 189.

Chapter Thirteen: Treason of the Blackest Dye

1. "Treason of the blackest dye was yesterday discovered. General Arnold, who commanded at West Point, lost to every sentiment of honor, of public and private obligation, was about to deliver up that important fort into the hands of the enemy. Such an event must have given the American cause a deadly wound if not a fatal stab." General Nathanael Greene's Order of the Day, September 26, 1780, Commager and Morris, 755.
2. Chernow, *Washington.*, 377
3. Cook, *The Long Fuse*, 327-328.
4. Randall, *Benedict Arnold: Patriot and Traitor*, 514.
5. For details of the time at Robinson House, see Randall, 493, 519, 523, 534, 537, 549, 551, 552, 557.
6. Cook, 331.
7. Lonergan, 134.
8. For a detailed account, see Thacher, Journal, September 26, 1780. Also, Randall, 558, and Harr, *Dark Eagle*, 493.
9. Chernow, *Hamilton*, 141.
10. Van Doren, *Secret History of the American Revolution*, 348-349.
11. Thacher, Journal, October 15, 1782.

Chapter Fourteen: The World Turned Upside Down

1. WE to John Warren, October 6, 1780, Warren Papers, MHS.
2. Ibid., October 6, 1780.
3. Chernow, *Washington.*, 388-389, 400.
4. Thacher, Journal; Crompond, March 1781.
5. Saffron, 123
6. Thacher, Journal; Crompond, Journal, March 1781.
7. Thacher, Journal, April 12, 1781.
8. Thacher, Journal, April 30, 1781.
9. Chernow, *Washington.*, 399.
10. Ibid., 404.
11. Richard Borkow, *George Washington's Westchester Gamble*, 96.
12. Saffron, 142.
13. For details of Benjamin Eustis's duel see *The Scotch-Irish in America: Proceedings of the Scotch-Irish Congress.* Vol. 10, 247-48.
14. Saffron, 155.

Chapter Fifteen: Never Ending

1. William M. Fowler Jr., *American Crisis,* 15-17.
2. Orders, January 6, 1782, Heath Papers, MHS. See also Fowler, 54.
3. Saffron, 111.
4. Ibid., July 23, 1781, 203-204.
5. Notice, January 7, 1782, Eustis Papers, LOC.
6. WE to George Washington, Letters, online at founders.archives.gov.
7. WE to William Heath, March 3, 1782, Heath Papers, MHS.
8. Thacher, Journal, April 5 and May 30, 1782.

9. WE to Henry Knox, September 6, 1782, Knox Papers, MHS.

10. Petition to Congress from William Eustis and other officers, December 1782. Journals of the Continental Congress, 1774-89. Ed. Worthington C. Ford. Government Printing Office, 1904-37. Vol. 24, 291-293. LOC. "We have borne all that men can bear – our property is expended – our private resources are at an end, and our friends are wearied out and disgusted with our incessant applications. We, therefore, most seriously and earnestly beg that a supply of money be forwarded to the army as soon as possible. The uneasiness of the soldiers, for want of pay, is great and dangerous; any further experiments on their patience may have fatal effects."

11. Thacher, Journal, December 15 and 19, 1782.

12. Chernow, *Hamilton*, 1276.

13. Flexner, 406.

14. Anonymous letter to Hudson Highlands encampments, March 12, 1783, LOC.

15. Richard Beeman, *Plain, Honest Men,* 4-5.

16. Ibid., 6.

17. Flexner, 413.

18. See the organization's history, Collection of Society of Cincinnati, Massachusetts Chapter, online at societyofthecincinnati.org.

Chapter Sixteen: Moving On

1. Saffron, 250.

2. Chernow, *Washington,* 448.

3. Palmer, 32.

4. Alexander, 268.

5. Chernow, *Washington*, 451.

6. Palmer, 39.

7. Ian W Toll, *Six Frigates: The Epic History of the Founding of the U.S. Navy*, 19.

8. Palmer, 33.

9. Thacher, Journal, June 1, 1782. See also Mark Puls, *Samuel Adams: Father of the American Revolution*, 171.

PART II: FORGING A COUNTRY, 1783 - 1810

Chapter Seventeen: Shays' Rebellion

1. Boston Street Directory, 1785.

2. Eustis Papers, Letter, 1790, MHS.

3. Samuel Adams to Richard Henry Lee, 1785, LOC.

4. WE to William North, November 4, 1785, North Letters, Duane Collection, N-YHS. William North, originally from Maine, had moved to Boston with his mother. He was a captain in Colonel Henry Jackson's Sixteenth Massachusetts Regiment. After the war, he established a farm in Duanesburg, New York, and married Mary Duane, with whom he had six children. He was appointed as a Federalist to the United States Senate in 1798 to fill a vacancy. Baron von Steuben and North stayed in touch, and von Steuben bequeathed

his property to him. There is some speculation about a romantic relationship between North and von Steuben. Eustis and North, at the least, were very close friends.

6. Saffron, 247.
7. Massachusetts Resolves 1785, February Session, C134, March 17, 1786.
8. Knox Papers, February 3, 1785, MHS.
9. Palmer, 78. See also Richard Beeman, *Plain, Honest Men: The Making of the American Constitution*, 17, 18.
10. Palmer, 78.
11. Maier, 16.
12. Palmer, 81.
13. Knox Papers, February 1, 1787, MHS.

Chapter Eighteen: E Pluribus Unum

Appreciation and credit go to Pauline Maier for details about the Massachusetts convention from her book *Ratification: The People Debate the Constitution, 1787-1788.*

1. Beeman, 18. For further discussion, see Maier, 14.
2. Abigail Adams, March 2, 1788, cited in *Connecticut College Times,* June 16, 2011.
3. Palmer, 89.
4. Maier, 150.
5. *Massachusetts Gazette*, January 18, 1788.
6. John K. Alexander, *Samuel Adams: The Life of an American Revolutionary*, 284.

For coverage of the Constitutional Convention, see Maier, 159, 165, 166, 207.

7. Boston Town Records, 1789.
8. WE to William North, March 9, 1778, North Letters, Duane Collection, N-YHS.
9. WE to William N., June 24, 1789, North Letters, Duane Collection, N-YHS.
10. Lonergan, 195.
11. Chernow, *Washington.*, 608.
12. Boston Town Records, 1789. See also Alexander, 260.
13. George Washington, Diary, October 23, 1789.
14. Nathaniel Eustis to WE, December 9, 1789, Eustis Papers, LOC.

Chapter Nineteen: 1790s: A New Country

1. Jacqueline Barbara Carr, *After the Siege: A Social History of Boston, 1775-1800*, 202-210, 220.
2. Eustis Papers, April 22, 1790, LOC.
3. Commonwealth of Massachusetts Resolves, May 1791, No. 40.
4. WE to William North, July 14, 1791, North Letters., Duane Collection, N-YHS.
5. Dolan, 90-91.
6. WE to William North, July 14, 1791, North Letters, Duane Collection, N-YHS.
7. Ibid.

8. Cochran, 67.
9. Henry Langdon to WE, October 1791, Eustis Papers, MHS.
10. *American Apollo*, Vol. II, December 21, 1792.

Chapter Twenty: Striving Toward the New Century

1. Augmenting Washington's concerns about remaining neutral were fears about the welfare of the Marquis de Lafayette, who was actively involved protecting King Louis XVI. As Jacobin extremism grew, Lafayette seemed too moderate. He was denounced and fled for his life to Belgium, intending to escape to the United States. Captured in August 1792, before the Reign of Terror set in, he was imprisoned in Prussia, then transferred and chained to a wall in a prison in Olmütz, Moravia, now the western part of the Czech Republic.
2. Goodman, Paul. *The Democratic-Republicans of Massachusetts: Politics in a Young Republic*, 57.
3. WE to David Cobb, February 1794, Cobb Papers, MHS.
4. WE to David Cobb, March 2, 1794, Cobb Papers, MHS.
5. WE to David Cobb, March 10, 1794, Cobb Papers, MHS.
6. WE to David Cobb, March 16, 1794, Cobb Papers, MHS.
7. WE to David Cobb, March 30, 1794, Cobb Papers, MHS.
8. Ibid.
9. WE to David Cobb, April 6, 1794; WE to David Cobb, April 24, 1794, Cobb Papers, MHS.
10. WE to David Cobb, November 16, 1794, Cobb Papers, MHS.
11. WE to David Cobb, December 1, 1794, Cobb Papers, MHS.
12. *Columbian Centinel* , Boston, April 29, 1795.
13. Walter Muir Whitehill, *Boston: A Topographical History,* Ch. 4, 73-94.
14. Ellis, *Founding Brothers*, 121. See also 162-163 and 169-170.
15. Ibid., 186.
16. WE to David Cobb, January 29, 1795; February 2, 1795, Cobb Papers, MHS.
17. Boston City Directory, 1796.
18. WE to WN, October 15, 1799, North Letters, Duane Collection, N-YHS.

Chapter Twenty-One: Business ... and Burr

1. Aaron Burr to WE, October 4, 1777, Burr Papers, Box 1, Folder 1, MHS.
2. Aaron Burr to WE, November 30, 1796, Burr Papers, Box 1, Folder 1, MHS.
3. Aaron Burr to WE, June 12, 1797, Burr Papers, Box 1, Folder 1, MHS.
4. Aaron Burr to WE, July 16, 1797, Burr Papers, Box 1, Folder 1, MHS.
5. Nancy Isenberg, *Fallen Founder: The Life of Aaron Burr,* 239.
6. Ibid., 35.
7. Aaron Burr to WE, June 13, 1800, Burr Papers, Box 1, Folder 3, MHS. Two letters in the collection of the Massachusetts Historical Society are completely in cipher or code.
8. Eustis Papers, November 6, 1797, LOC.
9. WE to William North, October 15, 1799, North Letters, Duane Collection, N-YHS.

10. Eustis Papers, November 29, 1799, LOC.
11. Eustis Papers, December 28, 1799, LOC.
12. Boston Town Records, Vol. 31.
13. Mary Wollstonecraft, *Vindication of the Rights of Women,* Ch. 3.
14. Gordon S. Wood, *Empire of Liberty: A History of the Early Republic, 1789-1815,* 500.
15. Norman K. Risjord, *Jefferson's America: 1760-1815,* 182.
16. WE to William North, October 15, 1799, North Letters, Duane Collection, N-YHS.
17. WE to William North, February 16, 1798, North Letters, Duane Collection, N-YHS. See also Rep-Dem, 101.
18. Aaron Burr to WE, December 1800, Burr Papers, Box 1, Folder 4, MHS.

Chapter Twenty-Two: Election of 1800

1. Paul Goodman, *The Democratic-Republicans of Massachusetts: Politics in a Young Republic,* 100.
2. Ibid., 149.
3. May 13, 1801, Mary-Jo Kline, ed., *Political Correspondence & Public Papers of Aaron Burr,* I:579, 501.
4. David O. Stewart, *American Emperor: Aaron Burr's Challenge to Jefferson's America,* 25.
5. Isenberg, 217. Citing Burr to Eustis, January 16, 1801, Kline, Burr Papers, I:479, 490-91.
6. *Independent Chronicle*, October 27, 1800.
7. Goodman, 128.
8. Ibid., 105.
9. *Constitutional Telegraph*, November 8, 1800.
10. Henry Jackson to David Cobb, November 5 and 8, 1800, MHS.
11. WE to William North, September 25, 1801, North Letters, Duane Collection, N-YHS.
12. John Adams to Abigail Adams, Adams Letters, MHS.
13. Fisher Ames to Christopher Gore, December 29, 1800, Fisher Ames, *Works, Vol. I,* 289, MHS.
14. Aaron Burr to WE, August 10, 1800, MHS.
15. Aaron Burr to WE, January 26, 1801, MHS. See also Isenberg, 236.
16. For a discussion about the condition of the interior of the country, see Stephen E. Ambrose, *Undaunted Courage: The Pioneering First Mission to Explore America's Wild Frontier,* 39-40.
17. For societal changes, see Gordon S. Wood, *Empire of Liberty, A History of the Early Republic, 1789-1815,* 303, 308.
18. John Adams to William Tudor, December 13, 1800, founders.archives.gov.

Chapter Twenty-Three: A Capital Life

Descriptions about the early settlement of Washington City and about the early days of Congress are in James Young's book, *The Washington Community 1800-1828,* 50–87.

1. Aaron Burr to WE, April 1801, Burr papers, MHS.
2. WE to William North, September 25, 1801, North Letters, Duane Collection, N-YHS.
3. Catherine Allgor, *A Perfect Union: Dolley Madison and the Creation of the American Nation*, 46.
4. For the description of a singular city built for politics alone, see Jay Winik, *The Great Upheaval: American and the Birth of the Modern World, 1788-1800*, 578. See also James Sterling Young, *The Washington Community 1800-1828*, 44.
5. Young, 41.
6. Thomas Fleming, *The Intimate Lives of the Founding Fathers*, 372.
7. Richard Brookhiser, *Gentleman Revolutionary: Gouverneur Morris – The Rake Who Wrote the Constitution*, 162.
8. Young, 87.
9. Ibid., 77.
10. Ibid., 72.
11. Historical Society of Washington, DC, formerly Columbia Historical Society (www.dchistory.org). Also, Thomas Froncek, ed., *The City of Washington: An Illustrated History*.
12. Ibid., 150.
13. Ron Chernow, *Alexander Hamilton,* 314.
14. Winik, 470.
15. For a discussion about residents and boarding houses, see Young, 100-101.
16. Ibid., 97. For further information about activity in Congress, 94-95.
17. Ibid., 111. See also Wood, 307.
18. WE to William North, September 25, 1801, North Letters, Duane Collection, N-YHS.
19. Ibid., September 25, 1801.

Chapter Twenty-Four: Whiskey and Reelection

1. Samuel Adams to Thomas Jefferson, November 18, 1801, founders.archives.gov.
2. Eustis Papers, February 21, 1802, LOC.
3. David Townsend to WE, March 18, 1802, Eustis Papers, LOC.
4. Henry Jackson to WE, March 28, 1802, Eustis Papers, LOC.
5. WE to William North, February 26, 1803, North Letters, Duane Collection, N-YHS.
6. Henry Dearborn to J. Bowdoin, March 3, 1802, *Sibley's Harvard Graduates*, 76.
7. See pbs.org/wgbh/amex/duel/peopleevents/pande14.html.
8. Thomas Jefferson to Granger, August 15, 1802, www.founders.archives.gov.
9. T. Law to WE in Boston, August 1802, Eustis Papers, LOC.
10. Alan Taylor,. *The Civil War of 1812*, 342.
11. Jacob Eustis to WE, October 30, 1802, Eustis Papers, LOC. See also Paul Goodman, *The Democratic-Republicans of Massachusetts: Politics in a*

Young Republic, 147.
12. Boston Town Records
13. John Quincy Adams, *Writings*, W.C. Ford, III, ed., 1914, 10.
14. Susan Binney to WE, December 9, 1802, Eustis Papers, reel 1, LOC.
15. Ibid., LOC.
16. Jacob Eustis to WE, December 8, 1802, Eustis Papers, LOC.
17. WE to William North, January 26, 1803, North Letters, Duane Collection, N-YHS.
18. Jacob Eustis to WE, December 19, 1802, Eustis Papers, LOC.
19. Joseph Wheaton to WE, March 13, 1802, Eustis Papers, LOC.
20. Jacob Eustis to WE, December 29, 1802, LOC.
21. Jacob Eustis to WE, December 27, 1802, LOC.
22. Jacob Eustis to WE, December 30, 1802, February 10, 1803, and February 20, 1803, LOC.
23. Jacob Eustis to WE, December 25, 1802, Ibid., LOC.
24. WE to Jacob Eustis, January 9, 1804, and January 11, 1804, LOC.
25. William Benemann, *Male-Male Intimacy in Early America: Beyond Romantic Friendships*, 166.
26. Isenberg, 234.
27. Lynn Cheney, *James Madison: A Life Reconsidered,* 315.
28. Gordon S. Wood, *Empire of Liberty: A History of the Early Republic, 1789-1815*, 300. For further descriptions about the dinners, see Wood, 128, 169.

Chapter Twenty-Five: Beyond Measure

1. WE to William North, January 26, 1803, North Letters, Duane Collection, N-YHS.
2. Stephen E. Ambrose, *Undaunted Courage: The Pioneering First Mission to Explore America's Wild Frontier*, 69.
3. Ibid., 90.
4. Allgor, 55.
5. Invitation, Thomas Jefferson to WE, October 19, 1803, MHS.
6. Ambrose, 82.
7. Elbridge Gerry to WE, October 24, 1803, MHS.
8. Joseph Sullivan to WE, November 17, 1803, MHS.
9. WE to Aaron Burr, 11/12/03, Special Collections, Louisiana State University.
10. Manasseh Cutler to Fitch Poole, December 30, 1803, *Sibley's Harvard Graduates,* Vol XVIII – 1772-1774, 76.
11. Eustis Papers, January 22, 1804, LOC.
12. WE to Jacob Eustis, March 9, 1804, Eustis Papers, LOC.
13. WE to Jacob Eustis, March 21, 1804, Eustis Papers, LOC.
14. Eustis Papers, Lexington Historical Society, 102.
15. Dueling evolved as a means of resolving disputes between individual members of the gentry beginning with the medieval practice of "judicial combat." Duels were governed by principles that had changed little over the centuries. A version of the code widely adopted in America was the Clonmel

Code, a set of twenty-six specific rules that were established in 1777. These rules specified how challenges were to be made, how many shots must be fired for each type of offense, how weapons and distances were chosen, and so on. Despite public disapproval of duels by the major political figures in America, including Washington and Franklin, they still remained a last resort to uphold one's honor.

16. Isenberg, 263.
17. Although Burr was not impeached while vice president, it isn't as if impeachments never occurred. Early in 1803, the House of Representatives appointed William Eustis to the committee conducting impeachment proceedings against Judge John Pickering—the first impeached official who was actually convicted. Years before, in April 1795, Pickering had been appointed to the Federal District Court of New Hampshire by President George Washington—the result of political infighting and a compromise to get him off the New Hampshire Supreme Court for negligence of duties. Serious problems began in 1800 when Pickering stopped performing his job at the federal court. By 1803, it was generally thought he was insane.
18. WE to William North, August 15, 1804, North Letters, Duane Collection, N-YHS; WE to Thomas Jefferson, October 3, 1804, LOC.
19. Lawrence Park, *Gilbert Stuart: An Illustrated Descriptive List of His Work*, Vol. 1, 1926.

Chapter Twenty-Six: Uncertainties of Life

1. WE to William North, January 14, 1806, North Letters, Duane Collection, N-YHS.
2. WE to Thomas Jefferson, June 1805, Jefferson Papers, LOC.
3. Boston Directory, 1806.
4. WE to William North, January 14, 1806, North Letters, Duane Collection, N-YHS.
5. John B Blake, *Benjamin Waterhouse and the Introduction of Vaccination: A Reappraisal*, 56-57.
6. Ibid., 67.
7. WE to William North, November 2, 1806, North Letters, Duane Collection, N-YHS.
8. Caners Papers, June 25, 1805, Shirley-Eustis House Association.
9. Stephen E. Ambrose, *Undaunted Courage: The Pioneering First Mission to Explore America's Wild Frontier*, 448, 456, 473.
10. David O. Stewart, *American Emperor: Aaron Burr's Challenge to Jefferson's America*, 131.
11. Andro Linklater, *An Artist in Treason: The Extraordinary Double Life of General James Wilkinson*, 260.
12. Henry Dearborn to WE, April 5, 1807, MHS.
13. *Boston Gazette*, April 16, 1807.
14. WE to William North, July 19, 1807, North Letters, Duane Collection, N-YHS.
15. For details about the trial, see Linklater, 268, 273.

16. Orchard Cook to WE, December 24, 1807. See also John Brazer to WE, December 13, 1807, LOC.

Chapter Twenty-Seven: Preparations for War

1. WE to William North, April 26, 1807, North Letters, Duane Collection, N-YHS.
2. Ian W. Toll, *Six Frigates: The Epic History of the Founding of the U.S. Navy*, 273.
3. Ibid., 305.
4. WE to William North, April 26, 1807, North Letters, Duane Collection, N-YHS.
5. WE to William North, July 19, 1807, North Letters, Duane Collection, N-YHS.
6. Ibid., July 19, 1807.
7. WE to Nicolas Gilman, November 29, 1807, Ch. C.1.135, BPL.
8. Alan Taylor, *The Civil War of 1812*, 117.
9. Toll, 31.
10. Ibid., 310.
11. Stephen Budiansky, *Perilous Fight: America's Intrepid War with Britain on the High Seas, 1812-1815*, 8.
12. WE to Nicolas Gilman, January 12, 1808, Ch. C.7.49, BPL.
13. WE to Nicolas Gilman, March 8, 1808, Ch. B.2.46, BPL.
14. WE to Henry Dearborn, April 10, 1808, Ch. C.7.50, BPL.
15. WE to Henry Dearborn, April 29, 1808, Mss. Col. AHMC, N-YHS. William Eustis's nephew, Abraham Eustis, followed the family tradition of serving in the artillery. By 1803, he was captain of light artillery in the militia. Abraham was the only child of William's brother, Abraham, born some five months after his father died.
16. Ibid.
17. Eustis Papers, March 21, 1809, LOC.
18. Federal Census, 1810.
19. Catherine Allgor, *A Perfect Union: Dolley Madison and the Creation of the American Nation*, 175.

Chapter Twenty-Eight: The War Office

1. Catherine Allgor, *A Perfect Union: Dolley Madison and the Creation of the American Nation*, 124.
2. WE to William North, January 4, 1809, North Letters, Duane Collection, N-YHS.
3. Budiansky, 89.
4. Allgor, 137. For further references to Dolley Madison, see 142, citing Margaret Bayard Smith's letter, March 8, 1809.
5. *Family Letters of Mrs. Samuel Harrison Smith (Margaret Bayard)*, March 1809, 58.
6. Gaillard Hunt, ed. *First Forty Years of Washington Society.*
7. WE to William North, March 3, 1809, North Letters, Duane Collection, N-YHS.

8. WE to James Madison, March 7, 1809, March 18, 1809, Madison Papers, LOC.
9. WE to William North, March 19, 1809, North Letters, Duane Collection, N-YHS.
10. *Independent Chronicle & Boston Patriot*, March 28, 1809.
11. Thomas Jefferson to WE, October 6, 1809, MHS.
12. Thomas Fleming, *The Intimate Lives of the Founding Fathers,* 376.
13. Allgor, 179. An appealing fictional characterization of Eustis appears in author David Nevin's historical novel, *1812,* at one of Dolley Madison's Wednesday evenings, describing him working the room, pausing to whisper a joke to someone, patting backs, and laughing as he moves to Madison's side. David Nevin, *1812*, 49.
14. Stephen E. Ambrose, *Undaunted Courage: The Pioneering First Mission to Explore America's Wild Frontier*, 505.
15. Ibid., 510-511, citing Clarence E. Carter, ed., The Territorial Papers of the United States, vol. XIV; The Territory of Louisiana – Missouri 1806-1814, Washington, D.C.: Government Printing Office, 1949, 285-86.
16. Ambrose, 512-513.
17. Richard Dillon, *Meriwether Lewis*, 331. Also see Ambrose, 520.
18. Ibid., 345.

Chapter Twenty-Nine: Secretary of War

1. Garry Wills, *James Madison*, 66.
2. Toll, 331.
3. Wood, 65.
4. Toll, 285.
5. Budiansky, 49.
6. *American & Commercial Daily Advertiser*, May 15, 1809.
7. Allgor, 148.
8. For a discussion of conditions, see Linklater, 284-289.
9. James Wilkinson to WE, Ibid., 285.
10. WE to James Wilkinson, Ibid., 285.
11. Alan Taylor, *The Civil War of 1812*, 281.
12. James Madison to WE, 1809, Madison Papers, LOC.
13. *Boston Gazette*, February 15, 1810.
14. James Wilkinson to WE, July 14, 1810, Madison Papers, LOC.
15. WE to James Madison, July 16, 1810, Madison Papers, LOC.
16. Taylor, 126.
17. Langguth, A.J., *Union 1812: The Americans Who Fought the Second War of Independence*, 61.
18. Ibid., 30.
19. WE to James Madison, June 11, 1810, Madison papers, LOC.
20. Langguth, 167.
21. WE to James Madison, August 19, 1810, Madison Papers, LOC.
22. James Madison to WE, July 29, 1810, Madison Papers, LOC.
23. WE to James Madison, August 26, 1810, WE to James Madison, September 7, 1810, WE to James Madison, September 14, 1810,

founders.archives.gov.

24. James Madison to WE, August 26, 1810, Madison Papers, LOC.

Chapter Thirty: A Fine Sensible Woman

1. *Portsmouth Oracle*, September 29, 1810.
2. Caroline Langdon to WE, 1803, Eustis Papers, MHS.
3. Abraham Eustis to WE, Eustis Papers, 1810, MHS. Abraham Eustis wrote to his uncle often. Shortly after the wedding, he was more serious and passed along his frustrations with his temporary command and his military assignment, Fort Wolcott's preparations. He asked if his uncle knew about the deficiency of the barracks and reported that the post had no grape or canister shot of any kind. Abraham Eustis to WE, October 24, 1811, MS. Am. 158, BPL.
4. William and Caroline's cake likely was made in the Langdon kitchen or could have been purchased locally. In 1810, a French pastry maker, M. Labatut, opened a confectionery shop in Portsmouth, a town with about five thousand inhabitants and large enough to support his business. He offered "the best jelly of all kinds, as well as wedding cakes and refreshments in general." *Portsmouth Oracle,* November 24, 1810.
5. Laurel Thatcher Ulrich, *A Midwife's Tale: The Life of Martha Ballard Based on Her Diary, 1785-1812,* 142.
6. WE to John Langdon, December 11, 1810, Portsmouth Athenaeum.
7. Mary Lee Mann, ed. *A Yankee Jeffersonian: Selections from the Diary and Letters of William Lee of Massachusetts, Written from 1796 to 1840,* 130.
8. Eustis Papers, Lexington Historical Society, 105.
9. Thomas A Foster, *Sex and the Eighteenth-Century Man: Massachusetts and the History of Sexuality in America*, 126.
10. Ibid., 109.
11. Megan Marshall, *The Peabody Sisters*, 26. Some women found the bonds of matrimony difficult, as did Grace Growden Galloway, c. 1760, when she wrote a poem: "Never get tyed to a Man / for when once you are Yoked / 'Tis all a Mere Joke / of seeing your freedom again." Cited in Carol Berkin, *Revolutionary Women in the Struggle for America's Independence.* (New York, Alfred A. Knopf, 2005), 94.
12. Sarah Langdon's portrait graces the staircase landing in the John Langdon House in Portsmouth, now owned by Historic New England and open seasonally to the public.
13. Seacoast.com/framers/wlangdon/html.
14. William Benemann, *Male-Male Intimacy in Early America: Beyond Romantic Friendships,* 107.
15. Ibid., 102-3. Benemann writes that the two men, Walker and North, developed a romantic relationship while in von Steuben's household or quarters, and that it is inaccurate to assume that all men wrote to each other with the deep affection occasionally found in letters.
16. Ibid., 107-108.

17. Ibid., 114. As Benemann notes, in 1789, less than two years into his marriage, North wrote to von Steuben: "My wife is the best Woman possible, my boy is good but I am not happy ... I shall come to New York, kiss you & Ben, go to Boston [to] comfort my old mother & return here to drudge on in getting my living."
18. Ibid., 116.
19. WE to William North, September 25, 1801, North Letters, Duane Collection, N-YHS.
20. WE to William North, February 26, 1803, North Letters, Duane Collection, N-YHS.

PART III: FULFILLMENT, 1810 - 1825

Chapter Thirty-One: Miscalculations
1. WE to James Madison, August 13, 1811, Madison papers, LOC.
2. Andro Linklater, *An Artist in Treason: The Extraordinary Double Life of General James Wilkinson*, 91. Linklater's account of the Wilkinson trial on pages 292-295 are helpful in understanding what Eustis was up against with this general.
3. Peter Gansevoort to WE, Madison Papers, LOC.
4. WE to James Madison, September 9, 1811, Madison Papers, LOC.
5. WE to James Madison, Madison Papers, LOC.
6. WE to James Madison, Madison Papers, LOC.
7. Eustis Papers, Shirley-Eustis House.
8. Eustis Papers, October 8, 1811, LOC.
9. Madison Papers, August 21, 1811, LOC. Also see Walter R. Borneman, *1812: The War That Forged a Nation*, 33.
10. For discussion about Harrison's activities, see A.J. Langguth, *Union 1812: The Americans Who Fought the Second War of Independence*, 170. Also helpful was Garry Wills's *James Madison*, 92-98, and David S. and Jeanne T. Heidler's *Henry Clay: The Essential American,* 89.
11. Walter Bournemn, *1812: The War That Forged a Nation*, 28.
12. Toll, 324.
13. Young, 182.
14. Gordon S. Wood, *Empire of Liberty, A History of the Early Republic, 1789-1815,* 672.
15. Stephen Budiansky, *Perilous Fight: America's Intrepid War with Britain on the High Seas, 1812-1815*, 95.
16. Taylor, 56.
17. WE to James Madison, April 9, 1812, Madison papers, LOC. www.founders.archives.com.
18. WE to Joseph Bloomfield, May 27, 1812, MHS.
19. WE to James Madison, April 1, 1812, Madison/Eustis Letters, LOC. Also, WE to JM, March 27, 1812, www.founders.archives.com.
20. Abner Lacock to WE, April 7, 1812, Madison Papers, LOC.

Chapter Thirty-Two: Rally Round Our Standard

1. Stephen Budiansky, *Perilous Fight: America's Intrepid War with Britain on the High Seas, 1812-1815*, 113. For campaign, see Budiansky's prologue, *x*.
2. David S. and Jeanne T. Heidler, *Henry Clay: The Essential American*, 95-99.
3. Wood, 674.
4. A.J. Langguth, *Union 1812: The Americans Who Fought the Second War of Independence,* 174.
5. Borneman, 52.
6. Linklater, 298.
7. Langguth, 174.
8. Ibid., June 18, 1812, 177.
9. Ibid., July 9, 1812, 178.
10. Garry Wills. *James Madison*, 133-134.
11. Langguth, 182.
12. S. B. Young to WE, July 21, 1812, Dearborn Papers, MHS.
13. Colonel David Fitz-Enz, USA, Ret., *Hacks, Sycophants, Adventurers & Heroes: Madison's Commanders in the War of 1812*, 98. See also Wills, 100.
14. William Hull to WE, August 7, 1812, Hull Collection, Clarke Historical Library, Central Michigan University.
15. WE to William Hull, August 12, 1812, Mss. Coll. AHMC Eustis, N-YHS.
16. Taylor, 169. See also Langguth, 192.
17. WE to James Madison, September 5, 1812, Madison Papers, LC.
18. WE to Henry Dearborn, September 8, 1812, Dearborn Papers, MHS.
19. William Hull to WE, Hull Collection, Clarke Historical Library, Central Michigan University.
20. Henry Clay to James Monroe, August 12, 1812. Cited in Taylor, 169. See also David and Jeanne Heidler, *Henry Clay: The Essential American.*
21. Ibid.
22. Wills, 104.

Chapter Thirty-Three: Difficulties Peculiarly Arduous

1. *Niles Weekly Register,* Baltimore, September 1, 1812.
2. Papers of James and Dolley Madison, Cutts Collection, LOC.
3. Allgor, 292.
4. WE to James Madison, October 29, 1812, Madison Papers, LOC.
5. Letters to the Secretary of War, vol. 49, internet archives through openlibrary.org and archive.org.
6. H. Johnson to WE, November 6, 1812, Eustis Papers, LOC.
7. *Whig Chronicle*, October 18, 1812.
8. Zebulon Pike to WE, November 11, 1812, Ch. A.9.37, BPPL.
9. Wills, 106.
10. Langguth, 206.
11. Wills, 111.
12. Ibid., 116.
13. Channing, 459.

14. Heidler, 100-101.

15. Eustis wrote his letter of resignation to President Madison in December. He hoped that "some other citizen might be selected, possessing greater military knowledge, and commanding in a higher degree the public confidence."

16. James Madison to WE, December 4, 1812, Madison Papers, LOC.

17. Jonathan Roberts to W. Jones, Eustis Papers, LOC.

18. Wills, 117.

19. Cited in Allgor, 329, Letters of Dolley Madison to Hannah Gallatin.

20. Anonymous to A. Cutts, January 4, 1813, Papers of James and Dolley Madison, Cutts Collection, LOC.

21. James Grant Forbes and William Hull, *Report of the Trial of Brigadier General William Hull Commanding the Northwestern Army of the United States by Court Martial held at Albany on January 30, 1814,* 3-5, appendix.

22. Nicole Eustace, *1812: War and the Passions of Patriotism,* 46.

23. Hugh Howard, *Mr. and Mrs. Madison's War: America's First Couple and the Second War of Independence,* 295. See also Eustace, 74.

Chapter Thirty-Four: Washington Burning

1. *Building Old Cambridge: Architecture and Development* (MIT Press, 2016). Courtesy of the Cambridge Historical Commission. See also Jenks Letters, Cambridge Historical Society.

2. WE to William North, May 27, 1813, North Letters, Duane Collection, N-YHS.

3. *Boston Gazette,* May 6, 1813.

4. Taylor, 415.

5. Howard, 30.

6. WE to James Madison, November 7, 1813, Madison Papers, LOC.

7. James Madison to WE, November 12, 1813, Madison Papers, LOC.

8. WE to James Madison, November 21, 1813, Madison Papers, LOC.

9. Budiansky, 252.

10. WE to James Madison, January 1, 1814, Madison Papers, LOC.

11. Publication describing this event is available at Lexington Historical Society.

12. A very thorough description can be found in Walter R Borneman, *1812: The War That Forged a Nation,* 220–227.

13. WE to William North, September 5, 1814, North Letters, Duane Collection, N-YHS.

14. John Greaton to WE, November 18, 1814, and December 17, 1814, Eustis Papers, Reel 2, LOC.

Chapter Thirty-Five: O Say Can You See

1. WE to William North, September 5, 1814, North Letters, Duane Collection, N-YHS.

2. Heidler, 123. See also Toll, 455.

3. Quoted in *National Intelligencer,* November 15, 1814, Eustis Papers, Reel 2, LOC.

4. JBC to WE, November 20, 1814, Eustis Papers, Reel 2, LOC.

5. Borneman, 254.

6. Richard Cutts to WE, December 14, 1814, Eustis Papers, Reel 2, LOC.
7. James Madison to WE, December 15, 1814, Eustis Papers, Reel 2, LOC. See also Madison Papers.
8. WE to James Madison, December 21, 1814, Eustis Papers, Reel 2, LOC.
9. C. Cutts to WE, December 17, 1814, Eustis Papers, Reel 2, LOC.
10. WE to James Madison, December 29, 1814, Eustis Papers, Reel 2, LOC.
11. WE to William North, 1799, North Letters, Duane Collection, N-YHS.
12. WE to James Madison, February 14, 1815, Madison Papers, LOC.

Chapter Thirty-Six: A New Europe

1. Thomson, David. *Europe Since Napoleon*. Second Edition. (New York: Alfred A. Knopf, 1962). 71-74.
2. WE to James Madison, January 14, 1815, Madison Papers, LOC.
3. WE to JM, Ibid.
4. WE to James Madison, March 19, 1815, Madison Papers, LOC.
5. WE to James Madison, May 2, 1815, Madison Papers, LOC.
6. WE to JM, Ibid.
7. Caroline Langdon Eustis to Dolley Madison, May 11, 1815, Haven-Pugh Letter Collection, 6 vol., thehavensisters.com.
8. For the full story of Mme. Bonaparte, see Carol Berkin's *Wondrous Beauty: The Life and Adventures of Elizabeth Patterson Bonaparte*, 80.
9. Caroline Langdon Eustis to Dolley Madison, May 11, 1815, Haven-Pugh Letter Collection, 6 vol., thehavensisters.com.
10. WE to William North, June 10, 1815, North Letters, Duane Collection, N-YHS.
11. Eustis, Diary, MHS.
12. Charles Morris, *Autobiography of Commodore Charles Morris, U. S. Navy*, 83-84.
13. Log Book for USS *Congress,* Entry 118, Vol. 3, Logs of US Ships and Stations, 1801-1947.

Chapter Thirty-Seven: Life on the Edge of Royalty

1. Log Book for USS *Congress,* Entry 118, Vol. 3, Logs of US Ships and Stations, 1801-1947.
2. WE to Henry Langdon, October 21, 1815, Eustis Letters, MHS.
3. WE to James Madison, August 18, 1815, Madison Papers, LOC.
4. Ibid., Madison Papers, LOC.
5. WE to James Madison, August 10, 1815, Madison Papers, LOC.
6. WE to James Madison, August 18, 1815, Madison Papers, LOC.
7. WE to Jacob Eustis, September 1815, Eustis Papers, LOC.
8. WE Diary, Eustis Papers, MHS. The costliest food items in the Eustis household were meat, wine, and spirits. Flour and bread were next. Less expensive were vegetables, fruit, eggs, and butter; with coffee, tea, spices, and cheese, acquired through expansive Dutch markets, much less expensive than in the United States.
9. WE to James Madison, August 18, 1815, Madison Papers, LOC.

10. Caroline Langdon Eustis to Dolley Madison, September 9, 1815, MHS.
11. WE to James Madison, October 1815, Madison Papers, LOC.
13. WE to William North, North Letters, Duane Collection, N-YHS.
14. Sylvanus Bourne to WE, January 6, 1816, Eustis Papers, Reel 2, LOC.
15. WE to James Madison, January 19, 1816, Eustis Papers, Reel 2, LOC.
16. WE to James Madison, April 27, 1816, Eustis Papers, Reel 2, LOC.
17. WE to William North, January 11, 1816, North Letters, Duane Collection, N-YHS.
18. James Madison to WE, May 21, 1816, Eustis Papers, Reel 2, LOC.
19. Dolley Madison to Caroline Langdon Eustis, May 17, 1816, MHS.

Chapter Thirty-Eight: A Pilgrimage to Paris
1. Eustis Papers, MHS.
2. David McCullough, *John Adams*, 303.
3. Eustis Papers, MHS.
4. Cristin O'Keefe Aptowicz, *Dr. Mutter's Marvels: A True Tale of Intrigue and Innovation at the Dawn of Modern Medicine*, 13.
5. WE to William North, June 21, 1816, North Letters, Duane Collection, N-YHS.
6. WE to William North, Ibid. They took side trips to Versailles, Chateau de Malmaison, Chateau de St. Cloud, and Basilique Saint-Denis where all French kings were entombed. They walked in the Jardins des Tuileries, with its *allées* of graveled walks and chestnut trees, statues, fountains, and the large orangery housing the royal citrus trees.
7. Caroline Langdon Eustis to Dolley Madison, June 8, 1816, Eustis Letters, Reel 2, LOC.
8. WE to William North, June 21, 1816, North Letters, Duane Collection, N-YHS.
9. Eustis Diary, MHS.
10. Ibid. Morgan escorted them to more gardens and to see a painting by the famous French artist Jacques-Louis David. The artist had painted somewhat fictional historical scenes featuring Napoleon. David's huge 1807 classical painting of the "Coronation of the Emperor Napoleon I and Coronation of Empress Josephine" was exhibited in the Louvre. David, knowing that with the return of Bourbon royalty he would be in trouble as a former revolutionary, now lived in Brussels. The Eustises may have seen his smaller paintings displayed there.
11. Ibid., MHS.
12. WE to William North, June 21, 1816, North Letters, Duane Collection, N-YHS.
13. For general information about Lafayette, see Harlow Giles Unger, *Lafayette*.
14. Gray to WE, August 31, 1817, Eustis papers, Reel 2, LOC.
15. Eustis Collection, Shirley-Eustis House, October 25, 1816.
16. Caroline Langdon Eustis to Dolley Madison, October 6, 1816, Eustis Papers, MHS.
17. WE to James Monroe, October 28, 1816, Eustis papers, Reel 2, LOC, and WE to James Monroe, October 29, 1816, Eustis Letters, N-YHS.
18. Caroline Langdon Eustis to Dolley Madison, October 6, 1816, Eustis Papers,

MHS.

19. Anne Eustis Langdon to WE, November 18, 1816, Eustis Papers, MHS.
20. WE to Sylvanus Bourne, October 15, 1816, Eustis Papers, N-YHS.
21. James Monroe to WE, September 24, 1816, MHS.
22. Lafayette to WE, December 1, 1816, MHS.
23. WE to William North, January 11, 1816, North Letters, Duane Collection, N-YHS.

Chapter Thirty-Nine: Frustrations, Furniture, and France

1. Walter Lord. *The Dawn's Early Light*, 40.
2. Kate Williams, *Becoming Queen Victoria: The Tragic Death of Princess Charlotte and The Unexpected Rise of Britain's Greatest Monarch*, 143.
3. WE to Joshua Clebborn, February 25, 1817, and February 27, 1817, Eustis Papers, Reel 2, LOC.
4. Eustis Papers, February 20, 1817, MHS.
5. James Madison to WE, March 1817, Madison Papers, LOC.
6. James Madison to WE, March 1817, Madison Papers, LOC.
7. W. Gray to WE, August 31, 1817, Eustis Papers, Reel 2, LOC.
8. Thomas Aspinwall to WE, March 13, 1817, Eustis Papers, Reel 2, LOC.
9. WE to James Madison, September 13, 1817, Madison Papers, LOC.
10. Joshua Clebborn to WE, July 5, 1817, Eustis Papers, Reel 2, LOC.
11. Joshua Clebborn to WE, July15, 1817, Eustis Papers, Reel 2, LOC.
12. Albert Gallatin to WE, July 11, 1817, and July 23, 1817, Eustis Papers, Reel 2, LOC.
13. Albert Gallatin to WE, October 9, 1817, Eustis Papers, Reel 2, LOC.
14. WE to James Madison, September 13, 1817, Eustis Papers, Reel 2, LOC.
15. JAS to WE, November 6, 1817, Eustis Papers, Reel 2, LOC.
16. Eustis Diary, MHS. One lot contained a looking glass, three parcels of china, three bundles of carpets, two boxes of wine and, surprisingly, one box of cheese. In a bundle were bed linens, clothes, books and pictures. Another collection at The Hague, wrapped and ready to go, included a boxed large looking glass and a crate containing "marbles" for two pier tables. There was also a secretary, a round table, and two dozen chairs. In the middle of this clearing and packing, the Duke of Kent exchanged furniture with them. A dozen chairs with green striped plush upholstery was traded for the Eustises' red ones, evidently a color more to the duke's taste. A pair of the duke's card tables followed his chairs into the Eustis household. Today, there are two card tables noted as formerly owned by the duke; one in the collection of the Langdon House in Portsmouth, New Hampshire, and one at Shirley Place, the Eustis house near Boston, Massachusetts.
17. Eustis Diary, MHS.
18. John Quincy Adams to WE, November 8, 1817, Eustis Papers, Reel 2, LOC.
19. For Appleton's correspondence: J. J. Appleton to WE, October 22, 1817, JJA to WE, October 27, 1817, JJA to WE, November 21, 1817, Eustis Papers, Reel 2, LOC
20. Albert Gallatin to WE, December 5, 1817, Eustis Papers, Reel 2, LOC.

21. WE to John Quincy Adams, December 13, 1817, and WE to John Quincy Adams, December 24, 1817, Eustis Papers, Reel 2, LOC.
22. WE to Thomas Aspinwall, April 16, 1818, Eustis Papers, Reel 2, LOC.
23. For departure activities, see Eustis Papers, MHS.
24. *Niles Register*, March 7, 1818.
25. William Eustis Langdon to WE, March 31, 1818, Eustis Papers, Portsmouth Athenaeum. See also A. Hill to WE, April 11, 1818, Eustis Papers, MHS.
26. Thomas Aspinwall was appointed by Madison in 1816 and served the longest of any consul in London. He was finally recalled by Franklin Pierce in 1854.
27. Thomas Aspinwall to WE, February 1, 1819, Mss. Acc. 754, BPL.

Chapter Forty: Shirley Place
1. *American Beacon*, Norfolk, Virginia, July 23, 1818, *Columbian Centinel*, July 31, 1818, and the *Boston Daily Advertiser,* August 1, 1818.
2. Among the tenants were a blacksmith, a soapstone workshop, a ship joiner, a house wright, merchant Benjamin Thompson's office, and Samuel Spear's boarding house.
3. WE to John Adams, August 10, 1818, Adams Papers, Founders online documents/Adams/99-02-02-6957, MHS.
4. The weekly cost for each full boarder was fourteen dollars; a parlor and a separate table in the dining room with five more candles could be added for another fourteen dollars, and there was an additional charge of three dollars if a fire was desired in their bedroom. Guests for dinner would pay one dollar each, and a guest for tea was charged twenty-five cents.
5. James Madison to Isaac Winston III, December 3, 1818, MS 2 M2655a, Virginia Historical Society.
6. James Madison to James Monroe, December 11, 1881, Papers of James Monroe, LOC.
7. WE to James Madison, December 27, 1818, James Madison Papers, LOC
8. James Madison to WE, Williamsburg, January 25, 1819, Eustis Papers, MHS.
9. William North to WE, May 21, 1819, Eustis Papers, MHS.
10. Diary, June 1819, Eustis Papers, MHS.
11. James Magee to WE, July 1, 1819, Eustis Papers, LOC.
12. Papers, Lexington Historical Society, 106.
13. WE to William North, February 16, 1798, Eustis Papers, N-YHS. See also Paul Goodman, *The Democratic-Republicans of Massachusetts: Politics in a Young Republic,* 101.
14. WE to Tristram Barnard, July 25, 1819, Smith-Carter Papers, MHS.
15. Tristram Barnard to WE, July 29, 1819, Mss. Acc. 750, BPL.
16. Henry S. Langdon to WE, August 3, 1819, Mss. Acc. 749, BPL.
17. For descriptions of settling into Shirley Place: WE to Tristram Barnard, September 5, 1819, Smith-Carter Papers, MHS.
18. WE to Tristram Barnard, October 31, 1819, Smith-Carter Papers, MHS.
19. WE to Tristram Barnard, December 5, 1819, Smith-Carter Papers, MHS.

Chapter Forty-One: Congressman Redux: The Missouri Question

1. Invaluable background for understanding the political situation and the U. S. Congress at this time is *Henry Clay: The Essential American* by David S. and Jeanne T. Heidler, 146-151.
2. *Columbian Centinel*, December 4, 1819.
3. WE to Tristram Barnard, December 5, 1819, Smith-Carter papers, MHS.
4. This imaginary demarcation line was named for two British surveyors, Charles Mason and Jeremiah Dixon, who marked out the boundary between Pennsylvania and Maryland.
5. WE to Tristram Barnard, May 20, 1820, Smith-Carter papers, MHS.
6. *Niles Weekly Register,* September 1820.
7. James Sterling Young, *The Washington Community 1800-1828,* 28, 31.
8. Annals 37:635-38, House of Representatives, December 12, 1820.
9. Annals 37, House of Representatives, January 24, 1821.
10. WE to J. Austin, January 28, 1821, Mss. Coll. AHMC Eustis, N-YHS.
11. WE to Tristram Barnard, January 30, 1821, Smith-Carter Papers, MHS.
12. *American Beacon and Norfolk Daily Advertiser*, December 18, 1820.
13. WE to Tristram Barnard, March 5, 1821, Smith-Carter Papers, MHS.
14. WE to Tristram Barnard, November 13, 1821, Smith-Carter Papers, MHS.
15. Boston Residence Directory, 1822.
16. Young, 223-226.
17. Young, 289, citing Adams Memoirs, IV, 279-80, 509.

Chapter Forty-Two: Patriot Governor

1. David Townsend to WE, September 23, 1823, Eustis Papers, MHS.
2. *New Hampshire Patriot and States Gazette*, March 4, 1823, Concord, New Hampshire.
3. *Independent Chronicle & Boston Patriot,* April 9, 1823, Boston.
4. American Athenaeum, Newspaper Collection, ID #253-888, April 1823.
5. *Essex Register,* April 14, 1823, Salem, Massachusetts, Vol. XXIII, Issue 30.
6. *Boston Commercial Gazette,* April 9, 1823.
7. WE to James Madison, May 10, 1823, Madison Papers, LOC.
8. General William H. Sumner, *Reminiscences of La Fayette's Visit to Boston, Gov. Brooks, Gov. Eustis and Others.* N-YHS.
9. *Boston Patriot,* May 24, 1823.
10. *Boston Commercial Gazette*, June 5, 1823.
11. WE to James Madison, June 6, 1823, Madison Papers, LOC.
12. James Madison to WE, June 14, 1823, Madison papers, LOC.
13. *Boston Commercial Gazette,* June 5, 1823.
14. *Bowen's Boston News-Letter and City Record,*1825-1827; January-July 1826; 1,1; American Periodicals Series Online, 155.
15. James Swan to WE, August 30, 1823, MS. Am. 2060, BPL.
16. Legislative Records, 1823, Massachusetts State Archives.
17. Monroe letter reprinted, *Boston Patriot,* February 23, 1824.
18. Broadside, Collection of Shirley-Eustis House.

19. *Boston Patriot*, February 23, 1824.
20. Resolves of the General Court of the Commonwealth of Massachusetts, June 1824-March 1825, Massachusetts State Archives.

Chapter Forty-Three: Lengthening Shadows

1. *Columbian Centinel*, Aug. 28, 1824. An outstanding resource for this visit, E.E. Brandon's *Lafayette: Guest of the Nation*, with details written at the time, has substantial, practically hour-by-hour details about Lafayette's visit, 105-128. Another resource is the journal written by Lafayette's secretary, Auguste Lavasseur, *Lafayette in America, 1824-1825*, translated, then printed in Philadelphia, 1829. Unger's biography, *Lafayette*, also covers the visit, 352.
2. Caner Papers, Collection, Shirley-Eustis House.
3. Unger, *Lafayette*, 352.
4. Brandon's *Lafayette: Guest of the Nation*. The Exchange Coffee House dinner's first course offered fish, fowl, and meats ranging from halibut to veal to beef and goose; roasted, boiled, and baked. Birds were featured for the second course including woodcock, pigeon, snipe, duck, and chicken, with the curious addition of calves' feet (possibly calves-foot jelly). Small side dishes of vegetables, pickles, and chutneys complimented the main menu. A third course of puddings, pastries, custards, and blancmange preceded the grand finale—ice cream.
5. General William H. Sumner, *Reminiscences of La Fayette's Visit to Boston, Gov. Brooks, Gov. Eustis and Others*, N-YHS.
6. Unger, *Lafayette*, 354.
7. Charles Francis Adams, Diary, August 29, 1824, Adams Papers Digital Edition, DCA01d269, MHS.
8. Resolves of the General Court of the Commonwealth of Massachusetts, 1824.
9. Eustis Papers, MHS.
10. WE to William North, December 15, 1824, North Letters, Duane Collection, N-YHS.
11. Resolves of the General Court of the Commonwealth of Massachusetts, 1825, 83-92; also *Boston Patriot*.
12. Reverend G. W. Porter, "A Sketch of the Life and Character of the Late William Eustis," Proceedings of the Lexington Historical Society Vol. 1 (1886-1889),107.
13. *Essex Register*, "Another Revolutionary Worthy Departed," February 10, 1825.
14. Sumner, *Reminiscences*, N-YHS.
15. Ibid.

Epilogue

1. Resolves of the General Court of the Commonwealth of Massachusetts (1825), February 7, 1825.
2. *Columbian Centinel*, February 9, 1825, Issue 4261, and February 14, 1825.
3. General William H. Sumner, *Reminiscences,* N-YHS.
4. *Columbian Centinel,* February 12, 1825.
5. Sumner, *Reminiscences,* N-YHS.

6. Ibid.
7. Reverend Thomas Gray, Sermon, February 13, 1825. A special anthem composed for John Hancock was performed at Caroline Eustis's request. Eustis Papers, MHS.
8. Eustis Papers, P-094, MHS.
9. "William Eustis," Read by Rev. G. W. Porter, 1887, 108, Proceedings of Lexington Historical Society, Vol. 1, 1890. Also, Massachusetts State House Reference Library biographical card. See also *Columbian Centinel*, February 12, 1825, and *Vermont Gazette*, December 6, 1825.
10. *Boston Gazette*, July 7, 1825.
11. Caroline Langdon Eustis to Jacob Eustis, Eustis papers, MHS.
12. Eustis Papers, MHS.
13. Norfolk County Probate File #6297.
14. Eustis Papers, March 19, 1826, LOC.
15. Mary Caroline Crawford, *The Romance of Old New England Rooftrees*, 1903.
16. Ibid.
17. Eustis Papers, MHS. Also, for household help, see Federal Census 1860.
18. George Eustis married Louis Corcoran Eustis and died in France, never returning to the United States. His son, William Corcoran Eustis, born in France, purchased the plantation, Oatlands, in Leesburg, Virginia, in 1903. It is now open to the public.
19. Crawford, 43.

Bibliography

The papers of William Eustis are scattered. The largest collection is at the Library of Congress and consists mostly of incoming correspondence from his tenures as secretary of war and minister to the Netherlands. Smaller collections are at the Massachusetts Historical Society, the New-York Historical Society, and the Boston Public Library. Much of his correspondence concerning Indian affairs while secretary of war is printed in Carter and Bloom, *Territorial Papers of the United States*. Correspondence between President James Madison and Eustis during this period is found in "The Papers of James Madison (Presidential Series)." Gilbert Stuart painted a portrait of Eustis about 1806, now at Shirley Place. Another portrait of Eustis by Henry Williams, painted in 1823, hangs in the Massachusetts State House. A copy by Mary Neal Richardson was commissioned by a relative and is now at Oatlands in Leesburg, Virginia.

Primary Sources

Ames, Dr. Nathaniel. *Ledger/Diary,* 1778. Dedham Historical Society. Dedham, MA.

Bugbee, James M., ed., *Memorials of the Massachusetts Society of the Cincinnati.* Boston: 1890.

Cobb, David. Papers. Massachusetts Historical Society.

Conrad, Edick Wright, and Edward W. Hanson, eds., *Sibley's Harvard Graduates,* Vol. XVIII, 1772-1774, Biographical Sketches of Those who Attended Harvard College in the Classes of 1772-1774. Boston: Massachusetts Historical Society, Northeastern Press, 1999.

Coolidge-Dworkin Family Papers. Massachusetts Historical Society.

Cooper, Reverend Samuel. *Diary of Rev. Samuel Cooper, of Boston.* New England Historical and Genealogical Register, 1887.

Eustis/Hull Correspondence. Michigan Pioneer and Historical Collections, Clarke Historical Library, Central Michigan University.

Eustis, William. Letters, 1775-1825, and Eustis, William. Papers, 1775-1864. Massachusetts Historical Society.

Eustis, William. *Journal, 1812-1817.* W. Eustis III. Massachusetts Historical Society.

Eustis, William. Papers, MMC-0329, Microfilm 18, 710-2P. Library of Congress.

Eustis, William to Nathaniel Ames. August 28, 1778. Dedham Historical Society.

Eustis-Langdon Letters. Massachusetts Historical Society.

Eustis, William Papers. New-York Historical Society.

Forbes, James Grant, and William Hull. *Report of the Trial of Brigadier General William Hull, Commanding the Northwestern Army of the United States By a Court Martial Held at Albany on Monday, January 30, 1814 and Succeeding Days.* Boston: Eastburn, Kirk & Co., 1824.

Gray, the Reverend Thomas. *Sermon on the Death of His Excellency, William*

Eustis. Preached in the First Church in Roxbury, February 13, 1825. Boston: Office of the Christian Register, 1825.

Hanson, Robert Brand, ed. *Diary of Dr. Nathanial Ames of Dedham, Massachusetts, 1758 – 1822*, Vol. I. Camden, ME: Picton Press, 1998.

Hunt, Gaillard, ed., *First Forty Years of Washington Society, Portrayed in the Family Letters of Mrs. Samuel Harrison Smith (Margaret Bayard)*. From the Collection of her grandson, J. Henley Smith. New York: Charles Scribner's Sons, 1906.

Jenks, Henry F. *Catalogue of the Boston Public Latin School*, Pt. 2. Boston: 1886.

Kline, Mary-Jo, and Joanne Wood Ryan, eds. *Political Correspondence and Public Papers of Aaron Burr,* Vol. 1. Princeton University Press, 1983.

Letters to the Secretary of War. 1812. Vol. 49, Vol. 56, no. 429. Internet Archives through http: //openlibrary.org and archive.org.

Levasseur, Auguste. *Lafayette in America in 1824-1825;* or *Journal of a Voyage to the United States.* Translated by John D. Godman, M.D. Philadelphia: Carey & Lea, 1829.

Log book for USS *Congress,* Vol. 3, June 4, 1815 – January 3, 1816. Entry 118, Logs of US Ships and Stations, 1801-1947. Naval Record Groups 19 and 24.

Loring, James Spear. *The Hundred Boston Orators Appointed by the Municipal Authorities and Other Public Bodies from 1770 to 1852.* Boston: J.P. Jewett & Co. 1854. 48-49, http: //archive.org.

Massachusetts Soldiers and Sailors of the Revolutionary War. Boston: 1896-1908.

Morris, Charles. *The Autobiography of Commodore Charles Morris, U.S. Navy.* Annapolis: Naval Institute Press, 2002.

National Cyclopedia of American Biography, Vol. II. Ann Arbor, Michigan: University Microfilms, 1967. Boston Public Library.

New England Historical & Genealogical Register & Antiquarian Journal, Volume XXIII. N.E. Historical & Genealogical Society. Boston: David Clapp & Son Printers, 1869.

North, William. North Letters, Duane Collection, New-York Historical Society.

Porter, G.W. *A Sketch of the Life and Character of the Late William Eustis*, Proceedings of the Lexington Historical Society, Vol. 1, 1886-1889. pp. 104-109. Published by the Historical Society, 1890.

Resolves of the General Court of the Commonwealth of Massachusetts, Vol. 16B. Boston: True and Greene, printers, June 1824-March 1825. Massachusetts State Archives.

Roberts, Oliver Ayer. *History of the Military Company of the Massachusetts now called The Ancient and Honorable Artillery Company of Massachusetts, 1637-1888.* Vol. II, *1738-1821.* Boston: Alfred Mudge & Son, printers,1897.

The Scotch-Irish in America: Proceedings of the Scotch-Irish Congress, Vol. 10. The Scotch-Irish Society of America, 1901. 247-248.

Sizer, Theodore, ed., *The Autobiography of Colonel John Trumbull, Patriot-Artist, 1756-1843.* New Haven: 1953.

Sumner, General William H. *Reminiscences of La Fayette's Visit to Boston, Gov.*

Brooks, Gov. Eustis and Others. New England Historical and Genealogical Register, April 1859. New-York Historical Society.

Thacher, James. *American Medical Biography*, Boston: 1828.

——— *A Military Journal, during the American Revolutionary War, from 1775 to 1783.* Plymouth, Massachusetts: 1823. Reprinted by Nabu Public Domain Reprints.

Warren, Edward. *The Life of John Warren, M.D.* Boston: 1874.

Wollstonecraft, Mary. *A Vindication of the Rights of Women: With Strictures on Political and Moral Subjects.* Boston: Peter Edes, printer, 1792.

Secondary Sources

Achenbach, Joel. *The Grand Idea: George Washington's Potomac and the Race to the West.* New York: Simon & Schuster, 2004.

Abbott, William, ed., *Memoirs of Major General William Heath.* New York: 1901. Originally printed Boston: 1798. University of California Digital Library.

Alexander, John K. *Samuel Adams: The Life of an American Revolutionary.* New York: Rowman & Littlefield Publishers Inc., 2011.

Allgor, Catherine. *A Perfect Union: Dolley Madison and the Creation of the American Nation.* New York: Henry Holt and Company, 2006.

Ambrose, Stephen E. *Undaunted Courage: The Pioneering First Mission to Explore America's Wild Frontier.* London: Simon & Schuster UK Ltd, 1997.

Aptowicz, Cristin O'Keefe. *Dr. Mutter's Marvels: A True Tale of Intrigue and Innovation at the Dawn of Modern Medicine.* New York: Gotham Books, Penguin Group, 2014.

Archer, Richard. *As If an Enemy's Country: the British Occupation of Boston and the Origins of Revolution.* New York: Oxford University Press, 2010.

Atkinson, Rick. *The British Are Coming: The War for America, Lexington to Princeton, 1775-1777.* Vol. 1. New York: Henry Holt and Company, 2019.

Beeman, Richard. *Plain, Honest Men: The Making of the American Constitution.* New York: Random House, 2009.

Benemann, William. *Male-Male Intimacy in Early America: Beyond Romantic Friendships.* New York: Harrington Park Press, 2006.

Berkin, Carol. *Wondrous Beauty: The Life and Adventures of Elizabeth Patterson Bonaparte.* New York: Alfred A. Knopf, 2014.

Bierce, Ambrose. *The Devil's Dictionary.* New York: Oxford University Press, 1999, 2002. Introduction by Bierce biographer Roy Morris Jr.

Philadelphia: University of Pennsylvania Press, 1958. Department of the History of Medicine, Yale University, Monograph Series, No. 33.

Borneman, Walter R. *1812: The War That Forged a Nation.* New York: HarperCollins, 2004.

Brandon, E.E. *Lafayette, Guest of the Nation: A Contemporary Account of the Triumphal Tour of General Lafayette through the United States in 1824-5.* Vol. 1. Oxford Historical Press, 1950.

Brookhiser, Richard. *Gentleman Revolutionary: Gouverneur Morris – The Rake*

Who Wrote the Constitution. New York: Free Press, 2003.

Budiansky, Stephen. *Perilous Fight: America's Intrepid War with Britain on the High Seas, 1812-1815.* New York: Alfred A. Knopf, 2010.

Butterfield, L.H., Marc Friedlaender, and Mary-Jo Kline, eds., *The Book of Abigail & John: Selected Letters of the Adams Family, 1762-1784.* Boston: Northeastern University Press, 2002.

Carr, Jacqueline Barbara. *After the Siege: A Social History of Boston, 1775-1800.* Boston: Northeastern University Press, 2005.

Carter, Clarence Edwin, and John Porter Bloom, eds., *Territorial Papers of the United States,* Washington 1938-1969.

Chadwick, Bruce. *The First American Army: The Untold Story of George Washington and the Men Behind America's First Fight for Freedom.* Naperville, IL: Sourcebooks Inc., 2005.

Cheney, Lynn. *James Madison: A Life Reconsidered.* New York: Viking, 2014.

Chernow, Ron. *Washington, A Life*, New York: Penguin Press, 2010.

——— *Alexander Hamilton*, New York: Penguin Press, 2004.

Cook, Don. *The Long Fuse: How England Lost the American Colonies, 1760-1785.* New York: Atlantic Monthly Press, 1995.

Côté, Richard N. *Strength and Honor: The Life of Dolley Madison.* Mount Pleasant, SC: Corinthian Books, 2005.

Craughwell, Thomas J. *Thomas Jefferson's Crème Brûleé.* Philadelphia: Quirk Books, 2012.

Crawford, Mary Caroline. *The Romance of Old New England Rooftrees.* Boston: L.C. Page & Company, 1903.

Dallas, Gregor. *1815: The Roads to Waterloo.* London: Pimlico/Random House, 2001.

DeVoto, Bernard, ed. *The Journals of Lewis and Clark.* Boston/New York: Houghton Mifflin, 1997.

Dillon, Richard. *Meriwether Lewis.* New York: Coward-McCann Inc., 1965.

Di Spigna, Christian. *Founding Martyr: The Life and Death of Dr. Joseph Warren, the American Revolution's Lost Hero.* New York: Crown Publishing Group, 2018.

Dolan, Eric Jay. *When America First Met China: An Exotic History of Tea, Drugs, and Money in the Age of Sail.* New York: Liveright Publishing Corp., W.W. Norton & Co., 2012.

Dudley, William S., ed., *The Naval War of 1812: A Documentary History.* Washington: Naval Historical Center, Dept. of the Navy, 1985.

Drake, Francis S. *The Town of Roxbury: Its Memorable Persons and Places, Its History and Antiquities with Numerous Illustrations of its old Landmarks and Noted Personages.* Boston: Municipal Printing Office, 1905.

Ellis, James H. *A Ruinous and Unhappy War: New England and the War of 1812.* New York: Algora Publishing, 2009.

Ellis, Joseph J. *American Sphinx: The Character of Thomas Jefferson.* New York: Vintage Books, Random House Inc., 1996.

——— *Founding Brothers: The Revolutionary Generation.* New York: Vintage

346

Books, Random House Inc., 2000.

Eustace, Nicole. *1812: War and the Passions of Patriotism*. Philadelphia: University of Pennsylvania Press, 2012.

Fenn, Elizabeth A. *Pox Americana: The Great Smallpox Epidemic of 1775-82*. New York: Hill and Wang, 2001.

Fischer, David Hackett. *Paul Revere's Ride*. New York: Oxford University Press, 1994.

——— *Liberty and Freedom*. New York: Oxford University Press, 2005.

Fitz-Enz, David, Colonel, USA Ret. *Hacks, Sycophants, Adventurers & Heroes: Madison's Commanders in the War of 1812*. Lanham, MD: Taylor Trade Publishing, 2012.

Fleming, Thomas. *The Intimate Lives of the Founding Fathers*. New York: HarperCollins, 2009.

——— *Duel: Alexander Hamilton, Aaron Burr and the Future of America*. New York: Basic Books, 1999.

Flexner, James Thomas. *Young Hamilton: A Biography*. New York: Fordham University Press, 1997.

Forbes, Allan. *Taverns and Stagecoaches of New England: Anecdotes and Tales*. R.M. Eastman, ed., Boston: State Street Trust Company, 1953.

Forbes, Esther. *Paul Revere and the World He Lived In*. Boston, New York: Houghton Mifflin, a Mariner Books reprint, 1999.

Forman, Samuel. *Dr. Joseph Warren: The Boston Tea Party, Bunker Hill, and the Birth of American Liberty*. Gretna, LA: Pelican Publishing Company, 2011.

Foster, Thomas A. *Sex and the Eighteenth-Century Man: Massachusetts and the History of Sexuality in America*. Boston: Beacon Press, 2006.

Fowler, William M., Jr. *American Crisis: George Washington and the Dangerous Two Years after Yorktown, 1781-1783*. New York: Walker & Company, 2011.

Froncek, Thomas, ed., *The City of Washington, An Illustrated History*. The Junior League of Washington. New York: Alfred A. Knopf, 1977.

Frothingham, Richard, Jr. *History of the Siege of Boston, and of the Battles of Lexington, Concord and Bunker Hill*. Boston: Charles C. Little and James Brown, 1849.

Gillmor, Don, and Pierre Turgeon. *Canada: A Peoples' History*. Toronto, Ontario: McClelland & Stewart Ltd., 2001.

Goodman, Paul. *The Democratic-Republicans of Massachusetts: Politics in a Young Republic*. Cambridge: Harvard University Press, 1964.

Greenburg, Michael M. *The Court-Martial of Paul Revere: A Son of Liberty & America's Forgotten Military Disaster*. Lebanon, NH: Fore Edge, an imprint of University Press of New England, 2014.

Gutzman, Kevin R. C. *James Madison and The Making of America*. New York: St. Martin's Press, 2012.

Harr, John Ensor. *Dark Eagle: Benedict Arnold and the American Revolution*. New York: Viking, 1999.

Hanson, Robert Brand, ed., *Diary of Dr. Nathanial Ames of Dedham,*

Massachusetts, 1758 – 1822. Vol. I. Camden, ME: Picton Press, 1998.

Heidler, David S., and Jeanne T. *Henry Clay: The Essential American*. New York: Random House, 2010.

Holton, Woody. *Abigail Adams*. New York: Free Press, 2009.

Howard, Brett. *Boston: A Social History*. New York: Hawthorn Books, 1976.

Howard, Hugh. *Mr. and Mrs. Madison's War: America's First Couple and the Second War of Independence*. New York: Bloomsbury Press, 2012.

Isenberg, Nancy. *Fallen·Founder: The Life of Aaron Burr*. New York: Viking Penguin, 2007.

Kilmeade, Brian, and Don Yaeger. *George Washington's Secret Six: The Spy Ring That Saved the American Revolution*. New York: Sentinel, Penguin Group (USA) LLC, 2013.

Lancaster, Bruce. *From Lexington to Liberty, the Story of the American Revolution*. New York: Doubleday, 1955.

Langguth, A.J. *Union 1812: The Americans Who Fought the Second War of Independence*. New York: Simon & Schuster, 2006.

Larson, Edward J. *The Return of George Washington 1783-1789*. New York: William Morrow, Imprint of HarperCollins Publishers, 2014.

Leavitt, Judith W., and Ronald L. Numbers, eds. *Sickness & Health in America: Readings in the History of Medicine and Public Health*. Madison: University of Wisconsin Press. 1978.

Lepore, Jill. *Book of Ages: The Life and Opinions of Jane Franklin*. New York: Vintage Books, A Division of Random House, 2013.

Linklater, Andro. *An Artist in Treason: The Extraordinary Double Life of General James Wilkinson*. New York: Walker Publishing Company, 2009.

Lockhart, Paul. *The Whites of Their Eyes: Bunker Hill, the First American Army, and the Emergence of George Washington*. New York: HarperCollins, 2011.

Lonergan, Thomas J. *Henry Knox: George Washington's Confidant, General of Artillery, and America's first Secretary of War*. Rockland, ME: Picton Press, 2003.

Lord, Walter. *The Dawn's Early Light*. New York: W.W. Norton & Company, 1972.

MacIntire, Jane Bacon. *Lafayette: The Guest of the Nation*. Newton, MA: 1967.

Maier, Pauline. *Ratification: The People Debate the Constitution, 1787-1788*. New York: Simon & Schuster, 2010.

Marshall, Megan. *The Peabody Sisters*. Boston: Houghton Mifflin, 2005.

Marten, James, ed., *Children in Colonial America*. New York: New York University Press, 2007.

Martin, James Kirby, ed. *Ordinary Courage: The Revolutionary War Adventures of Joseph Plumb Martin*. Malden, MA: Blackwell Publishing, 2008.

Mann, Mary Lee, ed. *A Yankee Jeffersonian: Selections from the Diary and Letters of William Lee of Massachusetts, Written from 1796 to 1840*. Cambridge: Belknap Press, Harvard University, 1958.

Mayer, Holly A. *Belonging to the Army*. Columbia: University of South Carolina Press, 1996.

McBurney, Christian M. *The Rhode Island Campaign: The First French and American Operation in the Revolutionary War*. Yardley, PA: Westholme Publishing LLC, 2011.

McCullough, David. *John Adams*. New York: Simon & Schuster, 2001.

—— *The Greater Journey: Americans in Paris*. New York: Simon & Schuster, 2011.

Morison, Samuel Eliot. *Three Centuries of Harvard: 1636-1936*. Cambridge, MA: The Belknap Press of Harvard University Press, 1936.

Murray, Stuart. *Washington's Farewell*. Bennington, VT: Images from the Past, 1999.

Nelson, James L. *With Fire and Sword: The Battle of Bunker Hill and the Beginning of the American Revolution*. New York: Thomas Dunn Books, St. Martin's Press, 2011.

Nevin, David. *1812*. New York: Tom Doherty Associates Inc., 1996.

—— *Treason*. New York: Tom Doherty Associates LLC, 2001.

Padover, Saul K. *Jefferson: A Great American's Life and Ideas*. New York: Penguin Books, 1970.

Palmer, Dave R. *1794: America, Its Army, and the Birth of the Nation*. Novato, CA: Presidio Press, 1994.

Palmer, Thomas. *The Admirable Secrets of Physick & Chyrurgery*. Thomas Rogers Forbes, ed. New Haven: Yale University Press. 1984.

Park, Lawrence. *Gilbert Stuart: An Illustrated Descriptive List of His Work*, Vol. 1, New York: Print House of William Edwin Rudge, 1926.

Pearson, Michael. *Those Damned Rebels: The American Revolution as Seen Through British Eyes*. Boston: Da Capo Press, 2000.

Peterson, Merrill D. *Thomas Jefferson and the New Nation*. London: Oxford University Press, 1975.

Philbrick, Nathaniel. *Bunker Hill: A City, a Siege, a Revolution*. New York: Penguin, 2013.

—— *Valiant Ambition: George Washington, Benedict Arnold and the Fate of the American Revolution*. New York: Viking, 2016.

Prucha, Francis Paul. *American Indian Treaties: The History of a Political Anomaly*. Berkeley, CA: University of California Press, 1994.

Puls, Mark. *Samuel Adams: Father of the American Revolution*. New York: St. Martin's Press, 2006.

Randall, Willard Sterne. *Benedict Arnold: Patriot and Traitor*. New York: William Morrow and Company Inc., 1990.

Raphael, Ray. *A People's History of the American Revolution: How Common People Shared the Fight for Independence*. New York: HarperCollins, 2002.

Rakove, Jack. *Revolutionaries: A New History of the Invention of America*. New York: Houghton Mifflin Harcourt Publishing Co., 2010.

Risjord, Norman K. *Jefferson's America: 1760-1815*. Madison, WI: Madison House Publishers Inc., 1991.

Rutland, Robert A. et al, eds. *The Papers of James Madison* (Presidential Series). Charlottesville: University of Virginia Press, 1984.

Saffron, Morris H. *Surgeon to Washington: Dr. John Cochran (1730-1807)*. New York: Columbia University Press, 1977.

Saunt, Claudio. *West of the Revolution: An Uncommon History of 1776.* New York: W.W. Norton, 2014.

Schama, Simon. *Rough Crossings: Britain, The Slaves and the American Revolution.* New York: HarperCollins, 2006.

Schecter, Barnet. *The Battle for New York: The City at the Heart of the Revolution.* New York: Walker & Company, 2002.

Schlesinger, Arthur M., Jr. *The Age of Jackson.* Boston: Little, Brown and Company, 1953.

Slaughter, Thomas P. *Independence: The Tangled Roots of the American Revolution.* New York: Hill and Wang, A Division of Farrar, Straus and Giroux, 2014.

Stewart, David O. *American Emperor: Aaron Burr's Challenge to Jefferson's America.* New York: Simon & Schuster, 2011.

Sizer, Theodore, ed. *The Autobiography of Colonel John Trumbull, Patriot-Artist, 1756-1843.* New Haven: 1953.

Taylor, Alan. *The Civil War of 1812.* New York: Alfred A. Knopf, 2010.

Thomson, David. *Europe Since Napoleon.* Second Edition. New York: Alfred A. Knopf, Inc., 1962.

Thorwald, Jurgen. *The Century of the Surgeon.* New York: Pantheon Books, 1956.

Toll, Ian W. *Six frigates: The Epic History of the Founding of the U.S. Navy.* New York: W.W. Norton & Company, 2006.

Truax, Rhoda. *The Doctors Warren of Boston: First Family of Surgery.* Boston: Houghton Mifflin Company, 1968.

Uhlar, Janet. *Liberty's Martyr: The Story of Dr. Joseph Warren.* Indianapolis: Dog Ear Publishing, 2009.

Ulrich, Laurel Thatcher. *A Midwife's Tale: The Life of Martha Ballard Based on Her Diary, 1785-1812.* New York: Vintage Books, Random House, 1990.

Unger, Harlow Giles. *American Tempest: How the Boston Tea Party Sparked a Revolution.* Philadelphia: Perseus Books Group, Da Capo Press, 2011.

———— *Lafayette.* Hoboken, NJ: John Wiley & Sons Inc., 2002.

———— *The Last Founding Father: James Monroe and A Nation's Call to Greatness.* Philadelphia: Perseus Books Group, Da Capo Press, 2009.

Van Doren, Mark, *Secret History of the American Revolution.* Clifton, NJ: Augustus M. Kelley, 1973.

Westermann, J.C. *The Netherlands and the United States: Their Relations in the Beginning of the Nineteenth Century.* Martinus Nyhoff: The Hague, 1935.

Wilbur, C. Keith, M.D. *Revolutionary Medicine, 1700 – 1800.* Guilford, CT: The Globe Pequot Press, 1997.

Williams, Kate. *Becoming Queen Victoria: The Tragic Death of Princess Charlotte and the Unexpected Rise of Britain's Greatest Monarch.* New York: Ballentine Books, 2008.

Wills, Garry. *James Madison.* The American Presidents Series. New York: Henry

Holt and Company, 2002.

Winik, Jay. *The Great Upheaval: America and the Birth of the Modern World, 1788-1800.* New York: HarperCollins, 2007.

Winsor, Justin, ed. *The Memorial History of Boston.* Boston: Tichnor, 1881, Vol. 3, 159, cited in Pail Revere's Boston 1975 Exhibition Catalog, Museum of Fine Arts, 1975.

Wood, Gordon S. *Empire of Liberty, A History of the Early Republic, 1789-1815.* New York: Oxford University Press, 2009.

——— *Radicalism of the American Revolution.* New York: Vintage Books, A Division of Random House, 1993.

Young, James Sterling. *The Washington Community, 1800-1828.* New York: Columbia University Press, 1966.

Zimmerman, Jean. *The Women of the House: How a Colonial She-Merchant Built a Mansion, a Fortune and a Dynasty.* New York: Harcourt Inc., 2006.

Reference Works

Bartlett, John. *Bartlett's Familiar Quotations.* Sixteenth Edition. Justin Kaplan, ed., Boston: Little, Brown and Company, 1992.

Channing, Edward. *A History of the United States,* IV. New York: The Macmillan Company, 1917.

Commager, Henry Steele, and Richard B. Morris, eds. *The Spirit of Seventy-Six: The Story of the American Revolution as told by its Participants.* New York: HarperCollins, 1967.

Conrad, Edick Wright, and Edward W. Hanson, eds. *Sibley's Harvard Graduates,* Vol. XVIII, 1772-1774, Biographical Sketches of Those who Attended Harvard College in the Classes of 1772-1774. Boston: Massachusetts Historical Society, Northeastern Press, 1999.

Newspapers/Magazines

American Beacon and Norfolk Daily Advertiser, (Norfolk, VA) *1818-1819.*
American Mercury, 1802.
Boston Weekly Messenger, 1823.
Columbian Centinel, (Boston, MA), *1818, 1823, 1825.*
Independent Chronicle & Boston Patriot, 1823-1825.
Independent Chronicle, 1791, 1800, 1802, 1815.
Massachusetts Register, 1799, 1808.
Niles Weekly Register, (Baltimore, MD).
The Whig Chronicle, 1812.
Roberts, Andrew. "Napoleon's Last Charge". *Smithsonian Magazine,* June 2015.

Internet Sources

George Washington's Visit to Boston, 1789. http: //www.teachhistory.com.
ProQuest LLC, information service
Wikipedia

Index

Treaty of Ghent, 248
Treaty of Paris, 106
Trenton, 67
tribal land rights, 202
Trinity Church, 127
Tsar Alexander, 254
Tudor, William, 153
Twelfth Amendment, 172

U

United Kingdom of the Netherlands, 247
uti possidetis, 94

V

van Rensselaer, General Stephen, 230
Varick , Colonel Richard, 85
Vassall, John, 49
Verplancks, fort, 77
victories at sea, War of 1812, 234
von Closen, Baron, 93
von Steuben, Baron Friedrich, 70
von Steuben, Baron Friedrich, 212

W

Walker, Captain Benjamin, 212
War Hawks, 218
War of 1812, 223, 225
Ward, General Artemas, 40
Warren, Dr. John (Jack), 46, 51, 75, 116, 132
Warren, Dr. John Collins, 304
Warren, Dr. Joseph, 14, 15, 23, 30, 31, 39, 45, 46, 295
Warren, Elizabeth Hooton, 14, 16
Washington City, 128, 155, 241, 242

Washington Street, Boston, 126
Washington, General George, 41, 48, 50, 58, 102, 103, 125, 138, 146
Washington, Martha, 61
water shortages, 100
Waterhouse, Dr. Benjamin, 178
Waterloo, Battle of, 253
Webster, Senator Daniel, 308, 311
Weehawken, New Jersey, 175
Wellesley, Arthur
    Duke of Wellington, 254
Wellington, Duke of
    Arthur Wellesley, 254
Wells, Catherine Eustis, 277
West End, Boston
    site of hospital and almshouse, 129
West Point, 84
whiskey, role in campaigning, 164
White, Private Hugh, 6
Wilkinson, General James, 180, 199, 201, 214, 241
William I
    First king of the United Netherlands, 258
William of Orange
    Dutch prince, 257
Williams, Henry, portraitist, 294
Williamsburg, Virginia, 95
Wilmington, North Carolina, 93
Wollstonecraft, Mary
    wrote *A Vindication of the Rights of Women*, 145

Y

York, William Clark's slave, 179
Yorktown, Cornwallis' Surrender, 96
Yorktown, Siege of, 96